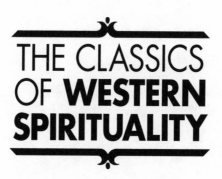

THE CLASSICS
OF **WESTERN
SPIRITUALITY**

THE CLASSICS OF WESTERN SPIRITUALITY
A Library of the Great Spiritual Masters

John Comenius

THE LABYRINTH OF THE WORLD AND THE PARADISE OF THE HEART

TRANSLATED AND INTRODUCED BY
HOWARD LOUTHAN AND ANDREA STERK

PREFACE BY
JAN MILIČ LOCHMAN

PAULIST PRESS
NEW YORK • MAHWAH

Cover art: This portrait, purported to be the best actual likeness of Comenius, is by J. Ovens (ca. 1660) and is used courtesy of Museum Catharijneconvent, Utrecht.

Library of Congress Cataloging-in-Publication Data

Comenius, Johann Amos, 1592–1670.
    [Labyrint světa a ráj srdce. English]
    Labyrinth of the world and the paradise of the heart / John Comenius ; translated and introduced by Howard Louthan and Andrea Sterk.
      p. cm. — (Classics of Western spirituality ; #90)
    Includes bibliographical references and index.
    ISBN 0-8091-3739-9 (alk. paper)—ISBN 0-8091-0489-X (cloth)
    1. Christian Life. I. Title. II. Series.
BV4509.C8C613   1997
248.4'846—dc121   97-16711
                                                      CIP

Published by Paulist Press
997 Macarthur Boulevard
Mahwah, New Jersey 07430

Printed and bound in the United States of America

Contents

CONTENTS

CONTENTS

Translators of This Volume

HOWARD LOUTHAN is an assistant professor of history at the University of Notre Dame. He received his Ph.D. from Princeton University in 1994. His area of specialization is early modern central Europe. He is the author of *Reforming a Counter-Reform Court: Johannis Crato and the Austrian Habsburgs* (Studies in Reformed Theology and History, Princeton Theological Seminary, 1994) and *The Quest for Compromise: Peacemakers in Counter-Reformation Vienna* (Cambridge, 1997).

ANDREA STERK received her Ph.D. from Princeton Theological Seminary in 1994. She has taught in the history department at Calvin College and as an adjunct professor at the University of Notre Dame. She specializes in the patristic period and is currently completing a book on the rise of monk-bishops in the Christian East. Her work on Comenius has enabled her to pursue broader interests in the history of spirituality and in Christianity in the Slavic world. Andrea and Howard are also the parents of three preschool boys.

Author of the Preface

JAN MILIČ LOCHMAN has been professor of theology at Basel University (Switzerland) since 1969. His distinguished career includes the following positions: professor at the Comenius Faculty (Prague) from 1950 to 1968; professor at the Union Theological Seminary (New York) from 1968 to 1969; and rector of Basel University from 1981 to 1983. Active in the international ecumenical movement since 1961, he has held many leading positions on both the World Council of Churches and the World Alliance of Reformed Churches. He has written extensively in Czechoslovakian, German and English. Among his most noted publications are *Encountering Marx: Bonds and Barriers between Christians and Marxists* (Books on Demand), *The Faith We Confess: An Ecumenical Dogmatics* (Augsburg Fortress) and *The Lord's Prayer* (Eerdmans).

Preface

John Amos Comenius (1592–1670) is widely acknowledged as one of the most important representatives of European pedagogy. It was with good reason, therefore, that he was honored throughout the world in 1992 on the four-hundredth anniversary of his birth. Much less known is the fact that he has also made a distinctive contribution to the history of ecumenical theology and spirituality. The present new English translation of one of the most significant works of Czech literature, *The Labyrinth of the World and the Paradise of the Heart,* shows that he has been served an injustice and that this text truly belongs among the "Classics of Western Spirituality."

Three emphases seem to me to be characteristic of Comenius and particularly relevant for contemporary ecumenical theology and spirituality: a personal relationship with Christ, ecumenical reformation, and a theology of hope.

Under the Scepter of Christ

Comenius's whole life and work has a crucial point of focus: his deep personal relationship to the living Christ. His early Czech work, *The Labyrinth of the World and the Paradise of the Heart,* already reflects this orientation. The Paradise of the Heart refers to the fellowship of the believer with his Savior. The same vision permeates the moving work of his later years in Amsterdam, *Unum necessarium* (The One Thing Necessary). The one thing necessary is a relationship to Christ. And along the way, in

1

the midst of his ecumenical effort, he could write, "Everything sways for the one not firmly anchored in Christ."[1]

All this sounds almost pietistic, and one can, in fact, trace lines of connection to later Pietism. It is no coincidence that manuscripts of Comenius's *Consultatio* were preserved in Halle, the center of German Pietism. The spiritual connection to Count Zinzendorf, the founder of the renewed Unity of Brethren, should also be considered in this context. Yet it seems to me that still more important than this continuity in the direction of Pietism is another connection or prior link, namely to the Czech Reformation. For there we find the other important axis of the Christ-relationship for Comenius: not only the personal relationship between I and Thou, the pious soul and Christ, but also the theme of the lordship of Christ, the *regnum Christi* or, as Comenius often called it, the *sceptrum Christi*.

This very point was clearly articulated in the Czech Reformation: Jesus Christ is the Lord. He is not only the savior of souls and the teacher of wisdom, but the king of the church and the world. He will reign! What really matters, then, is to live in conformity with his coming kingdom, and in this light to shape the alienated world, first within the church, and then also in society.

This legacy of the Bohemian Reformation is unequivocally and consciously adopted in the theology of Comenius. Precisely in this connection, he distinguishes himself from the other "unities," from different Protestant churches, which he otherwise values very highly. Listen to his voice: "Our forefathers sought to unite with all true Christians, especially with the German churches renewed through Luther. They were unable to achieve this end, however, because these churches had not yet truly begun to ensure that Christ would receive his proper place: not only the pulpit as a teacher and the altar as a priest, but a throne as the King."[2]

---

1. Comenius to Bartholomäus Nigrinus, December 7, 1643, *Jan Amos Komenský o sobě*, eds. Amedeo Molnár and Noemi Rejchrtová (Prague, 1987), 198.

2. Conclusion to Comenius's edition of Jan Laski's *History of the Brethren* (Amsterdam, 1660).

2

Another essential aspect of Comenius's Christology and theology in general is connected with his focus on Jesus Christ as the Coming One, the Lord of the future, *Christus Renovator*. Like his fathers and brothers in the faith, Comenius also lived in expectation of the eschatological promise. From this standpoint, one can understand both his patience and his impatience. I am referring to his perseverance, which kept him from despair or resignation despite the many attacks of fate, and also to his energetic drive toward world-transforming mission.

This foundation not only enables the most fervent believer to rest in the "Paradise of the Heart," but it also calls him in imitation of his Lord to mission in the "Labyrinth of the World"—first of all, to be sure, in the labyrinth of the church.

Toward an Ecumenical Reformation

This brings us to the second essential emphasis of Comenius's ecumenical theology: his program of an ecumenical reformation. Here I am using the word *ecumenical* in the narrower sense, with a focus on the unity of Christians. In this sense, Comenius is already a true *homo oecumenicus*. In his day, we find hardly any theological thinker who was as energetically involved for the unity and harmony of Christians as he. He suffered under the confessional hardening of his day, even among Protestants, and he did his best to reconcile the crippling divisions. His own bitter experiences in war and peace and the distinctive aspects of his confession point clearly in this direction. The Bohemian Brethren were of decidedly ecumenical orientation. They always refused to refer to themselves as a "church" and rather chose the name "unity," for they believed that the great name of the Church of Christ should be reserved only for the totality of Christians—the truly ecumenical church. The focus on the coming kingdom of Christ strengthened this ecumenical inclination. In the light of this eschatological promise, the historical distinctions between Christians faded or were relativized in importance.

This relativizing should not be understood as *relativism*. There are central truths of Christian faith that should never be abandoned. Comenius resolutely denied the thought of Michael Servetus that one could promote peace among Christians and even with the Turks if one would sacrifice trinitarian dogma. Unity must not be sought at the cost of the truth. "Therefore love truth and peace" (see Zec. 8:19). The two go hand in hand; indeed truth goes first. Here the classic distinction of the Unity of Brethren—namely that between *essentialia, ministerialia,* and *accessoria,* or what is essential, useful, and auxiliary (incidental) in the life of the church—came to Comenius's aid. This "hierarchy of truths" is to be respected. The essentials that would divide the church must be distinguished from the non-divisive incidentals.

What is essential and binding? We have just heard the answer: Jesus Christ, understood as the eschatological *Christus Renovator,* the Renewer of all things. Wherever this foundation or focus is present among Christians, then, even in the midst of the acknowledgment of remaining differences, communion is to be emphasized and brotherly conversation preferred to all other possible expedients. From this perspective, Comenius is one of the most compelling representatives of a Christian-motivated toleration. His is the *via pacis,* the path to peace followed by Christians, the "mutual tolerance, on which basis we do not slander, accuse of heresy, condemn or expel from the church those whom we cannot reform in everything, but rather accept them as weak in the faith (Rom 14:1) in the knowledge that each one stands and falls before his Lord, and that God himself is able to raise him up and establish him."[3]

Spirituality and Engagement Arising from Hope

Comenius is in many ways a theologian of hope. Hope marks the inner dimension of his life and work, the "omega point" at which most lines of his thought intersect. The question arises: Are not

---

3. *Cesta pokoje,* in Jan Kvačala, ed., *Veškeré spisy Jana Amosa Komenského,* Vol. 17 (Brno, 1912), 479.

the great themes of Comenius's life work an expression of a humanly impressive, if ultimately unguarded, optimism? His sketch of a perfect reformation and of a universal reform of all human things, his creed of the unity and equality of the human race, his vision of the all-embracing brotherhood of humanity—do not all these verge on pure utopia, beautiful and noble, to be sure, but in reality fanatical and unreal? Are human flaws and the imperfections of the world taken seriously enough? In his passionate striving for harmony is he dismissing all too easily the deep tensions and contradictions? Is he not, in the end, simply a pious dreamer?

Several contemporaries of Comenius already posed such questions, both theologians like Samuel Maresius and representatives of newer methods and fields of knowledge like René Descartes. In fact, there are still many unsettled questions in the intellectual world of Comenius. As a general criticism, however, these skeptical questions are hardly justified. This man was no dreamer. In his personal life, he had already experienced all too deeply the alienating forces and individuals of our world to simply disregard them. Also, his reflections are in many respects distinguished by a remarkable keenness of analytical insight. He has no illusions about the state of his world, either in the church or in "Christian" society. The world of men and women is indeed a labyrinth. But if, in spite of all he has experienced and reflected upon, he hesitates to surrender this world to the devil or to nihilism, if he resists the temptation, against all personal inclinations, to flee to the longed for paradise of the heart, there is a reason. The reason is his Christian hope.

In this perspective Comenius lived, suffered, and worked. If his thought has "utopian characteristics," it is this very world-transforming utopia of hope that takes seriously God in his promises and precisely for this reason hesitates to abandon the world in its status quo. Comenius supports unreservedly the renewal of human things because he knows the kingdom of God is coming. We are not its builders. Therefore, have no illusions! God is the Lord of his kingdom. But since this true God is coming, therefore also have no disillusionment! "Despair is an offence to God" *(Prodromus pansophicus)*. It makes sense to align and construct our little hopes on the basis of the Great Hope. This is precisely what Comenius does in his little projects: in his devotion to every individual and in his constant concern for improved pedagogical and didactic methods. But he does this also in his great projects: in his plans for a comprehensive reform. In this sense, I interpret his *consultatio catholica* not as triumphalistic fanaticism, but as a testimony that hope has far-reaching implications and that it is also to be practiced comprehensively for the transformation of the world. In other words, it is not the world that gives Comenius hope, but hope that gives him the world.

*　　*　　*

Comenius was the last bishop (elder) of the Bohemian Unity of Brethren. He clung to this treasure throughout his life. But he was forced to witness the sad fate of his "mother, the Unity," who lay dying, a victim of political intrigue. Despite these circumstances, he did not fall into despair but dared to interpret the collapse ecumenically, in the sense that "the wise, good God was tearing down his little house in order to prepare a place for a bigger one...that is, in place of his dear little Unity erecting a big one, even more beloved by him. In this way not only everywhere in the fatherland but among the peoples of the entire earth the candle, which hitherto only glimmered under a bushel of particular sects and unities, would now be placed on a high lampstand. From there it would shine brightly to all humanity in the houses of the church and in the houses of the world."[4] Comenius saw himself as a doorkeeper whose duty it was "to close behind me the door of the little Unity and to open before me the door of the great Unity":[5] a doorkeeper of ecumenical hope.

---

4. Comenius to the Brethren in Lednice, Puchov, and Skalice, October 2, 1670, *Jan Amos Komenský o sobě*, 327.

5. Ibid.

Introduction

*T*he study of Protestant spirituality in the late sixteenth and seventeenth centuries has long centered on Puritans and Pietists.
In Central Europe, the work of the German theologians Jacob
Boehme, Johann Arndt, and the later Pietist leaders has received
much attention.[1] The Slavic Protestant tradition has been virtually unnoticed; but with the collapse of communism in Eastern
Europe, the seventeenth-century Czech educator John Amos
Comenius has reemerged as one of this region's most prophetic
and relevant figures. As the Czech Republic is experiencing a new
golden age of letters, one is compelled to think back to the contributions of Comenius more than three centuries earlier. Many of
the questions Comenius wrestled with have found new life in the
cultural and intellectual chaos of post–Cold War Central Europe.
A champion of ecumenism and religious tolerance, Comenius
was a stalwart supporter of multinational states in the fractured
age of the seventeenth century. Caught in an ideological no-
man's-land, the countries of *Mitteleuropa* today are struggling des-
perately to integrate themselves into the larger and more
prosperous European community.

Without doubt it is Václav Havel who has inherited Comenius's
mantle. Both of these men made their mark in the world with the
pen. Both suffered and were persecuted for their beliefs. One was
forced into exile. The other spent time in prison and lived for
years under constant police surveillance. And in the end, both
rose to positions of power and influence. Comenius served as an
advisor to the Swedish chancellor Axel Oxenstierna; Havel led
the Velvet Revolution of 1989 and eventually became his coun-

try's president. Most important, however, is the profound spiritual link between the two men. A number of Havel's essays explore the ethical and spiritual dimensions of politics and power in the late twentieth century. In vivid terms, Havel depicts the moral quagmire in which the world has found itself with the collapse of the ideological rivalry of capitalism and communism.[2]

Long considered a classic by Slavic specialists, Comenius's *Labyrinth of the World* is especially relevant in the intellectual and spiritual climate of the modern era. Though the historical context is somewhat different, Comenius considers many of the issues that Havel discusses. Like the playwright, Comenius ponders the place of virtue and integrity in a world corrupt at its very core. Though he struggles with many of the same problems as Havel, Comenius poses a distinctly Christian response to these questions. His critique of materialism, biting satire of academic life, and search for ultimate meaning and happiness ring surprisingly true to the modern ear. Indeed, the message of the *Labyrinth* is just as timely now as when it was first written in 1623.

The introduction that follows is divided into three sections. The first reviews the life and career of John Amos Comenius. Though Comenius is a figure of critical importance for a small circle of educators and students of modern pedagogy, he is relatively unknown in the field of Christian spirituality. Moreover, the *Labyrinth* is replete with allusions to Comenius's own life and times. This biographical sketch will help the reader appreciate the personal experiences and historical events he incorporates in the text. Because Comenius is best known for his work as a pedagogical reformer, the second part examines the relationship of the *Labyrinth* to this aspect of his life's work. It also places his educational ideals in the broader context of his spirituality. The third section focuses on the spiritual themes of the *Labyrinth* itself. While Comenian research encompasses many facets of this polymath's career, his spirituality has received little or no attention. Though this Czech treatise has been inaccessible to many for linguistic reasons, the *Labyrinth* deserves to be recovered as a true classic of Protestant spirituality.

INTRODUCTION

Biographical Sketch

The *Labyrinth of the World* recounts the journey of a pilgrim through the marketplace of seventeenth-century Europe. It is no accident that Comenius chose a pilgrim as the central figure of his allegory. The *Labyrinth* has often been compared to John Bunyan's *Pilgrim's Progress*. Though there are many parallels between the two works, Comenius's treatise is more autobiographical. Its satirical and often caustic tone is rooted in the experiences of a man disillusioned and discouraged with the world. Throughout its pages, Comenius furnishes bits and pieces of biographical information that allow the reader to uncover the source of his frustrations. In the introduction he states explicitly:

> Reader, what you will read is no mere invention, even though it may bear resemblance to a fable; rather, these are true events that you will recognize once you have understood, especially you who know something of my life and circumstances. For the most part, I have described here adventures that I myself experienced over several years of my life. (To the Reader, 5)

A pilgrim is an outsider, a voluntary exile in search of a spiritual home. Like the protagonist of the *Labyrinth,* Comenius was both an outsider and a pilgrim. He was a wandering scholar who worked in seven countries over the course of his long career. Forced into exile by the victorious forces of the Catholic Habsburgs, Comenius was doggedly pursued by war and personal misfortune. In one of his last works he wrote concerning his trials, "My life was a continuous wandering. I never had a home. Without pause I was constantly tossed about. Nowhere did I ever find a secure place to live."[3] Though the first edition of the *Labyrinth* was written at the beginning of his career, Comenius's pilgrim anticipated much of the anguish his creator would later experience.

It is in many ways surprising that Comenius ever became a great scholar and social critic. He was born in the small Moravian village of Nivnice in 1592. Little is known about his family background. It is said that his father, Martin, was a miller.[4] It does

9

seem that Comenius was quite familiar with this profession, for in a number of passages in the *Labyrinth* he describes the machinery of a mill.[5] At the age of twelve, however, Comenius lost both his parents and two of his sisters to the plague. The family was divided, and John was sent off to his aunt in the nearby town of Strážnice. Up to this point, his formal education was spotty, and it seems likely that he tried out a number of different professions, for he writes in the *Labyrinth*, "I confess, however, that I secretly attempted to pursue first one, then another, then a third thing [occupation], but abandoned each one straight away, for I perceived (or so it seemed to me) difficulties and vanities in each." (1.4) It was not until he was sixteen and sent to the Latin school of Přerov that he began to develop his scholarly gifts.

With diligence and industry Comenius won the favor of his teacher, John Lánecký. It is said that Lánecký was so impressed with his pupil's love of knowledge that he gave Comenius the middle name Amos.[6] More importantly, Comenius's outstanding performance at the Přerov school caught the attention of the lord of the city, Charles the Elder of Žerotín. Žerotín himself had studied with Beza in Geneva and was eager to send capable students abroad.[7] Along with six other youths from the Czech lands, Comenius matriculated at the Reformed gymnasium of Herborn in March 1611.

The Herborn gymnasium was one of the most important Reformed centers of higher education in the early seventeenth century.[8] Though relatively small, it attracted a number of the leading scholars of the continent. Both Johann Fischer, the biblical exegete from Strassburg, and Johann Heinrich Alsted were among its faculty. Alsted had a profound influence on the young Comenius. A disciple of Peter Ramus, his anti-Aristotelian bias became an important part of Comenius's thinking. Comenius cynically attacked scholasticism throughout the *Labyrinth*, and Ramus himself makes a number of appearances in the text.[9] Alsted's emphasis on the Bible as the sole arbiter of truth also remained with Comenius.[10] Finally, Alsted was both a chiliast and an encyclopedist. His famous *Encyclopaedia*, published in 1630, would serve as Comenius's model in his later attempt to catalog all human knowledge. Comenius's millenarian views, first inspired by his teacher at Herborn, became an important part of his own theology.[11]

After completing his term at Herborn, Comenius continued his studies with a further year of work at Heidelberg.[12] There Comenius met the Reformed scholar David Pareus (1548–1622). During Comenius's tenure in Heidelberg, Pareus published his *Irenicum,* a treatise written for King Gustavus Adolphus of Sweden advocating the reunion of the Lutheran and Reformed communities.[13] Pareus's ecumenical spirit certainly had an effect on Comenius, who would himself later champion a number of plans for confessional reconciliation. In 1614 Comenius returned to Moravia. He first taught for two years at his alma mater in Přerov, and then in 1616 he was ordained a priest of the Unity of Brethren.

The Bohemian Brethren, or *Unitas Fratrum,* were an offshoot of the Hussite movement. During the middle decades of the fifteenth century, this group slowly distinguished itself from the Bohemian Utraquists, many of whom would fall under the sway of Martin Luther.[14] The differences between the Brethren and the Utraquists were less doctrinal than structural. The *Unitas Fratrum* bound themselves together through an efficient system of church discipline and close-knit organization. Following a credo of nonviolence articulated by Peter Chelčický (1390–1460), they initially opposed all civil commitment and pursued a humble and ascetic lifestyle.[15] They struggled to survive as a group and periodically suffered intense persecution. In an effort to defend themselves, they issued fifty different editions of their confession over the course of 160 years.[16]

Comenius's family were devout members of the Bohemian Brethren. His first patron, Count Žerotín, was one of the most prominent adherents of the group. Žerotín's decision to send Comenius to Herborn was largely motivated by his desire to help foster a new generation of learned and qualified leaders for the Brethren.

Comenius's first parish was in the town of Fulnek, a predominately Catholic area near the border of Moravia and Silesia. Just before accepting the post, he married Magdalena Vizovská, a young woman from a wealthy family in Přerov. By all accounts the marriage was a happy one. His professional duties in Fulnek, however, were not as successful. The pastor of a religious minority, Comenius suffered the taunts and insults of the local Catholic clergy and populace. In the *Labyrinth,* Comenius probably alludes to his time in Fulnek when he relates:

> Ubiquitous kept on urging me to join the clergy, assuring me that I was destined to belong to this profession...I allowed myself to be persuaded, assumed cap and cowl, and stepped onto a platform beside others until my own was allotted to me. But looking about me, I saw some turning their backs on me. A second group shook their heads, a third glowered at me, a fourth threatened with their fists, a fifth pointed their fingers. Finally, some attacked me, drove me off, and put someone else in my place, threatening that there was more to come. (18.18)

His abrupt departure from Fulnek was brought about by the Thirty Years' War, the decisive turning point in Comenius's life.

As a small and isolated religious community, the *Unitas Fratrum* had long been vulnerable to the whims of their Habsburg overlords. A crisis occurred in 1619 with the death of King Matthias, who left no direct heir. Many of the Protestants of the country, including the *Unitas Fratrum,* took advantage of this situation to elect a Protestant ruler, Frederick, the elector Palatine of the Rhine. The Calvinist prince hurriedly made his way to Prague. But the new Habsburg Emperor, Ferdinand II, had no intention of letting Bohemia slip into the hands of the Protestants. A decisive battle was fought between the two sides outside Prague at White Mountain in November 1620. The Habsburg armies carried the day, and the entourage of Protestant King Frederick was forced into a hurried exile.

In the *Labyrinth,* Comenius notes how he also supported Frederick in the aborted Bohemian rebellion.[17] After the Catholic victory, he was forced into hiding. Fulnek was sacked, and Comenius's house was burned. Though his library was spared for the moment, Capuchin friars would later order its destruction. War was not the only cause of Comenius's sufferings. Fleeing the imperial army, he was compelled to leave behind his wife, who was pregnant with another child. She returned to her mother in Přerov, and there, along with her two children, she died from the plague in 1622. Comenius devotes a few lines to this loss in the *Labyrinth:*

> Suddenly a terrible storm struck unexpectedly, with lightning, thunder, and frightful hail. Everyone around me scattered, except for those who were joined to me. Though I also ran into a corner with them, the arrows of Death struck my three companions. (8.8)

Emotionally and physically exhausted, he found refuge on the estate of his former patron, Count Žerotín. Under trying conditions, Comenius began work on the *Labyrinth,* which he completed in 1623.

Between 1623 and 1628 Comenius remained a fugitive in the Czech lands. Though the Brethren survived under difficult circumstances in Bohemia and Moravia, their fate was officially determined in July 1627. The Habsburgs issued a decree proclaiming Catholicism the only official religion of state. The Protestant nobility had six months to convert or leave the country. In the middle of the sixteenth century, a branch of the *Unitas Fratrum* had emigrated to Poland, finding refuge in the village of Leszno near the Silesian border. In the spring of 1628, Comenius joined the small band of believers and led them across the border to Leszno. Comenius's exile had begun. He would never again enter Moravia or Bohemia.

Comenius remained in Leszno until 1641. He served as pastor of his refugee band and also directed the local gymnasium. It was in this period that he wrote one of his most important works on education, *The Great Didactic.* In this treatise, he argued that formal schooling was only part of the pedagogical process. All of life was a school designed to prepare humanity for eternity. For this reason, girls and boys were to be educated together. They were to be taught in a spontaneous and natural manner. By looking to nature, Comenius developed a rigorous pedagogical science that drew its laws by analogy from life. He argued that failure to learn was an indication that the instructor, not the student, was at fault. True learning was a pleasant and stimulating experience. To this day, Comenius's groundbreaking work is widely respected by child psychologists and educators alike.

With these pedagogical contributions, Comenius quickly became a European celebrity. Cardinal Richelieu invited him to France, and John Winthrop may have hoped he would accept a position as the first president of Harvard College.[18] Comenius also began correspondence with the Englishman Samuel Hartlib. In 1637 Hartlib had published one of Comenius's manuscripts, entitled "Christian Pansophy." Pansophism was an important late-Renaissance concept attempting to unite religion, philosophy, and science in a coherent and unified system. Hartlib was part of a circle of English intellectuals who were fascinated by Comenius's ideas. They invited him to London to help establish a pansophic college. Comenius recounts his rough sea voyage to England in the *Labyrinth,* but long-term plans to work in this country were put to an end by the Irish Rebellion in 1641.[19]

Comenius hoped to return to England after its internal troubles were settled. In the meantime, however, he accepted an invitation from Louis de Geer to go to Sweden and lead a reform of the country's schools. De Geer, a wealthy industrialist of the Low Countries, was the principal arms merchant for Gustavus Adolphus. Apart from establishing Sweden's metallurgical industry, de Geer became one of Comenius's most important patrons. His financial support would give Comenius the freedom to write and to minister to the dispersed congregations of the *Unitas Fratrum.*

On his way to Sweden, Comenius stopped off in a village near Leiden and had an historic meeting with the French philosopher René Descartes. Though the two had an amiable conversation, they came to no agreement, for Descartes's division between mind and matter was unacceptable to Comenius. He would later describe their meeting in his *Continuatio:*

> We exchanged speech for about four hours, he expounding to us the mysteries of his philosophy, I myself maintaining all human knowledge, such as derives from senses alone and reasonings thereon, to be imperfect and defective. We parted in friendly

fashion: I begging him to publish the principles of his philosophy (which principles were published the year following), and he similarly urging me to mature my own thoughts adding this maxim: 'Beyond the things that appertain to philosophy I go not; mine therefore is that only in part, whereof yours is the whole.'[20]

Comenius's stay in Swedish territory was frustrating both for himself and his hosts. He had hoped that his relationship with Chancellor Axel Oxenstierna would help the *Unitas Fratrum*. Comenius was convinced that Sweden, the strongest Protestant power of Europe, could arrange a settlement that would allow the Brethren to return to the Czech lands. He was bitterly disappointed by the 1648 Peace of Westphalia. Oxenstierna supported no such provision, and Comenius and his flock remained exiles.[21] Comenius also had difficulties with the Swedish Lutheran community, many of whom questioned his theological orthodoxy. In the end, he returned to Leszno and in 1648 became the twentieth and last bishop of the Bohemian Brethren.

In 1650, Comenius was invited by Prince Sigismund Rákóczy of Transylvania to oversee the development of a school at Sarospatak. The new bishop spent four years in Transylvania; but despite his efforts, the pansophic school was not a success. During this time at Sarospatak, however, he did write the *Orbis sensualium pictus.* This first picture book for children was quickly translated into the major European languages. It was immediately prior to this Hungarian interlude that Comenius met his former classmate, Nicholas Drabík. Drabík, along with the Silesian tanner Christoph Kotter and the Polish woman Christina Poniatowska, formed a circle of prophets whom Comenius held in high regard. He eagerly listened to their predictions concerning the imminent collapse of Habsburg rule in Bohemia. In 1657 Comenius published *Light in Darkness,* a voluminous tome containing the prophecies of his three colleagues.[22] Even in his own time, Comenius's credulous attachment to Drabík's circle damaged his reputation.

Comenius returned to Poland in July 1655. Disaster awaited him the following year. Comenius seems to have had a premonition of the troubles ahead. Early in the year he wrote a sermon on the Old Testament figure of Enoch. He noted that 1,656 years after Creation, the great flood had destroyed the earth. He wondered what new catastrophe would strike 1,656 years after the birth of Christ.[23] The answer soon came. War had recently broken out between Poland and Sweden. Rampaging Polish troops entered Leszno and burned the city to the ground. Though Comenius had escaped earlier to Silesia, his library was completely destroyed. His Czech and Latin dictionaries, a project that he had been working on for almost half a century, were lost. At age 64, he was forced into exile once again.

This time the refugee moved to Holland. He spent the remaining years of his life in Amsterdam as the guest of Lawrence de Geer, the son of his former patron. It was in the Low Countries that he completed his seven-volume *De rerum humanarum emendatione consultatio catholica,* the crowning achievement of his career. He intended these volumes to serve as a blueprint for the unification of all knowledge and a universal system of education. He argued that education in turn would lead to both an ecumenical religious settlement and worldwide peace.[24] During this last phase of his life, Comenius sought practical applications to the ideas that he had articulated earlier in the *Labyrinth.* A new war between England and the Netherlands had broken out in 1665. Urging a cessation of hostilities between the two Protestant countries, Comenius himself attended the peace conference at Breda in May 1667[25]. For this occasion he wrote the *Angel of Peace,* an indictment of these two commercial rivals. Three years later he was dead. His idealistic vision of a unified Europe remained unfulfilled, but echoes of his mandate would be heard in the following centuries. Perhaps the most fitting epitaph for this man is the one he wrote for the *Unitas Fratrum* after the Thirty Years' War when it became apparent that they would not survive as a unified body. In *The Bequest of the Unity of Brethren,* Comenius spoke for his persecuted church:

> To all Christian churches together I bequeath a lively desire for unanimity of opinion and for reconciliation among themselves, and for union in faith, and love of the unity of spirit. May the spirit which was given to me from the very beginning by the Father of spirits be shed upon you all, so that you would desire as

sincerely as I did the union of all who call upon the name of Christ in truth.[26]

Educational Ideals and the Message of the Labyrinth

The *Labyrinth* was recognized almost immediately as a masterpiece of Czech literature. In one of their hymns, the *Unitas Fratrum* commemorated their 1628 exile with a verse honoring the *Labyrinth:*

> Naught have we taken with us,
> All to destruction is hurled,
> We have only our Kralice Bibles
> And our *Labyrinth of the World.*[27]

In a famous letter to Leibniz, Comenius's grandson, D. E. Jablonksy, highly praised his grandfather's allegory.[28] A century later, Bohemia's greatest linguist, Josef Jungmann, boasted that the *Labyrinth* was "one of the most beautiful books in all of Czech literature."[29] Nonetheless, the *Labyrinth* remains a puzzling text. Its pietist emphases, the rejection of worldly values and the retreat of the soul into the heart's quiet sanctuary, seem to stand in contrast to the frenetic activity of Comenius's own life. This Moravian polymath was an active reformer whose career took him from Hungary to England. He was such a prolific writer that scholars today have a difficult time categorizing his contributions. Contemporary Comenian research is broadly segregated into four major areas: philosophy, social reform, pedagogical reform, and theology.

Those who have studied the *Labyrinth* have had difficulty placing it in its proper context. Most twentieth-century Slavic specialists have examined it as a landmark of Czech literature,[30] and there is no doubt that the *Labyrinth* is a literary and linguistic masterpiece. Comenius stated in the letter of dedication to *Labyrinth* that one of the reasons he wrote the text was to preserve and expand the use of his native tongue.[31] It must be remembered that he wrote the *Labyrinth* immediately after the imperial victory of White Mountain when the Czech language itself was under attack. By the eighteenth century, it had practically ceased to be used as a literary language. Karel Kučera has remarked, "The Czech of Comenius has an extraordinary functional range, and it represents the culmination of efforts to create a formally perfect literary language capable of the widest communication."[32]

Despite the important contributions of Czech linguists and literary scholars, there has been little effort to explain how the *Labyrinth* fits into a larger conception of Comenius's life and accomplishments. The more recent editions of the treatise have emphasized its relationship with other works of utopian literature of the period, but again have neglected to integrate Comenius's early treatise with a broader understanding of his career.[33] Indeed, one Norwegian scholar has commented that the appearance of such a mature work so early in Comenius's career cannot be easily explained.[34] For an honest assessment of Comenius's life, however, it is essential to place the *Labyrinth* in its proper context.

Comenius is best known for his pioneering work in education. The publication of his two textbooks, *Janua linguarum reserata* (1629–1631) and *Orbis pictus* (1658), brought him almost instant notoriety. Comenius saw the teaching of language as particularly problematic and argued that methods of rote memory and recitation should be abandoned in favor of more natural means. He noted that the mind of the child is more concerned with concrete objects than with the more abstract notions of grammatical constructions. Toward this end he wrote the *Janua,* a textbook that presented useful facts about the world both in Czech and Latin. The book was received enthusiastically and was quickly translated into a number of European languages.

At first glance, it would appear that the utopian vision of the *Labyrinth* has very little to do with Comenius's work as a pedagogical reformer; however, under closer examination, the *Labyrinth* offers a number of fascinating insights into the more general reform project that occupied his entire lifetime. Comenius's views as an educator were informed by a pansophic presupposition. Throughout his career, he sought a basic principle by which all human knowledge could be united. Education provided humanity with the means to see beneath the chaos of the world and discover the underlying harmony of God's universe.

In the *Labyrinth's* letter of introduction, Comenius echoes a number of these same themes. He notes that philosophers from antiquity had debated the issue of life's highest good. This matter is not merely an intellectual and spiritual issue, but a practical problem that besets people in every age. True happiness and satisfaction is an elusive quarry. Humans need proper training to help them distinguish the good from the bad. The *Labyrinth* was written to assist in this task.[35] It is in essence an early *Bildungsroman,* an extended lesson of perception, a journey through the world of the seventeenth century designed to help the reader uncover falsehood and discover truth.

Upon entering the world, the *Labyrinth's* protagonist, the curious pilgrim, is encumbered with a number of impediments designed to impair his sensory perception. He is joined by two guides who carefully monitor and direct his journey. One of his escorts is aptly named Delusion. At the same time, the pilgrim is forced to wear a bridle that constrains his movement, and his sight is blurred by a pair of spectacles that his guides fix to his nose. The pilgrim acquires these accoutrements even before he begins his inspection of the world. In the marginal notes and the preface, Comenius explains his allegory. The pilgrim's guides are "insatiability of Mind, which pries into everything, and Custom, which lends a color of truth to all the frauds of the world" (To the Reader, 6). The bridle is Vanity, and the glasses are constructed from the rims of Habit and the lens of Assumption (4.3–5).

The bridle, glasses, and guides are not the only obstructions to the pilgrim's sight. His entire world is full of deception and deceit. He starts his tour in the marketplace, where he observes people of all nations and languages and of every age and profession. As he looks more closely, however, he sees that each person milling in the crowd wears a mask that hides his true appearance. The pilgrim finds that it is only in private, far from the gaze of others, that those in the marketplace would remove their disguise. Later in his journey, the pilgrim visits the beautiful castle of Wisdom. But upon reaching the fortress, he is sadly disappointed:

> Looking at the building of the castle itself, I saw its gleaming white walls, which they told me were of alabaster. But examining them more carefully and touching them with my hands, I saw that they were made of nothing but paper, the cracks revealing occasional patches of tow. From this I judged that the walls were partly hollow and filled with stuffing. I was amazed at this deception and laughed aloud. (29.3)

The pilgrim also surveys a number of professions whose primary concern is the discovery of truth. Here again, he meets with frustration. He visits the furnaces of the alchemists, those scholars seeking mastery over the natural world. Though they make great claims, the pilgrim finds that their attempts to discover the philosopher's stone are all in vain. They either scald themselves in their workshops, die from asphyxiation, or simply go bankrupt (12). Historians fare no better. Though the guild pledges itself to find truth through the events of antiquity, more often than not historians distort the past to serve their own interests. Expressing his disillusionment with this trade, the pilgrim notes, "The image of one whom I had seen handsome and graceful in life now appeared monstrous. Conversely, they painted the most beautiful pictures of those who were in actuality ugly" (27.5). The pilgrim also spends time examining the work of astronomers, astrologers, metaphysicians, rhetoricians, and dialecticians (11). Though he is initially attracted to these various occupations, he consistently uncovers the fraud and deception of each profession that he is investigating. Dejected by his futile search for knowledge, the pilgrim concludes, "I have seen, observed, and acknowledged that neither I nor anyone else is anything, knows anything, or possesses anything. We only imagine that we do. We grasp at shadows while the truth everywhere eludes us" (28.4).

In the *Labyrinth,* Comenius specifically faults the educational system of his day for failing to equip students properly in the pursuit of truth. He devotes a large section of the text to a critical assessment of Europe's schools and universities. In stark terms, he depicts the often cruel and inhumane pedagogical methods of teachers and schoolmasters.[36] Pupils are compelled to study in a forced and unnatural manner. They memorize innumerable terms and names, but never wrestle with weightier intellectual issues.[37] Instructors also encourage their students to engage in useless argumentation. Though carried on with weapons of paper and ink, these academic squabbles are conducted in such a terrible and violent fashion that the pilgrim remarks, "I observed here a cruelty unusual elsewhere. They spared neither the wounded nor the dead, but mercilessly hacked and lashed at them all the more, each more gladly proving his valor against one who did not defend himself" (10.10).

To acquire a proper understanding of the world, Comenius argued that one needed the help of nature and the tools of empiricism. It is not surprising, then, that he castigated the stale art of memory and an overdependence on the supposed wisdom of the ancients. In the *Labyrinth,* the pilgrim visits a library and observes the vain efforts of scholars seeking truth from the past:

> I saw some people who behaved very greedily, stuffing themselves with whatever came into their hands. Observing them more care-fully, I noticed that they neither improved their complexion nor gained flesh or fat, but their stomachs were swollen and never sat-isfied. I also saw that what they crammed down into themselves came out of them again undigested, either from above or from below. Some of them fainted from dizziness or went mad. Others grew pale, pined, and died. Many who saw these people pointed at them, indicating how dangerous it was to use books...(10.7)

Comenius argued that far too often students were forced to grapple with difficult abstract concepts when a simple analogy drawn from the natural world would suffice. He himself notes, "The picture of the elephant if I have seen the animal, were it only a single time—even as an effigy—will remain fixed in me more easily and more strongly than if it had been described to me ten times."[38]

21

Comenius has little good to say concerning those who have survived the grueling process of academic training. One of the stops on the pilgrim's tour is a university graduation ceremony. Impressed with the pomp and fanfare of the collegiate ritual, he approaches one of the graduates and begins quizzing him. To his great chagrin, he quickly discovers that though this new graduate claims he is a master of the seven liberal arts, he actually knows none of them (16.3). It is not surprising that one of the heroes in the *Labyrinth* is Peter Ramus, the great champion of educational reform. He appears in a number of places in the text and is portrayed as a valiant crusader, tirelessly combatting the sophistry and sterility of the academy.[39]

The connection between the *Labyrinth* and Comenius's pedagogical reforms may best be seen in a comparison with his popular textbook *Orbis Pictus*. There are remarkable parallels between these two works. The *Orbis Pictus* was the first illustrated children's book.[40] On each page is an engraving of an everyday object. Below the illustration are two passages describing the details of the picture, one in Latin and the other in the student's vernacular. Comenius believed that the child's natural curiosity would be captured by the engravings. An aroused interest would make the otherwise monotonous process of learning Latin an enjoyable experience.

Comenius maintained that for learning to be effective, all the senses needed to be engaged. True education was not an abstract exercise of the intellect. In the preface he notes:

> And therefore to exercise the senses well about the right perceiving of the differences of things will be to lay the grounds for all wisdom, all wise discourse and all discrete actions in one's course of life. Which, because it is commonly neglected in schools, and the things which are to be learned are offered to scholars without being understood or being rightly presented to the senses, it comes to pass that the work of teaching and learning goes heavily onward and affords little benefit.[41]

The *Orbis Pictus* was designed to activate the senses. The student who used it would be encouraged to imagine the heat of a roaring fire, the taste of sweet honey, the smell of daffodils, and the sights and sounds of a terrible storm at sea.[42]

The *Labyrinth* was constructed in much the same way. Comenius escorts the reader on a long search for truth. The pilgrim uses all his senses to detect the frauds of the world. With his eyes, he sees the hollow walls of the castle of Wisdom. He visits the musicians who claim they can approach the divine through their art; but after he hears the noise they create, he realizes that their profession too is a sham (11.12). With his nose, he detects the ultimate end of the hedonists he encounters. Though they hide in dark corners, the pilgrim smells the syphilitic stench of those whom the disease has infected (25.7). The pilgrim's graphic account of seasickness is an effective warning to those considering the profession of a sailor;[43] and when he is tempted by the pleasures of revellers, he discovers after tasting their food and sampling their beverages that "something began to gnaw under my coat, to sting under my cap, to force itself out of my throat; my legs began to stagger, my tongue to stutter, my head to spin" (26.5).

In the *Labyrinth,* the pilgrim surveys the world's broad theater. He visits humanity's every class, estate, and profession in an attempt to discover wisdom. This encyclopedic scope was characteristic of Comenius and was certainly an important aspect of the *Orbis Pictus* as well. In its preface, he states that he had designed this Latin primer as a "little encyclopedia of things subject to the senses."[44] In a manner similar to the *Labyrinth,* Comenius systematically leads the reader through the world of the seventeenth century. Comenius's textbook begins with a description of the four elements and continues with an exploration of the plant and animal kingdoms. He then proceeds by examining the human community. Starting simply by describing the body, he moves on to a thorough examination of the various professions of early modern society. He concludes the *Orbis Pictus* with a discussion of the western world's three major religions.

Although there are a number of structural parallels between the two texts, there is a more profound spiritual link between them. Comenius introduces the preface of the *Orbis Pictus* with a citation from Genesis:

INTRODUCTION

> The Lord God brought unto Adam every beast of the field, and
> every fowl of the air, to see what he would call them. And Adam
> gave names to all cattle, and to the fowl of the air and to every
> beast of the field.[45]

Comenius's Latin primer was designed as a basic naming exercise. A series of objects are numbered in each engraving. The student could find the appropriate name for the item by matching the number in the picture with the same number in the text. Comenius believed this drill would become an entertaining game of correspondence that would facilitate the learning process. But learning the proper word for everyday objects was only one aspect of the naming exercise. Ultimately, it had a moral and spiritual significance.

The first engraving of the *Orbis Pictus* depicts an elderly gentleman meeting his young student. This teacher does not encourage his pupil to study diligently or master his lessons perfectly, but instead greets him with the words, "Come, boy, learn to be wise."[46] The naming process becomes an ethical exercise of identifying vice and choosing virtue. The student first encounters a symbolic depiction of God, whom Comenius describes in the corresponding text as life's highest good.[47] Comenius scatters a number of moral lessons throughout the work. He devotes an entire section to the various virtues one should cultivate.[48] Prudence, diligence, and temperance are elevated for the student's emulation. The final portion of the book concerns itself with religion. Paganism, Judaism, and Islam are discussed, but Christianity is identified as the true path to God. The *Orbis Pictus* ends with an apocalyptic vision of the Last Judgment. The teacher reminds his pupil that God's wisdom is the final goal of true education.[49]

In the *Labyrinth,* the pilgrim is also involved in a naming exercise. His world is a place where titles deceive and names mislead. At one point on his journey, the pilgrim is brought to the palace of wisdom. Here a proclamation is issued that banishes the conspirators: Drunkenness, Greed, Usury, Lechery, Pride, Cruelty, Laziness, and Idleness. Heartened by this decree, the pilgrim is puzzled to hear that some of these exiles have supposedly slipped back into the kingdom:

24

[A commission] reported that they had indeed discovered some suspicious characters. These suspects did not consider themselves among the banished, however, and they also bore different names. One resembled Drunkenness, but he was called Intoxication or Merriment; the second resembled Greed, but was called Economy; the third resembled Usury, but was called Interest; the fourth was like Lechery, but they called him Graciousness; the fifth was similar to Pride, but was called Dignity; the sixth resembled Cruelty, but was called Severity; the seventh was like Laziness, but bore the name Good-naturedness; and so forth. (32.5)

This incident in the pilgrim's travels points to a larger project of the *Labyrinth*. Comenius's allegory was designed to help the reader name the phenomena of the world. Despite their misleading titles, the pilgrim learns how to distinguish virtue from vice and good from evil. This type of critical discernment was foundational for Comenius's pedagogical reforms; and though the *Labyrinth* and the *Orbis Pictus* were written for different audiences, they are united by this common goal.

Comenius outlined his educational principles in the *Panaugia* (Universal Dawn), the second volume of his magnum opus, the *Consultatio*. According to Comenius, God has provided humanity with three tools to learn wisdom: the five senses to discover the secrets of the natural world; reason and intelligence to increase their knowledge; and faith, for it is only with this spiritual gift that God's children may hear his voice through Scripture, meditation, or prayer. These three bases of Comenius's pedagogical reforms are central components of the *Labyrinth*.

By his senses and natural reason, the pilgrim begins to detect the fraud and hypocrisy of the world. His guides attempt to allure him with earthly riches and pleasures. Each time he is tempted, however, he is able to discover the moral flaw of the class he is examining. Although his sight is blurred by the spectacles Delusion has given him, the pilgrim can make these observations by surreptitiously peering under them (4.6). But human reason and sensory perception have their limits. With them, the pilgrim is only able to discover the deception and chaos of the world. The harmony and unity underlying this confusion can only be discerned through revelation. When the pilgrim meets Christ, he is given a new pair of spectacles. The Word of God and the Holy Spirit replace the lens of Assumption and rim of Habit (41.1). With these new aids, the pilgrim is able to reenter the world's labyrinth, confident in his ability to negotiate its tortuous passages successfully.

The labyrinth was one of Comenius's favorite metaphors to describe the world. He used it in his pedagogical works to depict the confused and twisted nature of human knowledge.[50] He also returned to it in *Unum necessarium* (1668), a spiritual treatise he wrote only a few years before his death. He explains that God's world was transformed by sin from a theater of his wisdom to a labyrinth of deception. There is only one exit from this maze, and that way out can only be discovered through the long process of education. Though this assertion may seem antithetical to the life of faith and grace, education was for Comenius a spiritual exercise. The pupil was not only to distinguish vice from virtue and falsehood from truth, but to turn away from the former and embrace the latter. Education, therefore, was a form of repentance. In *Unum necessarium,* Comenius turns to his own life and describes his pedagogical innovations as reforms intended to lead others out of the labyrinth.[51]

Bracketing his long career, the *Labyrinth of the World* and *Unum necessarium* express in different ways the central feature of his life's work. For Comenius, education was in essence a pastoral calling.[52] It was the process by which people could be trained to see beyond the apparent chaos of the world and discover the underlying harmony of God's universe. This pansophic pursuit lies at the heart of the *Labyrinth.* This work, then, is not simply an expression of narrow pietism, nor is it merely a utopian alternative composed in response to personal tragedy. On one level it is a pedagogical allegory, a creative examination of the educational process. It is an inchoate expression of ideas he would develop more fully in his later writings.

Comenius's Spirituality and the Themes of the Labyrinth

If the structure and message of the *Labyrinth* are closely connected with Comenius's lifelong work as a pedagogical reformer, it is equally true that he perceived his educational endeavors as part of his broader calling as a theologian. Concerning his *Great Didactic,* Comenius wrote in 1657, "What I have written for youth I have written, not as a pedagogue, but as a theologian."[53] Similarly, his preoccupation with the Greek concept *pan* is no mere philosophical fetish, for Comenius's entire pansophical program is undergirded by the theological conviction that all truth is God's truth.

Regarding the precise content of Comenius's theology, however, we find ourselves on less certain footing. The *Unitas Fratrum,* the church in which the Moravian was raised and with which he always identified, was more a tradition of confessions, catechisms, and hymns than of great speculative theologians whose doctrinal emphases can be traced in Comenius's writings.[54] Moreover, the Brethren were moving from attempts at rapprochement with the Lutherans toward a more Reformed expression of the Christian faith during the late sixteenth and early seventeenth centuries. Comenius himself was a conciliatory spirit who longed for the peaceful unification of the splintered Protestant confessions and was therefore less likely to emphasize sectarian distinctives. Some scholars have found his work as a theologian and pastor so puzzling or so disconnected from his better-known pedagogical efforts that they have chosen the phrase "der andere Comenius" to describe this aspect of his career.[55]

Although his theology has received more attention in recent years, Comenius's spirituality remains virtually unexplored terrain. In fact, two of his three main spiritual writings have not yet been published in English translation.[56] There is no single work devoted to his notion of spiritual life, and most treatments of spirituality in the seventeenth century either mention Comenius only in passing, if at all, or quickly dismiss him as a fanatic because of his chiliastic beliefs.[57]

Among those scholars who have touched on spiritual themes in his works, most have emphasized Comenius's indebtedness to the utopian writings of the German Lutheran John Valentin Andreae.[58] A few have connected his ideas with late medieval mystics, particularly Nicholas of Cusa.[59] Others have suggested the influence of Jakob Boehme and Johann Arndt or have seen Comenius as a precursor of the Pietists.[60] Elsewhere he has been linked with Count Nicholas von Zinzendorf or with certain Puritan spiritual writers.[61] There is some validity in all these associations.

In the three works central to his spirituality—*The Labyrinth of the World, Centrum securitatis,* and *Unum necessarium*—Comenius expresses a rich Protestant and biblical spirituality that drew from and contributed to several Christian traditions. In the *Labyrinth,* the earliest of these three treatises, the Moravian paints a vivid picture of humanity, the world, and the church gone wrong; Christ's rescue from the world's labyrinth; and the joyful experience of new birth and renewed life through union with the living God. We will examine these topics in turn while also considering the individuals and traditions that helped shape Comenius's spiritual perspective.

The overall theme of the work is pilgrimage to the place of the soul's rest and happiness. Here Comenius echoes a common theme of medieval spirituality. In his preface to the readers of the *Labyrinth,* the author suggests that all people naturally desire to attain to the highest good and inevitably seek the source of complete happiness. He explains, however, that "almost all people look outside themselves, seeking the means to calm and quiet their minds in the world and its possessions: this one in property and riches, that one in delights and pleasure; one in glory and status, another in wisdom and learning, yet another in merry companionship" (To the Reader, 2). Since God has opened his eyes to the deceptiveness and vanity of the world, he continues, his purpose in the *Labyrinth* is to expose this reality to others. Toward this end "I devised this journey or wandering through the world in which I recount the monstrous things I beheld or encountered and where and how I discovered the desired happiness that is vainly sought in the world" (To the Reader, 4).

INTRODUCTION

The pilgrim's spiritual journey in search of the highest good and the autobiographical nature of much of Comenius's allegory recall Augustine's *Confessions,* though his later *Unum necessarium* bears even greater resemblance to this work. Indeed, both works are scattered with tacit borrowings from Augustine. Although the journey is inward on one level—for the pilgrim must finally enter into the recesses of his own heart to find the peace and meaning he seeks—the first half of the *Labyrinth* does not really describe the inner development of the soul that so occupies the author of the *Confessions* and the medieval mystics. Comenius's education at the Reformed gymnasium in Herborn may have been influential in this regard, for his teachers would not have embraced such an understanding of the spiritual life. The journey through the labyrinth is not one of stages or degrees in the progress of the soul, but of observation, experience, and testing of the manifold professions and affairs of men and women. It is a journey that ultimately leads to despair.

Unlike Bunyan's Christian in *Pilgrim's Progress,* to which the protagonist of the *Labyrinth* has been compared, Comenius's pilgrim is not portrayed as a weak or easily beguiled victim of constant temptations.[62] Nor is he motivated to undertake his journey by fear of God's judgment or disgust with his former manner of life. He sets out with a sense of expectation and inquisitiveness, confident in his powers of reason and judgment. "I came to the decision that I would first observe all human affairs under the sun," relates the pilgrim. "Then, after having wisely compared one with another, I would choose a profession..." (1.5). Although the pilgrim allows himself to be led by the dubious guides Ubiquitous and Delusion and is at first favorably impressed by the seeming peace and order of each of the classes and occupations he observes, he is not completely deceived. By examining each scene more closely, he is soon able to discern the reality behind the harmonious facades he encounters. This portrayal of the pilgrim emphasizes the power of human reason, which Comenius considered, along with nature and Holy Scripture, one of the three books of divine truth.[63] Though imperfect and insufficient by itself to lead the pilgrim to his goal, reason is a wonderful gift of God that should be diligently employed for the discovery of truth. It equips the pilgrim to comprehend and critique the scenes he is shown.

The journey through the labyrinth is intended to depict the senselessness and chaos of a world that has lost sight of its Creator and his purposes for life. The pilgrim becomes increasingly disillusioned with what he observes, realizing that all the apparent harmony and order is a sham; all the allurements of his guides and enticements of individuals he meets along the way are only empty promises. The message of this half of the work is perhaps best expressed by the passage from Ecclesiastes that Comenius chose as an epigraph for the treatise: "I have seen all the works which are done under the sun, and behold, all is vanity and vexation of spirit" (Eccl. 1:14).

The notion of the labyrinth itself provides an apt metaphor for the confusion and deception of the world. Adapted from the classical myth to which Comenius alludes in the text (2.2), it was a common symbol in ancient and medieval sources.[64] Comenius employs it here, as in his later *Unum necessarium,* to portray the calamitous effects of sin.[65] The world has become a labyrinth in which its inhabitants are doomed to wander, confused, deceived, and alienated from God. They seek meaning in meaningless created things rather than in their Creator. Since God is the center and source of all being and harmony, a theme Comenius would develop more fully a few years later in his *Centrum securitatis,* the further human beings move away from this center, the more chaotic and unblessed their lives become.[66]

Comenius emphasizes the meaninglessness of this world by using the genre of *negative allegory.*[67] Whereas an allegory uses symbols to help explain the real meaning of objects, relationships, or ideals, the negative allegory employs the same technique to strip meaning away, to expose a reality devoid of significance. Thus, for example, in the marketplace of the world, people labor strenuously at such futile tasks as collecting and distributing garbage or chasing after their own shadows (7.6). Marriage is a process of weighing and shackling unhappy victims; and screaming, stinking children are attached to their parents with bridles,

30

which nonetheless fail to restrain their mischief. This technique of divesting reality of meaning is particularly prominent in the pilgrim's wanderings among the learned classes where historians look through backward-curved telescopes; poets weigh and measure syllables; mathematicians sort through, heap up, and separate piles of numbers; and lawyers scurry up to clients, ignoring their complaints but examining their purses. The books of academics are described as "little boxes" that scholars carry about for appropriate occasions, drawing from them "whatever was needed for their mouth or pen" (10.7). In similar terms, he describes the senseless labors of students:

> I saw others who did not bother carrying the boxes of books in their pockets, but brought them to their rooms. Going in after them, I saw that they prepared beautiful cases for them. They painted them in various colors, and some even adorned them with silver and gold. They looked at the books, putting them on and taking them off the shelves again. They packed and unpacked them, and approaching and withdrawing, they showed each other and strangers how beautiful they looked...Occasionally some also looked at the titles so that they would know what they were called. (10.8)

The use of this literary technique is similar to the treatment of the *civitas terrena* in sections of *City of God* in which the author attempts to portray the worthlessness of pagan civilization.[68] In fact, Comenius's presentation of two parallel and contrasting worlds, the labyrinth and paradise, recalls the Augustinian notion of two cities. Like Augustine, and unlike later Enlightenment thinkers who readily employed negative allegory, Comenius uses the device only to describe one side of reality, the city or the labyrinth of this world. His pilgrim finds everything in the world to be the opposite of what it ought to be; and the true church, which he will finally encounter in the second half of the work, is "the world turned upside down" (41.5).

In the first half of the treatise, however, neither the clergy nor the church at large are spared the pilgrim's examination and consequent disappointment. His critique of the Christian religion reveals many of the shortcomings Comenius found in the

31

various religious confessions of his day and his own longing for a simple expression of Christian spirituality and a pure, loving, and orderly Christian church. Among the clergy in the labyrinth, the pilgrim finds men indulging in all kinds of impious and wanton behavior. "They spend the least time with the Bible," he laments, "some hardly even picking it up, yet calling themselves teachers of the Word" (18.8). Some of them "preached very eloquent and pious sermons and were regarded by themselves and others as no less than angels fallen from heaven. Yet their lives were as dissolute as the rest" (18.9).

The pilgrim is particularly appalled by the constant disputes and quarrels that arose among the Christians he observed. Unable to agree about the gospel, they dispersed into different chapels. "Each drew a certain group of people after him and gave them rules regarding how they should differ from others" (18.14). Such descriptions allude to the hardening of orthodoxy and the rise of intolerance that had come to prevail in the Lutheran and Reformed traditions, as well as among the Catholic authorities who were purging Bohemia of all Protestants during the very time that Comenius was writing. It was against a background of confessional hostility that Comenius would develop his irenic plan for the unification of all Christendom.

The *Unitas Fratrum* was marked by a strong ecumenical orientation. Their very name was carefully chosen to avoid insinuating any exclusive claim to be the church. They emphasized the necessity of salvation in Christ and his lordship over the church and the world. Ecclesiology was always to be placed in the service of soteriology. The distinction between those elements that are essential, instrumental, and incidental to salvation was one of the most important principles of the Brethren's theology.[69] Comenius's thought reflects this threefold division, around which he would later organize the hymns he edited and composed for his 1659 revision of the Czech hymnbook.[70] His spiritual as well as his ecumenical writings insist on the need to cling to what is necessary and to put aside all else.

The Erasmian spirit of this theological notion has been noted, and indeed in several places the Moravian expressed admiration for the views of the great Christian humanist.[71] But an emphasis on the essential and practical over the speculative and theoretical was characteristic of Brethren theology already prior to the writings of Erasmus. It is in this spirit of simplicity that Comenius wrote the following words in *Unum necessarium:*

> If someone should ask about my theology, I would seize the Bible (with the dying Aquinas, for I myself am also about to die), and would say with all my heart and in a plain language: 'I believe all that is written in this book!' If someone should inquire more closely about my confession of faith, I would show him the Apostle's Creed, for I know nothing shorter, simpler, or pithier, nothing that could sooner bring me to a decision in all controversies and save me the endless labyrinths of disputation. If someone should ask me for a book of prayers, I would point him to the Lord's Prayer. For I am persuaded that no one can show a key that opens the Father's heart easier than the only-begotten Son who proceeded from the Father. If he should ask about my rules of life, I would show the Decalogue, for I am sure that no one can say better what is pleasing to God than God himself.[72]

The Christians the pilgrim observes in the *Labyrinth* stand in stark contrast to this profession. They are embroiled in endless labyrinths of disputation, squabbling over petty details and forgetting what is essential.

We are given a hint that true Christians do indeed dwell within the labyrinth, for the pilgrim catches sight of some who "walked silently, as if in deep thought, looking often to heaven and conducting themselves kindly toward all" (18.17). Unfortunately, his guide dissuades him from a closer examination of this group, and the pilgrim only realizes afterward how grievously he erred at this crucial juncture. Growing more and more disillusioned, he allows himself to be led further along the tangled streets of the world's maze.

Before the account of the pilgrim's exit from the labyrinth, Comenius includes an episode (chapters 31–35) that sheds light on his understanding of the plight of spiritual Christians. The account starts in a positive vein. King Solomon arrives with his retinue at the Palace of Wisdom, and the pilgrim is hopeful that he will now receive a trustworthy guide. Solomon begins to expose the vanities and deceptions of the world, starting with the Queen herself. He pulls off her expensive-looking veil, which turns out to be nothing but a spider's web, and discloses a pale, bloated, painted, and peeling face. He then proceeds to unmask the Queen's counselors, exposing the fraud beneath their assumed character. But before long, the Queen and her counselors conspire to outwit and seduce the wise king. Solomon is flattered by all the attention he receives, and his entanglement in worldly affairs eventually leads him to wanton behavior and crass idolatry. Chapter 35 describes the fate of his followers. Seeing Solomon so deluded, they are enraged and indignant. They vow to take no part in such abominations and warn others against them. As a result, they are deemed "public enemies of the world" and are brutally attacked and put to death before a cheering crowd (35.4).

The theme of "expelled Truth" that unfolds in this Solomon interlude has a long history in classical and medieval authors.[73] Christian writers found apt sources for this theme in the crucifixion of Christ and the martyrdom or persecution of faithful believers. It became particularly popular in the late Middle Ages. Certain Czech "Songs of Truth" even present the wanderings of Truth through the world, only to be driven away at every turn. The Hussites found an embodiment of the story in Jan Hus, and Hussite songs often incorporated the theme of expelled Truth. The parable was certainly known to Comenius, though he may not have drawn it from any one source in particular. Interestingly enough, the episode was only inserted into the text of the *Labyrinth* in the 1663 edition. Perhaps Comenius's bitter personal experience of exile and the expulsion of the Brethren from their homeland contributed to his reflections on this theme.

At this point in the text, Comenius's pilgrim is completely overcome by despair. Not only has he found the world devoid of truth and justice, but he now discovers that it is inimical to these values. The cruel death of the righteous at the end of this episode marks his final disgust with the world. He abandons all hope of ever reaching his goal. He attempts to flee the world, convinced that even a thousand deaths would be preferable to life in such a wretched place.

In the midst of his despair, however, he hears a "soft voice" bidding him to return (37.1). With this summons, Comenius begins to describe Christ's intervention to rescue the protagonist. The pilgrim does not know where to turn until the voice sounds a third time, giving the following command: "Return whence you came, to the home of your heart, and shut the door behind you!" Though still confused, the pilgrim obeys the voice as well as he can. After closing off all external passages, he confesses, "I entered into my heart and found that it was dark." What follows is Comenius's vivid, allegorical portrayal of corrupt human nature:

> I distinguished up above in the vault of this little chamber a large, round, glass window. But it was so dirty and smeared with grime that hardly any light could penetrate...I perceived some pictures on the walls, which seemed once to have been beautiful, but now the colors were faded and the limbs of some of the people were severed or broken. Approaching them more closely, I noticed the inscriptions: Prudence, Humility, Justice, Purity, Temperance, and so forth. In the middle of the chamber, I saw some broken and damaged ladders strewn about; likewise, broken pulleys and ropes, and large wings with broken feathers. Finally, clock-wheels with broken or bent cylinders, teeth and rods were all scattered randomly here and there. I wondered what was the purpose of these instruments, how and by whom they had been damaged and how they could be repaired. (37.3–5)

While he is pondering over this disrepair, Christ breaks into the dark chamber of the pilgrim's heart in a burst of brilliant light. Christ greets him with kindly words of welcome and a warm embrace. He then explains how the pilgrim has strayed by seeking happiness and rest in the world rather than in God. He assures him, however, that in his loving providence he has actually been guiding the pilgrim along the strange and circuitous paths of the labyrinth to himself. Through this wandering, says Christ, the pilgrim has learned that "Neither the world, nor your guides, nor Solomon could teach you anything; they could in no way enrich you, fulfill you, or satisfy the desires of your heart, for they did not have within them that which you sought. But I will teach you everything. I will enrich you. I will satisfy you" (39.1).

Christ continues by describing what it means to be united to himself, the theme that dominates the rest of the treatise. In a chapter entitled "Their Betrothal" Comenius employs bridal language to express the relationship between the Christian and his Lord. "The pilgrim should be joined only with Christ, the eternal bridegroom," he writes in the margin; and he ends this subsection of the text with Christ's loving call to his son, "Let us close ourselves together in this chamber, and you will experience truer pleasures than can be found in earthly marriage...Cling only to me, gaze only on me, converse sweetly with me, embrace me, kiss me; and in turn, expect all these things from me" (39.3). Assuming a more didactic tone, Christ reviews the experiences of the pilgrim in the labyrinth, describing how the world has perverted all his purposes and how in him the pilgrim will now find the goals, desires, and relationships he had sought in the world.

The pilgrim does not hesitate to describe the delight of his soul and a range of other emotions evoked by his encounter with the living Lord. Nevertheless, both in this chapter and throughout the *Paradise of the Heart,* he has less to say about the actual experience of union with Christ and much more to relate about its effects and fruit in the life of the Christian and the church. The gaze, the kiss, the embrace—common terms in descriptions of mystical union—are to be anticipated from Christ, but they are used here primarily to describe the pilgrim's response to God's tender love and care.

The Brethren as a group were not accustomed to introspection. Comenius is thus stepping beyond the framework of his tradition by focusing so closely on the heart and soul of the believer.[74] But it is the individual and total response of the believer to Christ's pledge of himself and his abundant blessings that is prominent here and that is fundamental to Comenius's spirituality. In keeping with this emphasis, the description of the "betrothal" concludes with the pilgrim's words of personal surrender and commitment to Christ:

Lord, my God, I understand that you alone are everything. Whoever has you can easily dispense with the whole world, because in possessing you there is more than one can desire. Now I understand that I erred, wandering through the world and seeking rest in created things. But from this hour I desire no delight apart from you. Now, at this moment, I submit myself wholly to you. Only strengthen me, that I might not again fall away from you to created things, committing once more those follies of which the world is full. (39.16)

The pilgrim's loving surrender to Christ in response to God's initiative brings about a radical transformation. Like Johann Arndt, whose devotional classic *True Christianity* (1606) had become extremely popular during Comenius's years of study in Herborn,[75] the Moravian places great emphasis on the new birth and the consequent renewal of the believer's life. Like Arndt, he speaks of the new birth in terms of the restoration of the ruined image of God in fallen humanity, a favorite metaphor of the Pietists.[76] The notion of human beings as the image of God plays a central role in Comenius's theology and educational reforms.[77] Here in the *Labyrinth*, however, he does not use theological language to explain the renewal of the image, but returns to the picture of the obscure and disorderly chamber of the heart, cited above. Where darkness once prevailed, a great light begins to shine; the scratched and deformed pictures are restored to their original wholeness and beauty; the scattered and broken wheels are joined together into a marvelous clock-like instrument; the broken ladders are repaired; and the plucked wings are restored with new, large feathers. Christ explains that the pilgrim will henceforth dwell in two places, for he himself dwells both "in heaven and in the penitent heart on earth." By means of the wings, Christ continues, "whenever you wish, you will be able to raise yourself up to me so that we may experience delight in one another" (40.1).

Lest the pilgrim begin to imagine that the Christian life consists only in such moments of rapture alone with his Lord, he is immediately sent to the invisible church. Christ explains that he has servants who "live in the world scattered among others, but the world does not know them" (41.1). He gives the pilgrim new glasses with which to discern more clearly the vanities of the world and the life of his servants. The pilgrim then returns to the place where he had earlier strayed. There, behind the exterior and interior curtain, called *Contemptus mundi* and *Amor Christi,* he beholds the community of "true Christians," as he is wont to call them throughout the *Paradise of the Heart.*

Unlike Schwenkfeld and other spiritualists, Comenius consistently links the renewed believer with the reformed church. The *Unitas Fratrum,* like both the Pietists and the Puritans after them, felt that the task of the Reformation was unfinished. It had rightly identified the errors of the papacy and corrected many doctrinal abuses, but it had failed to bring about the moral transformation of the church and society. The Bohemian Brethren embraced the Reformation of Luther and Calvin but also identified with the earlier reformation of Waldensians, Hussites, and Taborites.[78] For Comenius, therefore, not a second or third but a total reformation of the church was necessary.[79] His most extensive development of the theme of church reform occurs in his *Haggaeus redivivus* (1632). However, strong convictions are already evident in the *Labyrinth.*

In the remainder of the *Paradise of the Heart,* images of the transformed Christian life are interspersed with pictures of the true spiritual church. Comenius admits at the beginning of the treatise that his portrayal of true Christians is presented "more as an ideal rather than a full picture of what befalls all the elect." Nonetheless, he hopes it will motivate his readers "to desire the same degree of perfection" (To the Reader, 7). Certainly his treatment of the new creature and the new church in this section reveals many of his own spiritual ideals and longings.

Along with the necessity of new birth, Comenius stresses the necessity of a truly changed life. Though he does not deny that Christians have burdens to bear and hardships to endure, he insists that "all things are light and easy for hearts devoted to God" (45). Comenius's pilgrim is suspicious of those who claim to be Christians yet repeatedly yield to sin, or worse still, who attempt to excuse their misbehavior. Observing the joyful obedience of true believers, he affirms:

I understood that those who so often excuse themselves on the grounds that they are only human do not realize the power and effect of the new birth and perhaps have not experienced it. Therefore let them take heed! I did not see any among the true Christians who justified their sins by virtue of the weakness of the flesh or excused a misdeed committed because of the frailty of human nature. Rather, I saw that if a person committed his whole heart to the One who had created it, redeemed it, and sanctified it as a temple, his other limbs followed after his heart, willingly and gradually inclining in whichever direction God desired. (45.1)

Comenius's focus on outward obedience as the necessary expression of true inner transformation reflects no simple moralism. Rather it flows from the Christology of the Brethren, who emphasized the lordship of Christ and his kingly rule on earth. Christ's royal authority should be evident both in the personal life of the believer and in the church.[80] In keeping with this doctrinal conviction, in his *Bequest of the Unity of Brethren,* Comenius admonishes the Lutherans, for he feared they had undermined their treasured doctrine of justification by faith through the disorderly conduct of certain members and a general lack of discipline in their churches. He warns them that "knowledge of Christ without the following of Christ, and rejoicing in the gospel without the keeping of the law of love in which the gospel is founded, is nothing less than an abuse of the gospel."[81]

Indeed, the portrayal of the community of true Christians in the *Labyrinth* seems to be more akin to the Reformed vision of the church, with which Comenius had become well acquainted during his studies at Herborn. His description of the common life of believers emphasizes the harmonious order and loving discipline that he felt were best exemplified in the tradition of the *Unitas Fratrum.*[82] Such order reflects God's own orderly governance of the world, which true Christians, who have had their reason purified and sharpened by the Holy Spirit, can discern.

Comenius returns to his clock metaphor to describe God's marvelous, providential direction of both the world and its inhabitants. "Before me I saw the world as a great clock-like machine," recounts the pilgrim. It was composed of countless shafts, wheels, hooks, teeth, and notches, which were mysteriously kept in motion by the central and principal wheel. Despite the wobbling and slipping of various parts, the pilgrim is amazed and delighted to observe that "the general movement never stopped. It was maintained by some wondrous and mysterious means of direction that constantly replaced, restored, and renewed everything" (42.4).

The life of spiritual Christians should reflect this harmony, and this is precisely what the pilgrim observes in the true church. It stands in complete opposition to all that he saw and experienced in his journey through the labyrinth.

> In the world I had seen blindness and darkness everywhere, but here bright light; in the world deception, here truth; the world was full of disorder, here was marvelous order; in the world was striving, here peace; in the world were cares and concerns, here joy; in the world was want, here abundance; in the world were slavery and bondage, here freedom; in the world all was toilsome and difficult, here all was easy; there tragic accidents everywhere, here perfect safety. (41.5)

Likewise, in a chapter entitled "The Code of True Christians" (44), Comenius outlines the simple and orderly spiritual life of God's children. It is based on the Ten Commandments, the love of God and neighbor, unanimity among Christians, compassion, sharing of possessions, and mutual friendship.

The pilgrim also examines the classes and occupations of the true Christians; and again, in stark contrast to what he had seen in the world, he finds excellent order. He describes the joyful union of married Christians, the solicitude and reverence of rulers, the humility of the learned who "directed all their learning to Christ, the center" (50.4). Unlike the squabbling priests and theologians of the *Labyrinth,* here the clergy spent more time with God in prayer, reading, and meditation than with people. Endowed with truth, life, and vigor, their sermons consistently moved the hearts of believers. Having received the blessing of one of these elderly preachers, the pilgrim announces, "I truly understood that genuine theology is something more powerful and more penetrating than what is generally experienced" (50.5).[83]

It is the experience of Christ's loving presence that is paramount among true Christians. Comenius understood that it was possible to have the outward form and yet miss the inner reality of faith in Christ. It was this tendency that he observed among the Reformed. Although he praises the Swiss Church for its "love of order and discipline," in the *Bequest* he also expresses his desire "that thou mayest really possess the precious realities which thou imaginest to enjoy. Lest, deceiving thyself, thou mayest be content with the husks instead of penetrating to the kernel."[84] Accordingly, he admonishes them to demonstrate piety and discipline "not only in appearance but in reality," and to pursue a life of "more simplicity and less speculation," especially concerning the divine mysteries.[85] Comenius issued no warning to believers in the *Paradise of the Heart,* for their lives already encompassed both the form and the reality he so coveted for the church as a whole. The pilgrim can express only admiration. The lives of the true Christians he observes are not only marked by contentment, peace, and orderliness, but by constant joy in the experience of God's love. The pilgrim himself is caught up in this wonderful experience and can hardly express or contain his delight.

> I saw, perceived, recognized, and understood that to possess God and his heavenly treasures is so glorious that the glory, splendor, and brilliance of the whole world cannot be compared with it. It is so joyful that the whole world can neither add to nor detract from it. It is so lofty that the whole world can neither understand nor comprehend it...That is the sweetness that the world does not understand; that is the sweetness that if anyone but tastes, he must boldly attempt everything for its sake; the sweetness from which no other sweetness can entice, no bitterness drive away, no delight allure, no disaster, not even death itself, can divert us...Oh, Lord Jesus, how sweet you are to hearts that have tasted you! (49.1–3)

Toward the end of the *Labyrinth,* the pilgrim is given a vision of the glory of God enthroned in heaven. From the midst of this majestic scene, modeled on Revelation 4, the Lord Jesus speaks to the pilgrim for the last time in this treatise. Christ's message highlights an aspect of Comenius's spirituality that is not emphasized elsewhere in the *Labyrinth,* but is central to his thought and lifelong labors. After assuring the pilgrim of his forgiveness and his reception in God's household, the Lord commands him to return to the world. A transformed individual and a renewed church must bring about renewal in society. Confessional hostilities and particularly the tragedy of the Thirty Years' War caused many pious Christians to withdraw from the world into a more privatized religious life. But however much Comenius longed for the peaceful enjoyment of intimacy with Christ, retreat from the world was inconceivable. His own tradition was one of activism, for the Brethren stressed Christ's kingly authority over the world as well as the church and were convinced that the lifestyle of believers submitted to Christ would in turn change society.

The cry of the Hussite Reformation, *status mundi renovabitur,* was echoed by Comenius.[86] His controversial chiliastic views grew out of this eschatological orientation of the *Unitas Fratrum* as well as the influence of his teachers at Herborn.[87] He distinguished his beliefs from the "crude chiliasm" of certain fanatics, yet insisted on the necessity of a "true chiliasm" that had earthly implications.[88] Indeed, Comenius's chiliastic hope energized him for the wide-ranging reforms in the church and culture to which he devoted his life.

Thus, Comenius's spirituality led him from the paradise of the heart back into the labyrinth of the world.[89] But the pilgrim was not to return to the world alone, nor was he to take up permanent residence there. Rather, the Christian must live in two worlds at the same time. "Remain in the world as a pilgrim, a tenant, an alien, and a guest as long as I leave you there," (53.1) the Lord commands his servant. But only in Christ's household is he to be truly at home. Christ then offers final instructions for this task. His command to "make use of earthly things" but to "delight in heavenly things" is reminiscent of Augustine's *uti/frui* distinction. The pilgrim is not to despise the world. In fact for Comenius, the image of God in humankind seems to be related to the mission or task of humanity, especially the task of ruling over God's earth.[90]

Nonetheless, the Christian will find true rest and the fullness of joy only in the paradise of the heart where Christ dwells. Therefore, the Lord instructs the pilgrim, "Be unyielding toward the world, ever clinging to me. Be in the world with your body, but with me in your heart" (53.1). Union with Christ begins with the experience of new birth, but it continues in a daily, constant communion with the living Lord that empowers the believer to live in the labyrinth and to serve in God's world.

Comenius's allegory ends with the pilgrim's paean of praise to God, replete with quotations from Augustine and the Psalms. This prayer of worship provides a fitting conclusion to the work, for a spirit of joy and exultation marks every scene of the Christian community in the *Paradise of the Heart*. Though he does not deny the personal burdens believers must bear, for Comenius the Christian life was never a drudgery. While Puritan devotional writers tended to emphasize the agony and internal struggles of the believer, of which we find abundant testimony in Bunyan's popular spiritual classics *Pilgrim's Progress* and *Grace Abounding*, the *Labyrinth* represents the Christian life as consistently triumphant, peaceful, and blessed. We hear nothing about believers wrestling with sin, temptation, doubt, or trials. Disillusionment and despair occur only in the *Labyrinth of the World*, never in the *Paradise of the Heart*. One may accuse Comenius of idealism in his portrayal of spiritual life, but it is certainly not due to an absence of hardship and suffering in his own experience. Already at the time he wrote the *Labyrinth*, he had endured the death of his wife and two children, expulsion from his first pastoral position, and the loss of his precious library. The rest of his life would bring further hardships and frustrations. Yet the *Labyrinth* illustrates Comenius's profound experience of God's mercy and of intimacy with Christ, which served as a source of unsurpassable joy, strength, and hope for a better world.

* * *

Comenius certainly echoed spiritual themes that were influential in his day. The quest for unity, order, and harmony evident in the mystical writings of Nicholas of Cusa and the theosophic speculations of Jakob Boehme found expression in his spiritual and pansophical writings. The form, style, and even some of the wording of the *Labyrinth* were borrowed in part from the writings of Andreae. Comenius's Christocentric piety brought him near to Arndt and other early Pietists. His biblicism and his emphasis on the ordered and disciplined Christian life as an expression of true spirituality owes much to the German Reformed tradition in which he was educated and which he greatly admired.

But many elements in his spirituality originate in the theological emphases of his own church, the *Unitas Fratrum*. The Bohemian Brethren were an ecumenically oriented tradition long before the rise of an ecumenical movement. Identifying with Jan Hus, the Brethren stressed the authority of the Bible; the lordship of Christ and its implications for the individual believer, the church, and the world; and the important distinction between things essential, instrumental, and incidental for salvation. Comenius's writings echo these teachings. But in the *Labyrinth* and other spiritual treatises, he particularly developed the experiential aspect of the theology of the *Unitas Fratrum*. The distinctives of the Brethren as well as many aspects of his own spirituality are summed up in his *Bequest*. After exhorting all Christians to discern rightly the fundamentals of faith in Christ, Comenius emphasizes the experiential and practical nature of true Christianity:

> O, that ye may all be truly desirous of the genuine experience of God's mercy, and the true participation in the merits of Christ, and the genuine experience of the most sweet inward gifts of the Spirit which are attained through a true faith, true love, and a true trust in God, for in these the essence of Christianity is to be found!...May ye all understand the saying of the Lord: "The kingdom of God cometh not with observation, but is within you!"...Furthermore, I wish that all...might also form a single house of God which would be well ordered and united, and in it a single household living under one single law of God, helping each member in concord and love.[91]

The breadth of Comenius's spirituality was such that it could provide inspiration for two increasingly divergent trends within the Pietist movement—the educational and social thrust of Francke's "Halle Foundations" and the "religion of the heart" represented by Zinzendorf.[92] Intellectuals of the caliber of Leibniz and Herder recognized the genius of Comenius, and Slavic writers appropriated a number of the *Labyrinth*'s themes.[93] Surprisingly, however, the spiritual ideals of this man remain relatively unknown, particularly in the English-speaking community. It is hoped that the present volume will make John Amos Comenius more familiar to a variety of Christian traditions to which he himself expressed his debt and devoted his energy.

Notes to Introduction

1. See Johann Arndt, *True Christianity*, ed. Peter Erb, Classics of Western Spirituality (New York, 1979); Jacob Boehme, *Way to Christ*, ed. Peter Erb, Classics of Western Spirituality (New York, 1978); Philip Jacob Spener, *Pia Desideria*, ed. Theodore Tappert (Philadelphia, 1964).

2. See in particular Havel's famous essay, "The Power of the Powerless," in Václav Havel, *Living in Truth* (London, 1986), 36–122.

3. *Unum necessarium*, 10.10. Reprinted in *Johannis Amos Comenii Opera Omnia*, vol. 18 (Prague, 1974), 127.

4. Hans Aarslef, "John Comenius," in the *Dictionary of Scientific Biography* (New York, 1971) 3:359.

5. *Labyrinth*, 37.4, 40.1, 42.4.

6. The name Amos was a play on the Latin word *amare*. Comenius was also fond of the connection with the Old Testament prophet. Milada Blekastad, *Comenius* (Oslo, 1969), 23–24.

7. For Žerotín's connections with the Calvinist community of western Europe, see Otakar Odložilík, "Bohemian Protestants and the Calvinist Churches," *Church History* 8 (1939), 342–355.

8. See Gerhard Menk, *Die Hohe Schule Herborn in ihrer Frühzeit (1584–1660)* (Wiesbaden, 1981). For Comenius's experience specifically, see G. Michel, "Komenskýs Studien in Herborn und ihre Nachwirkungen in seinem Gesamtwerk," in *Comenius-Erkennen-Glauben-Handeln*, ed. K. Schaller (Sankt Augustin, 1985), 11–21.

9. *Labyrinth*, 10.11, 11.7.

10. *Labyrinth*, 39.5.

11. On this aspect of Comenius's theology, see Jan M. Lochman, "Chiliasmus verus: Eschatologie und Weltgestaltung in der Perspektive des Comenius," *Theologische Zeitschrift* 35 (1979), 275–282, and Josef Smolík, "Das eschatologische Denken des Johann Amos Comenius," *Evangelische Theologie* 43 (1983), 191–202.

12. See H. Röhrs, "Die Studienzeit des Comenius in Heidelberg," in *Comenius: Erkennen-Glauben-Handeln*, 30–37.

13. See Howard Hotson, "Irenicism and Dogmatics in the Confessional Age: Pareus and Comenius in Heidelberg, 1614," *Journal of Ecclesiastical History* 46 (1995), 432–453.

14. The Brethren began to differentiate themselves from the Utraquists through the settlement of Kunval in 1457–58, the Unity Constitution of 1464, and the establishment of a separate priesthood in 1467. For an English overview concerning the evolution of the Bohemian Brethren, see Peter Brock, *The Political and Social Doctrines of the Unity of Czech Brethren in the Fifteenth and Early Sixteenth Centuries* (The Hague, 1957).

By Comenius's period, the Utraquists were divided into two groups. The old Utraquists simply heeded Hus's teaching concerning the eucharist. The new Utraquists followed the Augsburg Confession.

15. One important exception to their simple lifestyle was music. In 1505 they published their first hymnbook. Gustav Vožda, "Jan Blahoslav-Musicus," in *Sborník Jan Blahoslav Přerovský* (Přerov, 1971), 69.

16. Of these fifty versions, twenty were substantially different in form and content. Anton Gindely, *Geschichte der Böhmischen Brüder*, vol. 1 (Osnabruck, 1861), 39. For a list of these confessional statements, see the appendix to Miloš Strupl's, "Confessional Theology of the Unitas Fratrum," *Church History* 33 (1964), 291–293.

17. "Turning to look at them, I observed that they led forth another prince [Frederick] and placed him on the throne, rejoicing that affairs would now be better than they had been. Dancing around the throne, whoever could, steadied and strengthened it. Considering that it was fitting to help support the common welfare (as they called it), I approached and drove in a wedge or two." *Labyrinth*, 19.11.

18. Comenius's relationship with Winthrop and Harvard remains somewhat murky. See J.H. Blodgett, "Was Comenius called to the presidency of Harvard?" *Educational Review*, 8 (1898). His connection with Harvard is based in part by a comment of Cotton Mather: "That brave old man, Johannes Amos Comenius, the fame of whose worth hath been trumpeted as far as more than three languages (whereof everyone is indebted unto his *Janua*) could carry it, was indeed agreed withall, by our Mr. Winthrop in his travels through the low countries, to come over into New England and illuminate this College [i.e., Harvard] and country in the quality of a President. But the solicitations of the Swedish Ambassador, diverting him another way, that incomparable Moravian became not an American." Cited in Matthew Spinka, *John Amos Comenius: That Incomparable Moravian* (Chicago, 1943), vi.

19. *Labyrinth*, 9,11–18. Also useful for Comenius's trip to England is Hugh Trevor-Roper's "Three Foreigners: The Philosophers of the

Puritan Revolution" in his *Religion, the Reformation and Social Change* (London, 1967), 237–293.

20. Cited in Daniel Murphy, *Comenius* (Dublin, 1995), 29–30.

21. See Comenius's reaction to the Peace of Westphalia in *The Bequest of the Unity of Brethren*, trans. and ed. Matthew Spinka (Chicago, 1940), 10.

22. Comenius expanded this work and published it in 1665 with the new title, *Lux e tenebris*.

23. Spinka, *John Amos Comenius: That Incomparable Moravian*, 136.

24. Matthew Spinka presents an excellent summary of the *Consultatio* in "Comenian Pansophic Principles," *Church History* 22 (1953), 155–165.

25. See Comenius's description of soldiers and warfare, *Labyrinth*, 20.5–6. Concerning his desire for confessional reconciliation, see 17.16.

26. Comenius, *The Bequest of the Unity of Brethren*, 29–30.

27. Cited in *Christian History* 6 (1987), 6.

28. "His *Labyrinthus Mundi* is an ingenious apologue and at the same time a masterpiece in the Bohemian language, of which Comenius had an extraordinary command. On account of the special derivatives and compounds which the Bohemian language employs it will be difficult to translate certain words into German or other languages." Cited in Dmitry Čiževsky, "Comenius' *Labyrinth of the World*: Its Themes and Their Sources," *Harvard Slavic Studies* 1 (1953), 84.

29. Josef Jungmann, *Historie literatury české* (Prague, 1849), 282.

30. In this context, see Dmitry Čiževsky's article above (n. 28). Also relevant is Jan Lehár "'Labyrintu světa'(The Labyrinth of the World) and its Characters," *Acta Comeniana* 4 (1979), 225–251, and Karel Kučera, "An Analysis of the Vocabulary of the Labyrinth of the World and the Paradise of the Heart," *Acta Comeniana* 4 (1979), 329–352. Čiževsky's analysis is strictly linguistic in his article "'Das Labyrinth der Welt und das Paradies des Herzens' des J. A. Comenius," *Wiener Slavistisches Jahrbuch* 5 (1956), 59–85. For other linguistic studies of the *Labyrinth*, see Lubomír Doležel, "Kompozice 'Labyrintu světa a ráje srdce' J. A. Komenského," *Česká Literatura* 17 (1969), 37–54; Hana Mirvaldová, "Alegoričnost v Labyrintu světa a ráji srdce J. A. Komenského" *Slovo a Slovesnost* 31 (1970), 353–365. J. B. Čapek's article, "K Otázkám Kořenů, Stavby a Funkce 'Labyrintu' Komenského" (*Archiv Pro Bádáni o Životě a Díle Jana Amose Komenského* 22 [1963], 255–271), gives more of a historical context for the treatise but still falls short of presenting it in

a more comprehensive portrayal of Comenius's career. For more bibliographic details, see *Johannis Amos Comenii: Opera Omnia*, 3:398–400.

31. Also indicative of Comenius's concern for the preservation of the Czech language are his later remarks in *The Bequest of the Unity of Brethren*, 36:

> In the fifth place, I bequeath thee and thy sons an eagerness for the enrichment, purification, and development of our beloved, melodious, mother tongue. In this endeavor the zeal of my sons was known of old, when it was said by competent judges that no purer Czech existed than that in use among the Brethren and in their books.

32. Kučera, 329.

33. See Matthew Spinka's two editions of the *Labyrinth* (Chicago, 1942; Ann Arbor, 1972) and the earlier translation of Count Lützow (New York, 1905). Also relevant are the remarks of Miriam Eliav-Feldon in *Realistic Utopias: The Ideal Imaginary Societies of the Renaissance* (Oxford, 1982), 4.

34. Blekastad, *Comenius,* 7.

35. "If you follow after them [the deceits of the world] with reason, you will perceive, as I did, the miserable confusion of our race. If it should seem otherwise, know that on your nose are the eyeglasses of general deception through which you see everything upside down." *Labyrinth*, To the Reader, 6.

36. *Labyrinth,* 10.3.

37. See his encounter with the natural scientists on this point. *Labyrinth*, 11.6.

38. Cited in Jean-Claude Margolin, "The Method of 'Words and Things' in Erasmus's *De Pueris Instituendis* (1529) and Comenius's *Orbis Sensualium Pictus* (1658)," in *Essays on the Works of Erasmus*, ed. R. L. DeMolen (New Haven, 1978), 223.

39. See in particular *Labyrinth*, 11.7. Peter Ramus (1515–1572) was a French philosopher and rhetorician whose reformed version of Aristotelian logic was enormously popular in Europe during the sixteenth and seventeenth centuries. On Ramus, see Walter Ong, *Ramus: Method and the Decay of Dialogue; from the Art of Discourse to the Art of Reason* (Cambridge, 1958).

40. See the remarks of C. W. Bardeen in the preface of the English edition of *Orbis sensualium pictus* (Syracuse, 1887), iii.

41. *Orbis sensualium pictus*, xiv. In another passage in the introduction,

Comenius refers to the senses as "the main guides of childhood." *Orbis sensualium pictus*, xv.

42. *Orbis sensualium pictus*, 8, 61, 20, 111.

43. "Then a raw stench began to overcome me, penetrating my brain and all my inward parts so that I fell down. I rolled and shrieked (as did others unaccustomed to this experience), not knowing what to do. Everything in me dissolved and poured out of me. It seemed to me as though we would dissolve there on the water like a snail shrivels in the sun" (*Labyrinth*, 9.14). This description of seasickness was based on Comenius's own voyage to England in 1641. For a letter detailing this experience see *Comenius in England*, ed. R. F. Young (London, 1932), 64. This passage was not in the original version of the *Labyrinth* but was added to the 1663 edition.

44. *Orbis sensualium pictus*, xviii.

45. Genesis 2:19, 20.

46. *Orbis sensualium pictus*, 1.

47. For another fascinating parallel with his earlier work, see also Comenius's discussion of the *summum bonum* in the *Labyrinth*, To the Reader, 1.

48. *Orbis sensualium pictus*, 136–148.

49. *Orbis sensualium pictus*, 193–194.

50. Margolin, "The Method," 230.

51. *Unum necessarium*, 10.3.

52. See Comenius's comments in *The Bequest of the Unity of Brethren*, 36, 37.

53. *Opera didactica omnia* IV, 27: "Ego quae pro iuventate scripsi, non ut paedagogus scripsi, sed ut theologus." Cited in Molnár, "Zum Theologieverständnis des Comenius," *Communio viatorum* 27 (1984), 227.

54. Amedeo Molnár, "The Brethren's Theology," in Rudolf Říčan, *The History of the Unity of Brethren*, trans. C. Daniel Crews (Bethlehem, Pa., 1992), 400. This chapter, pages 390–420, provides a substantial overview of the development and distinctives of Brethren theology.

55. For example, Renate Riemeck, *Der andere Comenius: Böhmischer Brüderbischof, Humanist, und Pädagoge* (Frankfurt am Main, 1970), and Jan Marinus van der Linde, "Der andere Comenius," *Unitas Fratrum* 8 (1980), 35–48.

56. There is an unpublished translation of *Unum necessarium* in Reeves Library, Moravian College, Bethlehem, Pa. We know of no English translation of *Centrum securitatis*.

57. An example of the former tendency is Louis Bouyer's mention of

Comenius in his *Orthodox Spirituality and Protestant and Anglican Spirituality*, A History of Christian Spirituality 3 (New York, 1969), 180–181. Bouyer comments in a footnote that Yves Congar fails to mention Comenius's "mystical allegory" in his article on the Moravian. Aside from this allusion to the *Labyrinth*, however, Bouyer himself says nothing more about Comenius's spirituality. The tendency to dismiss Comenius as a fanatic is evident in F. Ernest Stoeffler, *The Rise of Evangelical Pietism*, Studies in the History of Religions 9 (Leiden, 1965), 177.

58. See, for example, Čiževsky, "Comenius' *Labyrinth,*" 91–97.

59. Especially helpful on Comenius's connection to Nicholas of Cusa are several Czech articles of Jan Patočka in *Jan Komenský (II). Nachgelassene Schriften zur Comeniusforschung* (Sankt Augustin, 1984). See also the English article by the same author, "Cusanus and Comenius," *Pedagogik* 4 (1954), 508–523.

60. Lochman, *Comenius*, 12, notes the relation of Comenius's *Centrum securitatis* to certain themes in Boehme as well as Cusa. On Boehme's possible influence, see also Herwart Vorländer, "Der Theologe Johann Amos Comenius," *Zeitschrift für Kirchengeschichte* 79 (1968), 162. Blekastad, *Comenius*, 40–48, discusses the influence of Arndt, Boehme, and Andreae in his treatment of the intellectual currents of Comenius's day. He notes that Andreae, whose influence on Comenius is widely acknowledged, considered Arndt a spiritual father. Regarding links between Comenius and the Pietists, see Fritz Erlenbusch, "Komenský a němečti pietisté," in *Co daly naše země Evropě lidstvu* (Prague, 1940), 185–188.

61. See Bouyer, *Orthodox Spirituality and Protestant and Anglican Spirituality*, 180–181, for Comenius's connection with Zinzendorf. Puritan themes in the *Labyrinth* are examined by Th. B. Lubomír Balcar, "Theologické srovnání Komenského 'Labyrintu světa' s Bunyanovou knihou 'Pilgrims Progress,'" *Archiv pro Badání o Životě a Spisech J. A. Komenského* 14 (1938), 113–125.

62. For this and other points of comparison and contrast between the two pilgrims, see Balcar, "Theologické srovnání."

63. Lochman, *Comenius*, 18.

64. Čiževsky, 114. Čiževsky notes that it was not much used in Christian literature. Comenius likely borrowed it from Andreae, who was himself an ardent admirer of Arndt.

65. See *Unum necessarium* 1.6, where Comenius retells the myth and explains its significance.

66. Lochman, *Comenius*, 12, notes that the necessity of turning back

to the center, which is particularly emphasized in *Centrum securitatis*, is reminiscent of the writings of Nicholas of Cusa and the theosophic speculations of Boehme. *Centrum securitatis* expresses a more generally theistic spirituality in contrast to the strictly Christian perspective of the *Labyrinth* and other of Comenius's spiritual writings.

67. Čiževsky, 120.

68. See, for example, *City of God* II.4, 9, and 20, and VI.1f. and 7. This similarity is noted by Čiževsky, who also mentions Tertullian's use of the device.

69. A. Molnar, "The Brethren's Theology," 405.

70. For Comenius's own explanation of his choice of this structure for the hymnbook, see Jan Amos Komenský, *Duchovní písně*, ed. Antonín Škarka (Prague, 1952), 58.

71. A. Molnar, "Zum Theologieverständnis des Comenius," 236–237. Also see Comenius's own comments in *Unum necessarium* 8.8.

72. *Unum necessarium* 19.9; translation adapted from Spinka, *That Incomparable Moravian*, 147.

73. On the development of this theme from its classical roots through the twentieth century, see Čiževsky, 102–111. He sees Comenius's treatment of this parable as a possible model for later writers.

74. Vorländer, 174.

75. Molnar, "Zum Theologieverständnis des Comenius," 232.

76. See Albert C. Outler, "Pietism and Enlightenment: Alternatives to Tradition," in *Christian Spirituality: Post-Reformation and Modern*, ed. Louis Dupré and Don E. Saliers (New York, 1989), 244. For Arndt's description of the renewal of God's image in humanity, see in particular Johann Arndt, *True Christianity*, ed. Peter C. Erb (New York, 1979), 29–32.

77. See Lochman, *Comenius*, 40–41.

78. Comenius explicitly identifies with the Hussite reformation in several of his writings. In a 1647 letter to his Lutheran friend John Valentin Andreae, the Moravian refers to himself as "a member of the church whose reformation did not begin with Luther, or Calvin, but with Hus, one hundred years before yours, and which did not completely coalesce with you, because you split at the very beginning, not being interested in establishing discipline and a truly Christian, quiet life, but you were absorbed in excited dispute." Translated in Amedeo Molnár, ed., *J. A. Comenius: A Perfect Reformation* (Prague, 1957), 36–37.

79. On the interrelation of the two reformations in the tradition of the Unity of Brethren, see Molnár, "The Brethren's Theology," espe-

cially 390–392. For Comenius's own views on the reformation of the church, see *J. A. Comenius: The Perfect Reformation*, including Molnár's excellent introduction.

80. See Lochman, *Comenius*, 43–44, and Molnár, "The Brethren's Theology," 400.

81. Comenius, *The Bequest of the Unity of Brethren*, 27.

82. See Comenius's own comments in this regard, supra, n.78. On similar emphases in the German Reformed tradition in which Comenius had been educated, see Vorländer, 172–173.

83. Comenius emphasizes the important connection between theology and the life of the theologian or preacher in several other writings. For example, "Theologus vir, mysteriorum Dei rationes verbo et vita docens," in *De rerum humanarum emendatione consultatio catholica* 2 (Prague 1966), 1242; and "Theologia est scientia rerum divinarum: sed theologus vivat theologice," *Opera didactica omnia* III, 380. Both these passages are cited and discussed in Molnár, "Zum Theologieverständnis des Comenius," 228–229.

84. *The Bequest of the Unity of Brethren*, 28.

85. Ibid. Though Comenius himself believed in divine election (see, for example, *Labyrinth*, 39.1), he felt that certain Calvinists had gone too far in their speculations about the doctrine of predestination and had thereby provoked disruptions and divisions in the church.

86. Lochman, *Comenius*, 45.

87. The Calvinists Heinrich Alsted and Johann Fischer (Piscator), two of Comenius's most influential teachers, held strong millennial views. See Spinka, *That Incomparable Moravian*, 28, and Blekastad, *Comenius*, 33.

88. Comenius distinguished himself from fanatics who claimed the realization of the thousand-year reign of Christ's kingdom in their own church or political community. Vorländer, 175, notes that Comenius's millennial views also stand apart from Barth's criticism of chiliasm for its lack of an ethical dimension. For a fuller treatment of this important theme in Comenius's thought, see Lochman, "Chiliasmus verus. Eschatologie und Weltgestaltung in der Perspektive des Comenius," *Theologische Zeitschrift* 35 (1979), 275–282.

89. Lochman, *Comenius*, 56–57.

90. Both Vorländer, 174, and Lochman, *Comenius*, 40, speak of this notion of the *imago dei* in Comenius's thought and suggest its distinctiveness in the history of doctrine.

91. *The Bequest of the Unity of Brethren*, 30–31.

92. David W. Lotz, "Continental Pietism," in Cheslyn Jones et al., ed., *The Study of Spirituality* (Oxford, 1986), 451. These trends were not by any means mutually exclusive, but a difference in emphasis certainly existed. For Comenius's influence on Francke, especially in the area of pedagogy, see Dmitry Čiževsky, "Comenius und die deutschen Pietisten," *Aus zwei Welten* XI, 165–71, a German translation of Erlenbusch, "Komenský a němčtí pietisté." Zinzendorf was ordained a bishop in the revived *Unitas Fratrum* by Jablonsky, Comenius's grandson and devotee, who appears to have passed on some of the Moravian's ideals to the Count.

93. Čiževsky, "Comenius' *Labyrinth*: Themes and Sources," *passim*.

The Labyrinth of the World and the Paradise of the Heart

That is a vivid portrayal, showing that in this world and in all its affairs there is nothing but confusion and entanglement, floundering and drudgery, delusion and deception, misery and anxiety, and finally weariness and despair; but that whoever rests at home in his heart, alone with the Lord God, comes to true and complete joy and peace of mind.

Second Edition
Amsterdam, 1663

I have seen all the works which are done
    under the sun,
And, behold, all is vanity and vexation of
    spirit.
                                    –*Ecclesiastes 1:14*

I, liber, in lucem, rigidi secure Catonis,
i labyrinthaeis currere docte viis.
Cumque ibis curresque viis, dic: Optime
    lector,
ex me supremum non nisi disce bonum.[1]
                          –*M. Georg. Colsinius*[2]

---

1. Proceed, oh book, toward the light,
Wisely run the ways of the labyrinth
fearing not stern Cato.
While you hurry along the paths, say:
Good reader, learn nothing from me but the greatest good.

2. Jiří Kolsín (d. 1643), originally Kavka, was a Czech humanist writer and spiritual leader who worked with Comenius in Leszno, Poland.

To the most illustrious and truly noble lord,
Baron Charles the Elder of Žerotín, etc.,
most gracious lord of Moravia:[1]

*I*n these exceedingly turbulent and disturbing times I would
hesitate, most illustrious lord, to bother Your Grace with this
letter, even more with the dedication of a book, were it not the
type of work intended to encourage and to calm souls in God.[2]
Let me say something about it. While in my seclusion and unwel-
come leisure, removed from the concerns of my vocation, I neither could nor would be inactive. Thus, during the past few
months I began to reflect, among other things, on the vanity of
the world (since stimulus for such meditation has arisen from all
sides). As a result, this drama that I am offering to Your Grace
was born under my hands. The first part depicts, through a
series of scenes, the ludicrous and worthless things of the world.
It shows how the world, despite its great and far-reaching power,
accomplishes nothing and how all things end miserably either in
laughter or in grief. The second part describes, either figura-
tively or directly, the true and sure happiness of the children of
God; how they are truly blessed who, having completely abandoned the world and all worldly treasures, adhere, nay even
cling, to God alone. I admit that what is presented here is in
rough outline and not yet complete.[3] For I see that the material is
truly rich and extremely well-suited for sharpening intellect and
refining language, so that the themes can be continually
expanded by occasional new inventions.[4] Whatever the deficiencies of its present form, I wanted to offer Your Grace what I have
collected from these imperfect sketches. I do not venture to say
with what purpose I do so. However, Your Grace will either perceive its purpose in the course of reading, or it will be explained
at another time. I will indicate this one thing. I believe that this
book is not offered inappropriately to the one who has experienced in a thousand ways the waves and sorrows of the sea of this

world but who nevertheless finds peace in the most tranquil harbor of conscience. Hence I wish only that Your Grace may live safe from the world of Satan and pleasantly with his Christ, and that he may joyfully await the life that is rightfully his and that will follow this miserable one. Meanwhile, may the Spirit of our eternal and merciful God guide, encourage, comfort, and strengthen us. Amen.

Given under the Klopoty, on the Ides of December, 1623.

The devoted servant of Your Grace,
J. A. C.

To the Reader

1. Every creature, even an irrational one, is naturally inclined to indulge in and desire comfortable and pleasurable things. The human being, of course, endowed with innate rational power, aspires all the more to the good and the comfortable. Indeed, reason not only awakens him but also provokes him more heartily to seek and enjoy what is more pleasant and comfortable. Long ago a question arose among the wise concerning the source and nature of the highest good *(summum bonum)*, which is the goal of all human desire.⁵ Once that good has been obtained, one could and should put one's mind at rest, for there would be no more to desire.

2. Should we direct our attention to this matter, we would find not only that this problem has been and still is examined among philosophers who attempt to solve it, but that the thought of every human being turns to the question of where and how to attain complete happiness. We find that almost all people look outside themselves, seeking the means to calm and quiet their minds in the world and its possessions: this one in property and riches, that one in delights and pleasure, one in glory and status, another in wisdom and learning, yet another in merry companionship.

3. But the wisest of men, Solomon, is a witness that the highest good is not found in these attainments. After travelling through the whole world in search of rest for his mind, he finally concluded: "I hate this life. There is nothing under the sun that pleases me, for all is only vanity and misery."⁶ Having found true peace of mind, he declared that it consists in leaving the world such as it is, looking only to the Lord God, fearing him, and keep-

ing his commandments.[7] For, he said, everything depends on this one precept. Likewise, David discovered that the happiest person is the one who dismisses the world from sight and mind, holds to God alone, has God as his portion, and dwells with God in his heart.[8]

4. May the mercy of God be praised, for he opened my eyes also, enabling me to see the manifold vanities of this pompous world and the wretched deceit hiding everywhere under outward brilliance. I have learned to seek peace and security of mind elsewhere. Since I wanted both to set this truth more clearly before my own eyes and to show it to others, I devised this journey or wandering though the world in which I recount the monstrous things I beheld or encountered and where and how I discovered the desired happiness that is vainly sought in the world.[9] All this I have portrayed in the present treatise. How cleverly [I have composed this tract], I care not. May God only grant that it be profitable both for me and for my neighbors.

5. Reader, what you will read is no mere invention, even though it may bear resemblance to a fable; rather, these are true events that you will recognize once you have understood, especially you who know something of my life and circumstances. For the most part, I have described here adventures that I myself experienced over several years of my life.[10] For the rest, I have observed some incidents in the lives of others or have been told about them. I have not related all my adventures, however, partly for shame, and partly because I did not know how edifying it would be for others.

6. My guides, the guides of everyone who gropes about in the world, are indeed two: presumptuousness of mind, which examines everything, and inveterate custom, which gives a shade of truth to all the deceits of the world. If you follow after them with reason, you will perceive, as I did, the miserable confusion of our race. If it should seem otherwise, know that on your nose are the eyeglasses of general deception through which you see everything upside down.

7. As regards the portrayal of the happy course of hearts devoted to God, this is described more as an ideal rather than as

a full picture of what befalls all the elect. But the Lord God does not lack even such perfected spirits, and every truly devout person who reads this account will be bound to desire the same degree of perfection. Farewell, dear Christian, and may the leader of light, the Holy Spirit, show you better than I can both the vanity of the world and the glory, happiness, and joy of the elect whose hearts are united with God.

Chapter 1
On the Reasons for Wandering
in the World

1. When I had reached the age when human reason begins to discern the difference between good and evil, I saw the various estates, classes, callings, occupations, and endeavors in which people engage. It seemed important to me to consider well what group of people I ought to join and with what affairs I should occupy my life.

Fickleness of mind

2. Reflecting much and often on this matter and considering it diligently in my mind, I decided that I would be most pleased with that course of life which contained fewer cares and labors and more comfort, peace, and cheerfulness.

3. Yet it seemed difficult to know which profession this might be. Nor did I know with whom to take proper counsel, for I did not want to seek the advice of some unsuitable person, assuming that each one would praise his own profession. I dared not take hold of anything too hastily, for I feared that I would choose wrongly.

4. I confess, however, that I secretly attempted to pursue first one, then another, then a third thing,[11] but abandoned each one straightaway, for I perceived (or so it seemed to me) difficulties and vanities in each. Meanwhile, I feared lest my fickleness should bring me shame. And I did not know what to do.

5. After much struggle and inward deliberation, I came to the decision that I would first observe all human affairs under the sun. Then, after having wisely compared one with another, I would choose a profession that would somehow provide me with what was necessary for a peaceful and pleasant life. The more I thought about this course, the better it pleased me.

Chapter 2
The Pilgrim Receives Ubiquitous as a Guide

1. So I went out alone and began to consider where and how to begin. Then suddenly there appeared, from where I do not know, a certain man of brisk gait, spry appearance, and quick speech whose legs, eyes, and tongue all seemed to me to be in constant motion. He approached me and inquired from where I had come and where I was going. I answered that I had left my home and intended to wander through the world to gain experience.

2. He approved of this and said, "Where is your guide?"

"I have none," I answered. "I trust that God and my eyes will not lead me astray."

"You will accomplish nothing," said he. "Have you ever heard of the Cretan labyrinth?"

"I have heard something about it," I replied.

The world a labyrinth

"It was one of the wonders of the world," he explained, "a building with so many rooms, compartments, and passages that whoever entered it without a guide would wander and grope about without ever finding a way out. But that was a joke compared with the way the labyrinth of this world is arranged, especially in our day. Trust me, for I am an experienced man. I advise you not to enter it alone."

3. "But where shall I find such a guide?" I asked.

Description of an insolent man

"It is my task," he answered, "to lead those who desire to see and experience [the world] and to show them where everything is. That is why I have come to meet you."

"And who are you, my friend?" I asked, marvelling.

"My name is Searchall, but I am called Ubiquitous," he answered, "for I walk through the whole world, explore all corners, and inquire into the words and deeds of every person. I see all that is revealed and spy out and pursue all that is secret. In short, nothing should be done without me, for it is my duty to oversee everything. If you follow me, I will lead you to many secret places that otherwise you would never find."

4. Hearing these words, I began to rejoice within myself that I had found such a guide. I begged him not to consider it troublesome to lead me through the world. "As I gladly serve others in this way, I will gladly serve you also," he replied. After taking me by the hand, he said, "Let us go." So we set out.

Then I said, "I would like to observe the course of the world and whether there is anything in it on which one can safely rely."

Hearing these words, my companion stopped and said, "Friend, if you are setting out with the intention of passing judgment on what you see according to your own understanding, rather than being pleased merely to observe these things, I do not know whether Her Majesty, our Queen, will be satisfied."

Vanity, the Queen of the World

5. "And who is your queen?" I inquired.

"She who directs the whole world and its course from one end to the other," he answered. "Her name is Wisdom, though some cynics call her Vanity. Therefore I warn you beforehand, when we go there and investigate, do not philosophize too much, or you will come to evil and I along with you."

Chapter 3
Delusion Joins Them

1. While he was speaking with me, someone approached us from the side. I didn't see whether it was a man or a woman (for the person was strangely disguised and surrounded by something like a mist). He asked, "Where are you hurrying with this man, Ubiquitous?"

"I am leading him through the world," he replied, "for he is eager to examine it."

2. "But why without me?" he asked. "You know that it is your duty to guide, and mine to show what there is to see. For it is not Her Majesty's will that whoever enters her kingdom should interpret

what he sees and hears as he pleases or that he should philosophize about it. Rather, the nature and purpose of what he sees should be explained to him, and he should be content with this."

3. "Is anyone so insolent as not to comply with our rules as others do?" Ubiquitous responded. "However, I expect that this man will need a bridle. Well, then, come along!" Then he joined us, and we went on.

4. I, however, thought to myself, "I hope to God that I have not been misled. These men are deliberating about some bridle for my mouth." So I said to the new companion, "Friend, don't be angry, but I would like to know your name."

Practice of deluding the world in everything

"I am the interpreter of Wisdom, Queen of the World," he replied. "I have orders to teach how all things in the world should be understood. Therefore I place in the minds of all the people you will see—young and old, noble and common, ignorant and learned—everything that pertains to true worldly wisdom, and I lead them to joy and contentment. For without me, even kings, princes, lords, and the most distinguished people would be in strange difficulties and would spend their time on earth in sorrow."

5. To this I rejoined, "How fortunate that God should give me you as a guide, dear friend, if what you say is true. For I have set out into the world in order to seek and take hold of what is safest and most satisfying. Having you as my guide, I will be able to choose more easily."

"Do not doubt this," said he. "For though you will find everything in our kingdom excellently and finely ordered and merry, and will learn that all subjects obedient to our queen can live well, nevertheless it is true that one profession or trade has more comfort and leisure than another. You will be able to choose whatever you wish from among all of them. I will explain to you everything as it is."

"What, then, is your name?" I asked.

"My name is Delusion," he answered.

Chapter 4
The Pilgrim Receives a Bridle and Spectacles

1. Upon hearing this I was horrified and thought to myself, What fine companions I have received because of my sin! The first one (I mused) was speaking about some kind of bridle. The other one, named Delusion, called his queen Vanity (though I suspect that was an unguarded outburst). What is all this?

2. While I continued silently with downcast eyes and moved on with unwilling legs, Searchall said, "What is it, you fickle man? I suspect you want to turn back." Before I could answer, he threw some kind of bridle on my neck, the bit of which slipped suddenly into my mouth. And he said, "Now you will go compliantly whither you began."

The bridle of curiosity

3. I looked at the bridle and found that it was stitched together out of straps of curiosity and that its bit was made of tenacity in resolutions. Then I understood that in beholding the world I would no longer travel freely as before, but would be driven on forcibly by the fickleness and insatiable thirst of my own mind.

The spectacles of delusion

4. Then the second guide on the other side said, "I give you these spectacles through which you will view the world." And he thrust on my nose spectacles through which I immediately saw everything before me in a different manner.[12] Indeed, they had this power (as I tested many times afterwards) to present objects to the beholder in such a way that what was far seemed near, and what was near seemed far; what was small seemed large, and what was large seemed small; what was ugly, beautiful, and beautiful, ugly; what was black, white, and white, black; and so forth. Then I understood that he was rightly called Delusion since he was able to make such spectacles and put them on people.

Composed of presumption and habit

5. As I learned afterwards, these spectacles were fashioned out

of the glass of presumption; and the frames in which they were set were made of horn called habit.

6. Fortunately for me, he thrust them on my nose somewhat crookedly, so that they did not fit tightly against my eyes. Thus by raising my head and peering under them, I was able to see things clearly and naturally. This made me glad, and I thought to myself, "Though you have shut my mouth and covered my eyes, yet I trust God that you will not bind my mind and reason. I will go and see what this world is like that Lady Vanity wants one to examine on her own terms but not with one's own eyes."

Chapter 5
The Pilgrim Looks at the World from Above

Beyond the world there is nothing

1. While I was thinking about this matter, we suddenly appeared (I don't know how) on an exceedingly high tower, so that I seemed to be right under the clouds. Looking down from there, I saw on earth a certain city, beautiful and splendid in appearance and spread over an extremely wide expanse. Nevertheless, I was always able to distinguish its boundaries and limits on all sides. The city was constructed in a circle, arranged with walls and ramparts, but instead of moats there was a certain dark abyss that seemed to be without sides or bottom. There was light only above the city; beyond the walls it was pitch dark.

The situation of the world

2. I saw the city itself divided into innumerable streets, squares, houses, and buildings, some larger and some smaller; and people were scurrying everywhere like insects. On the eastern side, I saw a certain gate from which an alley led to another gate that faced the west. The second gate led into the different streets of the city. I counted six main streets, all running parallel to each other. In the midst of them was a square or very large circular marketplace. Further to the west on a steep and rocky hill

stood a high and splendid castle at which the inhabitants of the city often gazed.

The gate of entry and the gate of division

3. My guide Ubiquitous said to me, "Pilgrim, here you have that fine world that you were so anxious to behold. I brought you first to this height so you could survey the whole and understand its layout. That eastern gate is the gate of life through which all who live in the world enter. This second closer gate is the gate of division from which all turn to one or another calling as their lot falls.

The classes of the world are divided into six

4. The streets that you see are the various classes, orders, and callings in which people establish themselves. You see six main avenues. In the one to the south, dwells the domestic group—parents, children, and servants. In the next one are craftsmen and tradesmen; in the third, closest to the square, dwells the class of the learned, engaged with the labors of the mind; on the other side is the spiritual class, to which the others go to practice religion; beyond them is the class of rulers and magistrates of the world; farthest to the north is the knightly class, engaged in military affairs. Oh how excellent it is! The first class produces all; the second sustains all; the third teaches all; the fourth prays for all; the fifth judges and preserves all from disorder; the sixth fights for all. Thus all serve one another, and everything is harmonious.

The castle of fortune

5. The castle to the west is *Arx Fortunae,* the castle of fortune, in which the more distinguished people live, enjoying riches, pleasure, and fame.

The marketplace and castle of the world

The central marketplace is for everyone. Here people of all classes come together and manage their necessary affairs. In the middle of the marketplace, as the center of all, stands the residence of Wisdom, Queen of the World."

The beginning of confusion

6. This excellent arrangement pleased me, and I began to praise God that He had divided the estates of the world in such fine fashion. But it displeased me that these streets intersected and ran into each other at various points. This seemed to be an indication of confusion and a cause of straying. Moreover, when I looked at the round shape of the world, I clearly felt that it moved and turned in a circle, so that I feared dizziness. For wherever I cast my eyes, I saw that everything down to the smallest items swarmed about. When I listened, everything was filled with beating, banging, rustling, whispering, and shouting.

And delusion besides

7. My interpreter Delusion said, "You see, my dear man, how beautiful this world is, how excellent is everything in it even though you have only viewed it from afar. What will you say after examining it in its parts and with its delights? Who would not be pleased to dwell in it?"

"It pleases me from afar," I said. "I don't know how it will be afterwards."

"All will be well," he replied. "Only believe, and let us go onward."

The ways of childhood

8. "Wait until I show him from this vantage point those places where we do not intend to go," Ubiquitous interjected. "Look back toward the east. Do you see something crawling and creeping toward us from that dark gate?"

"I see," I replied.

And he added, "Those are people newly entering the world, though they do not know from where, nor do they yet realize that they are human. Therefore, darkness surrounds them, and there is nothing but wailing and crying. But as they continue along this street, the darkness gradually dissipates until it becomes light where they come to this gate under us. Let's go and see what happens there."

Chapter 6
Fate Distributes Callings

Fate, the guard of the world

1. We descended a dark winding staircase, and at the gate was a large hall full of young people. Sitting on the right side was a fierce-looking old man holding in his hand a large copper pot. I saw that all who came from the gate of life approached him, and each one reached into that pot, drew out a slip of paper with a message, and then continued on to one of the streets of the city. Some were running with joy and shouting. Others were creeping and looking back with groans and complaints.

Distributing callings

2. I approached nearer, looked at some of those slips of paper and saw that one drew out "Rule," another "Serve" or "Command" or "Obey" or "Write" or "Plow" or "Learn" or "Dig" or "Judge" or "Fight," and so forth. I was amazed at these proceedings. Searchall said to me, "Here the callings and occupations are distributed according to which each one must fulfill an assigned task. The one who oversees the lots is called Fate. From him everyone who enters the world must take his assignment in this manner."

The Pilgrim asks first to examine all

3. Then Delusion nudged me from the side, giving a signal that I also should draw. I asked that I not be forced to accept any one profession without first examining it so as not to commit myself to blind chance. But I was told that this would not be allowed without the knowledge and permission of the lord regent, Fate. Approaching him, I humbly submitted my request. I said that I came with the intention of investigating everything and choosing for myself only what pleased me.

And he receives permission

4. "Son, you see that others do not do this," he answered, "but accept whatever is offered or presented to them. But since you so eagerly desire this, so be it." Then, having written on a slip of

paper "Speculare" (i.e., Examine or Inquire), he gave it to me and dismissed me.

Chapter 7
The Pilgrim Examines the Marketplace of the World

He sees the diversity of people

1. "Since you have to examine everything," my guide said to me, "let us go first to the marketplace."[13] And he led me on. I saw countless multitudes that seemed like a mist, for here were people of all languages and nations, of every age, size, estate, class, and calling, and of both sexes. Looking at them, I saw them moving about here and there like swarming bees, but even more strangely.

Their various characteristics and gestures

2. For some walked, others ran or rode or stood or sat or lay down or stood up; still others reclined or turned in various directions. Some were alone whereas others were in larger or smaller groups. Their dress and appearance varied greatly. Some were even stark naked and gesticulated strangely. Whenever they met each other, they gestured in various ways with their hands, mouths, and knees or otherwise huddled and cuddled together in some other foolish manner. "Look," my interpreter announced, "here you have the noble human race, those delightful creatures who have been endowed with reason and immortality. They bear the image and likeness of immortal God, which can be recognized by the variety of their praiseworthy deeds. Here you can see as in a mirror the dignity of your race."

Hypocrisy in all of them

3. Then I looked at them more closely, and I saw first of all that each one walking among others in the crowd wore a mask on his face. When he went away, however, and was alone or among his equals, he removed it. But when he had to rejoin the crowd, he put it on again. I asked what this meant. "This, my dear son," the guide answered, "is human prudence. For each one does not reveal to

everyone who he really is. Alone one can be as one is, but among others, it is fitting to conform and to give a semblance of propriety in one's affairs." Then I desired to examine their appearance more thoroughly to see how they looked without this artificial covering.

Their strange deformities

4. And watching them carefully, I saw that all were deformed—not only their faces, but also their bodies. Most of them were pimply, scabby, or leprous; and besides, one had a pig lip, others dog teeth, ox horns, ass ears, lizard eyes, a fox tail, or wolf claws. I saw some with an outstretched peacock's neck, others with a bristling lapwing crest, still others with horse hooves, and so forth. For the most part they resembled monkeys.[14] I was horrified and said, "But it is as if I see monsters!"

"What monsters are you talking about, you busybody," said the interpreter, threatening me with his fist. "If you would only look properly through your glasses, you would see that they are human." Some of those going by overheard me calling them monsters. They stopped, growled, and threatened me.

When I realized that it was useless to argue, I kept silent, thinking to myself, "If they wish to consider themselves human, let them be; but I see what I see." But since I was afraid that my guide would readjust my glasses and deceive me, I determined to keep quiet and only wonder silently at these fine things of which I had seen only the beginning. Looking again, I saw how some manipulated their masks skillfully, removing and replacing them so nimbly that in a moment, when they saw the need, they were able to give themselves another appearance. Then I began to understand the course of the world. Nevertheless, I kept silent.

Common misunderstanding of all

5. I also observed and heard them speak to one other in different languages, so that for the most part they did not understand each other. They either did not answer, or each one responded differently. In some places, a whole crowd stood together. All were speaking their own language, and no one listened to anything, though they pulled at one another in an effort to gain a hearing.

But they were not successful and instead provoked fights and scuffles. "For God's sake, are we then in Babel?" I exclaimed. "Each one sings his own song.[15] Can there be any greater chaos?"

Preoccupation with useless affairs

6. There were few here who were idle, for all occupied themselves with some kind of work. Yet their work (and this I would have never expected) was nothing but children's games or at most drudgery. Indeed, some collected garbage and distributed it among themselves. Some were rolling logs and stones here and there or hoisting them on pulleys and setting them down again. Some were digging earth and conveying or carrying it from place to place. The rest were working with bells, mirrors, children's games, rattles, and other trinkets. Others were even playing with their own shadows—measuring, chasing, and trying to catch them. They did this so vigorously that many groaned and perspired, and some even collapsed from over-exertion. Moreover, almost everywhere there were officials who directed and distributed such tasks with great zeal, and still others obeyed them with no less enthusiasm. "But was humanity created to spend the keenness of its divinely endowed gifts on such vain and petty tasks?" I asked with wonder.

"What is so vain about them?" answered the interpreter. "Does it not seem as if looking in a mirror, everything is overcome by human ingenuity? One does this, and another something else."

"But all," I said, "work at useless tasks unbecoming their glorious dignity."

"Do not complain so much," he retorted, "for they are not yet in heaven but on earth, and they must engage in earthly affairs. You see how everything proceeds among them in such an orderly fashion."

Dreadful disorder

7. Looking again, I saw that nothing more disorderly could be imagined! For when someone staggered and strained with a burden, another interfered with him. This led to quarrels, brawls, and fights. Then they were reconciled, but in a moment they

73

were fighting again. Sometimes a few of them caught hold of the same thing; then they all dropped it and ran, each in his own direction. Those who were under the authority of officials and supervisors did what they were ordered halfheartedly because they had to; though even here, I saw a lot of confusion. Some broke rank and ran away. Some grumbled against their overseers, not wanting to do what they were ordered. Others snatched their overseers' clubs and took them away. Thus, everything was in a hubbub. But since they wanted to call this orderly, I dared not say anything to the contrary.

Many scandals and bad examples

8. I also perceived further disorder, blindness, and foolishness. The whole square (as well as the streets) was full of craters, pits, potholes, stones, logs, and other obstacles lying crisscross in every direction. No one cleared, straightened, or put them in order; nor did anyone avoid or bypass them. Rather, they walked about capriciously, bumped into one thing or another, fell, and were injured or killed. My heart shuddered upon seeing this scene. But none of them took notice of anything. Instead, when someone fell, they laughed at him. Seeing some climb blindly onto a branch, out on a beam, or into a pit, I began to warn some of them, but no one heeded me. Some even laughed at me or scolded me, and others wanted to beat me. One fell, not to rise again, another stood up and fell head over heels over and over again. They all had many callouses and bruises, yet no one paid attention to them. I could not but wonder at their apathy and disregard of their own falls and wounds. If one but touched another (as I observed elsewhere), they took to arms and began to fight.

Human fickleness and inconstancy in everything

9. I also observed their great delight in novelty and change with regard to clothing, architecture, speech, gait, and other matters. I saw some who did nothing but change clothes, putting on one costume after another. Others invented new building methods, but after a while they tore down what they built. They took up one task, then another, and finally abandoned all, showing

fickleness in everything. If anyone died from the burden he bore, or abandoned it, several others were found to squabble, dispute, and fight about it in an amazing way. Meanwhile, nobody could say, do, or build anything that would not be mocked, maligned, or destroyed by others. If somebody accomplished a task with significant toil or expense and expressed pleasure with it, another came and knocked it down, smashed, or ruined it. I did not see anyone anywhere who accomplished anything that someone else did not destroy. Some did not even wait for others, but destroyed it themselves. I was amazed at their senseless inconstancy and vain endeavors.

Pride and presumption

10. I saw that many wore elevated shoes and that some made stilts for themselves. (By raising themselves above all the others, they were able to observe everyone from a higher vantage point.) In this manner they strutted about. But whoever had higher stilts was more easily knocked down or tripped up by others (out of envy, I presume). Not a few people met this end, causing others to laugh. I observed many such instances.

Arrogance and self-approval

11. I also saw some who carried mirrors and looked at themselves in them while speaking with others, quarrelling, fighting, rolling logs, or even walking on stilts. They looked at themselves from the front, from the back, and from the side. Admiring their beauty, figure, gait, and actions, they gave their mirrors to others so that they too could look into them.

Death miserably destroying everyone

12. Finally, I saw Death stalking everywhere among them. Equipped with a sharp scythe and a bow and arrows, she warned all in a loud voice to remember that they were mortal. But nobody heeded her warning; each was concerned with his own foolishness and wickedness. Therefore, drawing arrows, she shot at them in all directions. Whomever she hit in the crowd—whether young, old, poor, rich, learned, or ignorant—fell to the ground. Each one who

was hit cried out, screamed, and shrieked. When others walking nearby saw the wound, they ran some distance away and then took no further notice. Some came and looked at the groaning, wounded person; and when his legs stiffened and he stopped breathing, they gathered together and sang around him, ate, drank, and made merry. At the same time, a few people grimaced a little. Then they grabbed, dragged, and threw him outside the enclosure into that dark pit which surrounds the world. Returning from there, they caroused again. No one avoided Death. They only took care not to look at her (although she brushed against them).

Various diseases

13. I also saw that not all whom Death hit fell immediately. Some she only wounded, lamed, blinded, deafened, or stunned. Some swelled like blisters from their wounds, others dried up like splinters, while still others trembled like aspen leaves. Thus there were more wounded people walking about with ulcerous and rotten limbs than healthy people.

Help sought in vain

14. I observed some running about and selling plasters, ointments, and potions for the wounds. All were buying these remedies from them, making merry, and defying Death. But she took no notice and continued shooting and striking them down, even the merchants. It was a sad spectacle to see how a creature prepared for immortality should fall prey to such sorry, sudden, and strange deaths. It was especially tragic when someone intended to live long, gather friends around himself, put his business in order, build houses, accumulate money, and otherwise work hard to provide for himself. For then almost always Death's flying arrow would put an end to it all. The one who has feathered his nest is torn away from it, and his preparations are brought to naught. When an heir succeeds him, the same fate befalls him also, and likewise to the third, tenth and hundredth generation. I saw then that no one wanted to consider or take to heart the uncertainties of life. Even standing in the face of Death, all behave as if certain of immortality (which nearly caused my heart

to burst from pity). I wanted to raise my voice in warning and entreaty, hoping that they would open their eyes, look at Death preparing her arrows, and avoid them somehow. I realized, however, that since Death herself was unable to accomplish anything either by her incessant warnings or by the repeated appearance of her ghastly form, my own feeble urging would be in vain. Nevertheless, I said softly, "Oh God, what eternal woe that we miserable mortals are so blind to our misfortune!"

"My dear friend," my interpreter responded, "would it be wise to trouble ourselves with the thought of Death? Since all know that Death is inescapable, it is better to ignore her and rather attend to one's business and think well of oneself. When Death comes, she comes. It is done in an hour, perhaps even in a minute. If one should die, should others cease being merry? How many others are born in place of the one who dies!"

To this I answered, "If this be wisdom, I understand it poorly." And I was silent.

People themselves are the cause of diseases and death

15. I do not want to conceal this matter. When I saw such a countless quantity of Death's flying arrows, the thought came to me, "Where does Death obtain such an inexhaustible supply of arrows?" I looked and saw clearly that she had no arrows of her own, but only a bow. She obtained the arrows from the people she intended to hit. I also observed that people themselves produced and prepared these arrows. Some even carried them to her foolishly and audaciously so that she needed only to take those they had prepared and to shoot them in the heart. I cried out, "I see that the saying is true, *'Et mortis faber est quilibet ipse suae.'*[16] I realized that no one dies who has not by his own intemperance, incontinence, foolhardiness, or carelessness brought upon himself tumors, sores, and internal and external wounds (for they are the arrows of Death). While I gazed attentively at Death and her pursuit of people, Delusion pulled me away and said, "What then, would you rather observe the dead than the living? When one dies, life is over. You, then, should strive to live."

Chapter 8
The Pilgrim Observes the State and
Order of Marriage

Preparation for this state is toilsome and full of unfulfilled desires

1. Then they directed me to a street in which they said the married people lived, and it gave me a pleasant picture of the manner of that delightful life. Behold, there stood a gate that my guide told me was called Engagement. Before it was a wide square crowded with people of both sexes walking about and looking into each others' eyes. Moreover, they examined each others' ears, noses, teeth, necks, tongues, arms, legs, and other limbs. Each measured how tall, broad, fat, or thin the other was. One approached, then drew away from another, looking at the person first from the front, then from the back, then from the right and left side, examining all that he or she saw. Most often I saw that they examined each other's pouches, money-bags, and purses, measuring and weighing how long, wide, full, heavy, or light they were. Sometimes several men pointed at one woman. At other times none took notice of her. If one drove off another, they quarreled, exchanged blows, and fought. Sometimes I even observed murders. One pushed another aside and then was himself pushed aside. Another drove away his rivals and then ran away himself. Some spent no time in examination, but grasped the nearest one he could. Then they led each other hand in hand toward the gate. Seeing such an abundance of trivial proceedings in this place, I asked what these people were doing.

"These people would gladly dwell on matrimonial street," my interpreter replied, "but since no one is permitted through the gate alone, rather only in couples, each one must choose a mate. The choosing takes place here, and each one seeks a mate suitable for himself. Whoever finds one, as you see, continues with his mate to the gate."

"Should not the choosing be somehow easier?" I asked. "How dreadfully wearisome it all is."

"Not wearisome, but delightful," he answered. "Don't you see how merry they are about this process, how they laugh, sing and shout? Believe me, no manner of life is more merry than this." So I looked and saw that indeed some people laughed and shouted. But I also observed that others went about depressed and hanging their heads. They were restlessly moping about here and there; they were troubled and could not sleep and eat; and some even became delirious.

"What about these people?" I inquired.

"Even this activity is a delight," he answered.

"So be it," I responded. "Let's go and see what happens further ahead."

Great uncertainty concerning the outcome

2. Forcing ourselves through the crowd, we came to the gate itself. But before we entered it, I saw hanging scales made of two baskets and people standing around them. They placed each pair on the scale in the baskets opposite each other and watched to see whether the scale balanced. There was much climbing in and out, and shaking and steadying of the scales. Only after they had spent much time weighing were they allowed to go through the gate. But not all fared equally well. For some fell through the baskets and were met with laughter. They were compelled to collect themselves with shame and to slip away from the place. Moreover, a hood or sack was thrust over their ears, and they were made a laughingstock. Looking at this, I asked, "What is happening here?"

He answered, "This is their engagement, when the circumstances are favorable. If the scale shows that they are equal and suitable, they are allowed to enter this state, as you see. If not, they separate."

"But what is considered equality here," I asked, "for I see that the scale shows that some are equal in age, class, and otherwise, but they allow one to fall through the basket. They place together others, however, who are extremely unequal: an old man with a young woman, a young man with a hag; one stands straight, and the other is bent with age, yet they say that this is permissible. How can this be?"

"You do not see all," he answered. "It is true that some of these old men and hags would not weigh a pound of tow, but when they have a fat purse or a cap before which other hats are doffed, or something similar (for all such things also go on the scale), matters do not turn out as one might judge."

Unbreakable bond between them regardless of the outcome

3. Following behind those who were permitted through the gate, I observed between the gates certain blacksmiths who bound each couple in shackles. Only so bound were they allowed to proceed further. Many people attended this fettering, invited purposely (as they said) in order to serve as witnesses. They played, sang, and urged the couples to be of good cheer. Looking carefully, I saw that the chains were not padlocked as on other prisoners, but forged, welded, and soldered together so that as long as they lived, they could neither unfasten them nor break them apart. This frightened me, and I said, "O most cruel prison! Whoever enters it has no hope of deliverance."

"Of course this union is the strongest of all human bonds," the interpreter responded, "but there is no reason to fear it. Because of the sweetness of this state, it is gladly undertaken. You see yourself how delightful this life is."

"Let us now go among them," I said, "that I might observe."

Little delight even when marriage is most successful

4. Then we entered the street and saw a great multitude of these people, all in pairs. It seemed to me, however, that many were unequally yoked, large with small, handsome with ugly, young with old, etc. Looking carefully at what they were doing, and seeing in what the sweetness of that state consisted, I observed that they looked at each other, talked with each other, and sometimes caressed or even kissed one another. "Here you see how fine a thing marriage is when it succeeds," said my interpreter.

"Is this then marriage at its best?" I asked.

"Of course," he replied. And I said, "This is but little pleasure, and I don't know whether marriage is worth such fetters."

Misery and drudgery of all married people generally

5. I looked further and saw how much work and anxiety the poor wretches had. The majority of them had a flock of children around them, attached to them with bridles. They screamed, shrieked, stank, quarrelled, and got sick and died, to say nothing of the pains, tears, and dangers to their own life with which they came into the world. If any should grow up, the parents had two tasks: first, to restrain them with a bridle; and second, to make them follow in their tracks by driving them on with spurs. Often they endured neither bridle nor spurs and caused such terrible mischief that they drove their parents to exhaustion and tears. If the parents gave them free rein, or they tore themselves away, shame or even the death of the parents resulted.

Observing this situation, I began to admonish both parents and children, warning the former against foolish love and over-indulgence, and exhorting the latter to virtue. But I had little success, save that some looked at me sullenly, jeered, or even threatened to kill me. Noticing some of the childless there, I blessed them, but they whined and complained and were without comfort. Therefore I understood that in marriage both to have and not to have children is misery.

Almost every couple had servants around them to attend to them and their families. Often they had to expend more effort on these servants than on themselves, at the cost of considerable annoyance. In addition, there was here, as also in the square, a lot of baggage, obstacles, timber, rocks, and pits. If one stumbled, fell, or was wounded, the other, unable to get away, had to howl, cry, and endure pain along with him. Thus I recognized that in the married state, instead of one care, concern, and danger, each one had as many cares, concerns, and dangers as those with whom he was joined. So I acquired a dislike for this state.

The awful tragedy of unsuccessful marriage

6. When I looked at some in this crowd, I observed tragedies. Indeed, not a few of those joined together were of differing dispositions. One wanted one thing, the other something else. One wanted to go here, the other there. So they argued, resented, and

81

bit one another. One complained to those passing by about one thing; the other about some other matter. When there was no one to arbitrate, and they were left to themselves, they fought and beat one another viciously with fists and cudgels. If someone pacified them, they were soon at each other again. Some argued about what direction to take. When each one set off in the direction he wished, one threw himself with all his strength in one direction, and the other in the opposite. As a result, there was a tug-of-war and a spectacle as to who would overcome the other. Sometimes the man won. In this case the woman, though she grasped at earth, grass, and anything else, was dragged after him. Sometimes, however, the man was dragged after the woman, which caused others to laugh. But to me it seemed a matter more worthy of pity than of laughter, especially when I saw how some in this misery wept, sighed, and wrung their hands toward heaven, declaring that they would redeem themselves with gold and silver from this bondage. And I said to my interpreter, "Cannot some help be given them? Cannot those who are so unequally matched be unbound and freed from one another?"

"This cannot be," he replied. "As long as they live, they must remain in this state."

"Is there anything more cruel than this bondage and slavery? It is worse than death itself," I said.

He responded again, "Why did they not consider this better at first? It serves them right!"

Voluntary slavery

7. I then observed that Death pierced and knocked some down with her arrows. The chains of each person who was struck down in this manner were immediately broken open. I was sincerely happy for them, thinking that they themselves desired such release and would be truly glad for this liberation. Almost every one of them broke into tears and wailing such as I had never heard before anywhere in the world. They wrung their hands and lamented these unfortunate events. As for those whom I had at first observed living peacefully together, I understood that one really grieved the loss of his or her spouse. As for the rest, I

thought that they were merely putting on a show before other people, although I wager that they wished they could repent and would advise others to avoid the chains. But then, before I realized it, wiping their eyes, they ran before the gate again and returned in chains once more. "Oh, you wretches, you are not worthy of pity!" I said angrily. To my guide I said, "Let us go from here. I see more futility in this state than anything else."

The pilgrim also receives fetters

8. Meanwhile (for I do not wish to conceal my own experiences), we returned to the gate of division. Though I had earlier intended to investigate all things in the world, my guides, Ubiquitous and Delusion, began urging me strongly to try this state myself. They argued that I would better understand its nature, saying that I was young, that bad examples had frightened me, that I had not yet seen everything. But finally, as if in jest, they tricked me into getting onto the scale. Then I received chains and walked about yoked as one of four. They then added to me a number of others (for the purpose of service and honor, they said). Thus, panting and gasping, I was hardly able to pull them after me.

Suddenly a terrible storm struck unexpectedly, with lightning, thunder, and frightful hail. Everyone around me scattered, except for those who were joined to me. Though I also ran into a corner with them, the arrows of Death struck my three companions.[17] Being left alone in anguish and stunned with terror, I did not know what to do. My guides said that I should take advantage of this moment to escape more easily. "Why, then, did you first advise me to marry?" I asked. They replied that it was not time to quarrel, but to flee. So I hurried on.

His judgment about this state

9. Although I escaped from this state, as a matter of fact, I do not know what to say about it. I know not whether there is more comfort in it when it succeeds (as I presume there would have been in my case) or more sorrows resulting from many different causes. This only I recall, that both outside it and in it, there is sorrow; and that even when it succeeds best, sweetness is mixed with bitterness.

Chapter 9
The Pilgrim Observes the Working Class

What he saw there generally

Proceeding further, we entered a street where trades were conducted. This street was divided into many smaller alleys and squares, and everywhere there were different halls, workshops, forges, workrooms, shops, and booths full of various unusual-looking tools. People used these tools in a curious fashion, all with crashing, banging, squeaking, squealing, whistling, piping, blowing, roaring, clattering, and rattling noises. I saw some here who dug and mined the earth, either by stripping its surface or by digging into its interior as moles. Others waded in the water, in rivers, or in the sea. Some tended fires, while others gaped at the air, fought with wild beasts, busied themselves with wood and stone, and conveyed goods to and fro. My interpreter said to me, "Behold, how brisk and cheerful this work is. What profession here pleases you the most?"

"It may be that there is some happiness here," I replied. "Along with it, however, I see much drudgery, and I hear much groaning."

"Not all of it is so arduous. Let us look closer at some of these occupations," he suggested. They led me through them one after another, and I viewed them all. I also tried one or the other of them for the sake of experience, but I am not able nor do I want to describe them all. However, I will not remain silent about what I examined in general.

Dangerous striving in every trade

1. First, I saw that all of these human enterprises are only toil and vain striving. Each had some discomfort and danger of its own. I saw that those who worked with fire were burnt and blackened like Moors. The clatter of hammers was always ringing in their ears and made them half deaf. The glow of the fire shone in their eyes, and their skin was continually singed. Those who worked underground had darkness and horrors as companions, and more than once it happened that they were buried alive.

84

Those who worked in water were as drenched as a wet thatched roof, and shook with cold like aspen leaves; their bowels were raw; and not a few of them fell prey to the deep. Those who occupied themselves with wood, stone, and other heavy objects were full of callouses and grunted with fatigue. Indeed, I saw how some engaged in asinine tasks, laboring and exerting themselves to the point of sweat, exhaustion, collapse, injury, and total breakdown. Nevertheless, even with their miserable labor, they were hardly able to earn bread. It is true that I saw others who lived more easily and with greater remuneration, but the less drudgery, the more vice and fraud there were.

Incessant striving

2. Second, I saw that the toil of all people is for the sake of food. For whatever they acquired, they crammed it all into their own mouths or those of their families. On rare occasions, however, they skimped on food in order to load their wallets. But I noticed that these were either full of holes, so that what had been gathered fell out again and others collected it; or someone came and tore the wallet away; or the owner himself tripped and dropped it, tore it, or lost it through some other mishap. I saw clearly that these human endeavors were like water flowing from one vessel into another, earning money and spending it again. The only difference was that money was more easily spent than earned, whether stuffed through the mouth or stored in chests. As a result, everywhere I looked I saw more needy than wealthy people.

Toilsome striving

3. Third, I observed that every occupation demanded the whole person. If anyone looked around or acted somewhat hesitantly, he remained behind and everything fell from his hands, and before he realized it, he found himself reduced to poverty.

Arduous striving

4. Fourth, I saw many difficulties everywhere. Before someone started in an occupation, a good part of his life had passed. Moreover, once having set out, if he did not give careful attention

to himself, everything turned against him. Finally, I noticed that even the most careful met with misfortune as often as with gain.

Striving that kindles envy

5. Fifth, I saw everywhere (especially among those in similar occupations) much envy and ill-will. If more work piled up for one person or more was bought from him, his neighbors gave him ugly looks. They gnashed their teeth, and if they could, they ruined his business. From such striving arose dissension, feuds, and cursing. Some, throwing their tools away out of impatience, gave themselves over to idleness and voluntary poverty in defiance of others.

Sinful striving

6. Sixth, I saw everywhere much falsehood and deception. Whatever anyone did, especially for someone else, he did shoddily and carelessly. At the same time, he exalted and praised his own work as much as he could.

Vain and pointless striving

7. Seventh, I found here much pointless vanity. I clearly acknowledged that the greater part of these occupations were nothing but mere vanity and useless foolishness. For the human body is preserved by plain and simple food and drink, is clad in plain and simple garments, is sheltered in a plain and simple dwelling; clearly it requires little and simple care and labor, even as in ancient times. Nevertheless, I recognized that the world either could not or would not comprehend this truth. People had become accustomed to stuffing and filling their bellies with so many and such unusual delicacies that a great number of them had to work on land and sea, staking their strength and even their lives to obtain them. To prepare such delicacies, special masters are required. Similarly, a significant number of people were busy gathering different materials for clothing and shelter and designing them in a variety of preposterous styles. All this is superfluous, vain, and often even sinful. Likewise I also saw craftsmen whose whole art and labor consisted in making child-

ish trifles or other games intended for amusement and wasting time. There were others whose work consisted in fashioning instruments of cruelty—swords, daggers, battle-maces, muskets, and so forth—all for the destruction of humanity. I do not know how people pursuing such livelihoods can have a clear conscience and such cheerful thoughts. But I do know that if what was unnecessary, superfluous, and sinful in people's occupations were to be removed or eliminated, that most businesses would collapse. Because of this, as well as the reasons noted above, my mind took no delight in anything here.

Striving more fitting for beasts than for humans

8. I felt this way especially when I saw that this work was only done by the body and for the body. However, humanity possesses something greater, the soul. Therefore one ought to labor most for the soul and to seek its gain above all else.[18]

9. I especially want to mention how I fared among the freight carriers on land and among the sailors on the sea. When I became depressed examining the workshops, Ubiquitous said to Delusion, "I see that this man is of a restless disposition, always wanting to move about like mercury. Not a single place smells good to him. He would not want to be tied down anywhere. Let us show him a freer occupation, commerce, where he could move throughout the world and fly about freely like a bird."

"I am not against trying this," I said. So we went on.

Striving of the freight carrier's life

10. I saw a crowd of people turning about here and there, gathering, collecting, hoisting, and tying into bundles all kinds of things, even kindling wood, soil, and manure. I asked what they were doing. They replied that they were preparing to travel through the world. "But why not without this load?" I asked. "They could proceed more easily."

"You are a fool," they replied. "How could they proceed? For these are their wings."

"Wings?" I asked.

"Certainly wings. These give them both resolve and courage,

as well as a passport and safe-conduct everywhere. Or do you think that everyone roams freely throughout the world without a purpose? From this they must earn a living, gain favor, and everything else."

Then I looked, and saw how they tied as many of these bundles as they could gather, and rolled and fastened them onto a type of dolly on wheels. Fastening beasts to them, they dragged all these bundles over hills and mountains, through valleys and ravines, rejoicing in what they considered a merry life. So it seemed to me in the beginning. But I saw how here and there they got stuck in the mud, wallowed in it, pushing and pulling, and how they endured the many discomforts of rain, snow, storms, blizzards, cold, and heat. On all the mountain passes, people lurked in ambush for them, attacked them, and emptied their purses (for neither anger, scuffling, nor threats were of any effect in such instances). When I observed such bands of robbers attacking them on the highways and saw that their lives were always in great danger, I became disgusted with their work.

Discomforts of the sailor's life

11. They then said that there is a more comfortable manner of flying about the world, that of navigation. By this means a person is not shaken about, spattered with mud, nor stuck in a rut; but he could be shot from one end of the world to the other, everywhere finding something new, unseen, or unheard of. They led me to the ends of the earth, where we saw before us nothing but sky and water.

Description of a ship

12. There they told me to enter a certain little cottage made of planks. It did not stand on the ground, nor was it based on a foundation, nor was it underpinned by braces, columns, or supports. Rather, it rested on the water and wobbled to and fro, so that one entered it with misgivings. But when others entered it, I went also, so that I would not appear cowardly, for they said that this was our vehicle. I was thinking then that we would set out, or as they put it, fly. But we stood there on the second, third, and

tenth day. "What's this?" I asked. "Didn't you say that we would be shot from one end of the world to another? Yet we are not able to move from this place at all."

They answered that our horses were coming and that these horses need neither inns, stables, fodder, spurs, nor whip. One need only harness them and drive off. Just wait and see. Meanwhile they showed me reins, ropes, traces, doubletrees, singletrees, shafts, axle-trees, fore-hounds, side-poles, and various levers, all different from those of the freight carriers' wagons. The carriage was lying flat on its back, with its shafts, made of two of the tallest pine trees, sticking upright in the air, and with ropes, rigging, and ladders running from their tops to the railing around.[19] The axle-tree of this vehicle was in the back, and a single man sitting beside it boasted that he could turn this monstrous contraption wherever he wished.

Description of navigation

13. Then the wind arose. Our crew got up, began running, jumping, shouting, and screaming. One grasped one thing, another something else. Some climbed up and down the ropes like squirrels, letting down the poles, letting out the rolled up sails, and doing other similar activities. "What is this?" I asked.

They answered that they were in the process of harnessing. And I saw our sails swell to the size of barns (they said that these were our wings). Then the wind above us began to whiz, and the water below us began to splash and spray. Before I knew it, the coast, the land, and everything else was lost from view. "Where are we going?" I asked. "What is going to happen?"

They said that we were flying. "Then in the name of God, let us fly," I exclaimed. I marveled, not without pleasure, yet also not without fear, at how fast we were moving. For if I went outside to look about, a fit of dizziness seized me, and when I went down to the bottom, I was overcome by fear of the water violently rushing against the sides. And I began to think, was it not great audacity to entrust one's life to such raging elements as water and wind, and purposely to cast oneself into the face of Death, from which we were separated by the space of merely two fingers? For such was the thickness of the board between me and the frightful abyss. But having resolved to conceal my fear, I remained silent.

Seasickness

14. Then a raw stench began to overcome me, penetrating my brain and all my inward parts so that I fell down. I rolled and shrieked (as did others unaccustomed to this experience), not knowing what to do. Everything in me dissolved and poured out of me. It seemed to me as though we would dissolve there on the water like a snail shrivels in the sun. I began to reproach myself and cry out against my guides, not believing that I could stay alive. But from them I got laughter instead of pity. For they knew from experience (as I did not) that this state would last but a few days. So it happened. My strength gradually returned to me again, and I realized that the raging sea had merely welcomed me.

Calm at sea

15. But what next? More difficult things then came upon us. The wind left us, our wings drooped, and we stood still, unable to move a hair's breadth. Again I knit my brow, wondering what would happen. We have been carried here to the wilderness of the sea. Will we ever get out again? Will we ever again see the land of the living? Oh, dear Mother Earth, Earth, dear mother, where are you? God the Creator gave fish to the sea, and to us he gave you. Fish prudently remain in their dwelling-place, but we foolishly abandon ours. Unless heaven hastens to help us, we will perish in this sad abyss. My soul did not cease to be troubled by such grievous thoughts until the sailors began to shout. Running out, I asked, "What is this?" They replied that the wind was coming. I looked, but saw nothing. They let out the sails. The wind came, seized us, and carried us on again. This brought joy to everyone, but our rejoicing soon turned bitter.

Storm at sea

16. Indeed, the storm grew so violent that not only we, but the depths beneath were shaken; and terror entered our hearts. The sea rolled with such waves on all sides that we were thrown as if

onto high mountains and into deep valleys, now upward, now downward. Sometimes we were shot up so high that it seemed as if we could reach the moon; then again we descended into the abyss. Then it seemed that a wave, coming against us or the sides of the boat, would rush upon us and sink us on the spot. But then it merely lifted us up, so that our wooden vessel was bounced about and tossed from one wave to another. It fell sometimes to this side, sometimes to the other side; the prow rose at one moment perpendicularly upward, then downward. Not only was the water sprayed on us and above us into the air, but we could neither stand nor lie down, but were pitched from side to side, standing one moment on our feet, one moment on our heads. This turbulence caused dizziness, and nausea seized us. One can well imagine what kind of horrors and fears we experienced as we were trapped in the storm day and night.

I thought to myself, "Of all people in the world, these sailors have reason to be devout, for they are not certain of their lives even for an hour." But looking around them to see how religious they were, I saw that they gorged themselves in the tavern, drinking, playing, howling with laughter, talking obscenely, blaspheming, and indulging in all manner of debauchery. Saddened by this sight, I began to upbraid them and entreated them to remember our situation at sea, to cease such behavior, and to call upon God. But to what avail? Some laughed at me, others snapped at me, threatened me, or prepared to throw me overboard. My guide Delusion told me to be silent and reminded me that I was a guest in a strange house where it was best to be deaf and blind. "But it is impossible that our situation will turn our well with such behavior," I said. Once again they broke out in laughter. Seeing such mischievousness, I decided to be silent, fearing some kind of beating from them.

Shipwreck

17. Then the storm intensified, and a terrible gale came upon us. The waves of the sea began to rise to the sky like smoke. They tossed us like a ball. The depths opened up, threatening one moment to devour us, the next to throw us up. The wind whirled

around us, carrying us here, then casting us there. Everything crashed, as if it would be shattered into a hundred thousand pieces. I considered myself dead, seeing nothing but destruction before me. Unable to resist the violence of the storm and fearing to be driven onto the rocks or shallows, they took down the wings and threw out large iron hooks on thick ropes. In this way they hoped to anchor the boat until the storm had passed. But in vain. Indeed, some of them who were climbing the ropes were thrown off and cast into the sea like caterpillars by the force of the wind. By this same force, the anchors were ripped away and sunk into the depths. Defenseless, both we and our boat began to be thrown about like a piece of wood on a river current. Then even the sailors, those iron-willed giants, lost heart. They turned pale, trembled, and did not know what to do. Only then did they remember God. They urged us to pray, and they themselves clasped their hands in prayer. Our boat began on the one hand to sink to the bottom of the sea, and also to strike against hidden rocks under the water, causing it to sink and break apart. Water poured into the boat through the cracks. Whoever was able, whether old or young, was ordered to bail it out; however, nothing was effective. The water pressed in on us forcefully and drew us in. There was weeping, shouting, and incessant cries. No one saw anything but cruel death before his eyes.

However, since life is dear, each one seized what he could—tables, planks, or poles—hoping that he could thereby save himself from drowning and perhaps somehow swim to safety. When the boat finally broke apart and everything sank, I also seized something and came with a few others to a shore. That frightful abyss had devoured everyone else.

Having hardly recovered from fear and horror, I began to reproach my guides for leading me here. They replied that nothing had harmed me. I should be of good cheer since we had survived. Good cheer indeed! To the day of my death I will not allow myself to be led into such a situation.

18. Looking around, I saw that those who had been saved with me ran and once again boarded ships. "You foolhardy people," I

exclaimed. "Return to all your unhappiness. I do not even want to look at this anymore."

My interpreter said, "Not everyone is so spoiled, dear brother, as to have property and wealth. To obtain them, one must risk even one's own life."

To this I replied, "Am I a beast that I should risk my life for the body and its pleasures? No, not even a beast does this. And humankind, possessing something even greater, the soul, should seek its gain and pleasure."

Chapter 10
The Pilgrim Examines the Learned Class: A General Survey

1. "I understand where your thoughts are pulling you," my guide said to me. "Among the learned with you, among the learned. You will surely be attracted by this easier, more peaceful, and more useful life for the mind."

"Indeed that is so," said the Interpreter. "For what can be more delightful than ignoring and neglecting the toils of the physical body in order to engage only in the examination of all manner of noble things? That is truly what makes mortal people similar, indeed almost equal, to immortal God. For they hope to become omniscient, knowing and pursuing all that was or will be in heaven, on earth, or in the depths. It is true, however, that not everyone reaches the same level of perfection."

"Lead me there," I said. "Why do you hesitate?"

First of all, a difficult examination

2. We came to a gate called Discipline. It was long, narrow, and dark, full of armed guards, to whom each one who wished to enter the street of the learned had to give account and seek their guidance. I saw that crowds of people, especially the young, came and immediately went through various rigorous examinations. The first examination for each person investigated what kind of purse, buttocks, head, brain (which they judged by the nasal mucus), and

skin they brought. If the head were of steel, the brain inside it of mercury, the buttocks of lead, the skin of iron, and the purse of gold, they praised the person and readily conducted him further. If he lacked one of these five qualities, they either ordered him to return or, foreboding an unhappy outcome, admitted him at random. Wondering at this, I said, "Does so much depend on these five metals that they are sought so diligently?"

"Very much, indeed," the interpreter answered. "If one does not have a head of steel, it will burst; without a brain of mercury, he would not have a mirror;[20] without skin of sheet iron, he would not endure the educational process; without a seat of lead, he would not endure sitting and would lose everything; and without a purse of gold, where would he obtain time and teachers, both living and dead? Or do you presume that such great things can be obtained without cost?"

I then understood the direction of his comments, that one must bring to this profession health, wits, perseverance, patience, and money. "It can be truly affirmed," I said, "*Non cuivis contingit adire Corinthum.*[21] Not all wood is sufficiently solid."

Entrance is difficult and painful

Memoria artificialis

3. We proceeded further to the gate, and I saw that each guard took one or more of the candidates and led them along. He blew something in their ears, rubbed their eyes, cleaned their noses and nostrils, pulled out and trimmed their tongues, folded and unfolded their hands and fingers, and I do not know what more. Some even tried to bore holes in their heads and pour something into them. Seeing me alarmed, my interpreter said, "Do not be amazed. The learned must possess hands, tongue, eyes, ears, brain, and all internal and external senses different from the masses of ignorant people. For this reason they are reshaped, and this cannot be done without toil and pain.

Then I looked and saw how much these poor wretches had to pay for their education. I am not talking about their purses, but about their skin, which they had to expose. Indeed, they were often struck with fists, pointers, rods, and canes on their face, head, back, and seat until they shed blood and were almost completely covered with stripes, scars, bruises, and callouses. Seeing this, before they surrendered themselves to the guards, some only looked through the gate and ran away. Others, tearing themselves free from the hands of their educators, also fled. A lesser number of them persevered until they were released. Desiring to enter this profession, I too underwent this education, though not without difficulty and bitterness.[22]

Every scholar is given a password

4. When we went through the gate, I saw that they gave to each who had undergone the preliminary training a stamp by which he could be recognized as belonging among the learned: an inkwell under his belt, a pen behind his ear, and for the hand an empty book for collecting knowledge. I too received these items. Searchall then said to me, "We have here four paths: philosophy, medicine, law, and theology. Where shall we go first?"

"What do you consider best?" I asked.

"Let us first go to the square where everyone assembles so that you can look at them all together. Then we will go to their various lecture halls."

Deficiencies even among the learned

5. He led me to a certain square where there was a mob of students, teachers, doctors, and priests—both youths and gray-haired men. Some of them gathered in groups, discussing and disputing among themselves. Others squeezed into corners out of the sight of the rest. Some (as I clearly perceived, though I dared not speak of it) had eyes, but no tongues; others had tongues, but no eyes; still others had only ears, without eyes or tongues. Thus I realized that here too there were deficiencies. Seeing that all were going out from and coming into a certain place, like bees swarming in and out of a hive, I asked that we also might enter.

Description of a library

6. So we entered. Here was a great hall, the end of which I could not see, but on all sides it was full of shelves, compartments, boxes,

and cartons. A hundred thousand wagons could not remove them, and each had its own inscription and title. "Into what kind of apothecary shop have we come?" I asked.

"Into an apothecary shop where medicines against ailments of the mind are kept," said the interpreter. "This place is properly called a library. Just look at these endless stores of wisdom!"

I looked around and saw groups of scholars coming and walking around these items. Some, choosing the finest and most sophisticated, tore off a piece and ate it, slowly chewing and digesting. Approaching one of these scholars, I asked what he was doing.

"I am improving myself," he answered.

"And how does it taste?" I inquired.

"As long as one chews, it tastes bitter or acidic, but later it turns sweet," he replied.[23]

"But why are you doing this?" I asked.

"It is easier for me to carry it inside," he answered, "and in this way I am surer of it. Do you not see its use?" I looked at him more carefully, and I saw that he was stout and fat, had a healthy color, his eyes shone like candles, his speech was careful, and everything about him was lively.

"Just look at these people!" the interpreter said to me.

The evils of studies

7. I saw some people who behaved very greedily, stuffing themselves with whatever came into their hands. Observing them more carefully, I noticed that they neither improved their complexion nor gained flesh or fat, but their stomachs were swollen and never satisfied. I also saw that what they crammed into themselves came out of them again undigested, either from above or from below. Some of them fainted from dizziness or went mad. Others grew pale, pined, and died. Many who saw these people pointed at them, indicating how dangerous it was to use books (as they called the boxes).[24] Thereupon some ran away, and others exhorted people to deal with those things cautiously. Hence this latter group did not eat the books. Rather they filled them in sacks and bags and carried them in front and in back.

(Most of the titles selected were Vocabulary, Dictionary, Lexicon, *Promtuarium, Florilegium, Loci communes,* Postils, Concordances, Herbaria, and so forth, according to what each judged most appropriate.) They carried these about, and whenever they had to speak or to write, they pulled them out of their pockets and drew forth whatever was needed for their mouth or pen. Noticing this, I said, "These people carry their knowledge in their pockets."

"Memoriae subsidia," my interpreter replied. "Haven't you heard of them?"

I had indeed heard this custom praised by some people, for it is said that they brought forth only knowledge that was sanctioned. This may very well be, but I also noticed other inconveniences. It happened in my presence that some scattered and lost their boxes, while those of others, who had laid them aside, caught fire. Oh, what running about, wringing of hands, lamenting and crying for help ensued. For the moment, no one wanted to dispute, write, or preach anymore; rather they walked about with downcast head, cringed, blushed, and sought another container from whomever they knew, with entreaty or with money. Those who had an inner store of knowledge did not fear such an incident.[25]

Students who do not study

8. Meanwhile, I saw others who did not bother carrying the boxes of books in their pockets but brought them to their rooms. Going in after them, I saw that they prepared beautiful cases for them. They painted them in various colors, and some even adorned them with silver and gold. They looked at the books, putting them on and taking them off the shelves again. They packed and unpacked them, and approaching and withdrawing, they showed each other and strangers how beautiful they looked. All this was done superficially. Occasionally some also looked at the titles so that they would know what they were called. "Why are these people playing such games?" I asked.

"Dear fellow," the interpreter answered, "it is a fine thing to have a beautiful library."

"Even if it is not used?" I questioned.

"Those who love libraries are reckoned among the learned," he explained.

I thought to myself, "This is like counting someone among blacksmiths who has heaps of hammers and tongs but doesn't know how to use them." But I did not dare say this for fear of suffering a blow.

Evils of writing books

9. Entering the hall again, I noticed that the apothecary containers on all sides were ever increasing, and I tried to see where they were coming from. I saw a certain closed off area. Entering it, I found many turners who vied with one another to shape more carefully and artistically the boxes from wood, bone, stone, and various other materials. They filled them with salve or medicine and offered them for general consumption. "These people are worthy of praise and all honor," the interpreter said to me, "for sparing no toil or effort for the increase of wisdom and knowledge, they share their glorious gifts with others."

I desired to examine how these potions (which are called gifts and wisdom) were made and prepared. I observed one or two people who gathered fragrant spices and herbs, then cut, ground, boiled, and distilled them, preparing various delightful remedies, cures, syrups, and other medicines useful for human life. On the other hand, I saw some who merely took from the vessels of others and transferred the contents to their own. Of these there were hundreds. "These people are only pouring water from one vessel into another," I exclaimed.

"And so is knowledge increased," my interpreter responded. "For is it not possible that one thing is prepared in different ways? And something can always be added to or improved in the original substance."

"And ruined as well," I answered angrily, seeing clearly that a fraud was being perpetrated. Indeed, some seized others' vessels in order to fill several of their own, then diluted the contents as much as possible, even with dirty dishwater. Still others thickened it with various odds and ends, even dust or refuse, so that it would appear as if something new had been made. Meanwhile, they added inscriptions more glorious than the original ones and, like other quacks, they shamelessly extolled their own work.

I was both amazed and angered (as I noted above) that few examined the true content of the substance, but took everything indiscriminately. And if they chose, they looked only at the outer appearance and inscriptions. Then I understood why it is that so few of them attained inner freshness of mind. For the more of these medicines a person gulped down, the more he vomited, turned pale, faded and wasted away.

I also observed that the great part of these fine remedies were never even used by human beings, but were only the portion of moths, worms, spiders and flies, dust and mildew, and were finally relegated to dusty shelves and back corners. Fearing this fate, some people, as soon as they had prepared their remedy (indeed some even before they had seriously begun to prepare it), ran to neighbors to beg for prefaces, verses, and anagrams. They also sought patrons who would lend their names and purses to the new preparations. They painted most ornate titles and inscriptions or embellished the various figures and engravings with decorative floral designs. They personally brought such potions to people, and crammed them down their throats against their will.

I saw, however, that this effort finally failed because the concoctions had been multiplied too much. Therefore, I pitied some who could have had complete peace, yet needlessly and uselessly gave themselves to this quackery, even at the risk of their own reputation and to the detriment of their neighbors. When I offered warnings in this regard, I gained only hatred, as if I had impeded the common good. I kept silent about how some prepared their quack remedies out of thoroughly toxic materials. As a result, as many poisons as medicines were being sold. Though I bore this evil with displeasure, there was no one to correct it.

Discord and strife

10. Then we returned to the square of the learned, and behold there were quarrels, strife, and fights between them. It was rare indeed for someone not to be involved in some type of scuffle.

Not only the young (whose impudence could be attributed to their age), but also the old, were fighting each other. For the more learned one considered himself or was esteemed by others, the more quarrels he began; and he fought, hacked, threw, and shot those around him until it was frightful to behold. He based his honor and esteem on such behavior.

"But dear God, what is this?" I asked. "For I thought and you had promised me that this profession was the most peaceful, yet I find so many quarrels."

"You do not understand, my son," the interpreter answered. "They are merely sharpening their wits."

"Sharpening their wits?" I retorted. "But I see wounds, blood, anger, and murderous hatred of one toward another. Even among the working class, I have seen nothing like this."

"Doubtless," said he, "for the arts of such people are manual and slavish, whereas these others are concerned with the liberal arts. Therefore, what is not permitted or even tolerated by the former group is freely granted to the latter."

"But how that can be called orderly I do not know," I said. It is true that their weapons did not appear fearful. For the spears, swords, and daggers with which they hacked and stabbed each other were made of leather, and they did not hold them in their hands but in their mouths. Their artillery was made of reeds and sand, loaded with dust dissolved in water,[26] and they shot at each other with paper. On the surface, as I said, none of this appeared fearful. However, seeing how one who was lightly wounded jerked, cried out, writhed, and fled, I clearly recognized that this was no joke, but a real fight. One individual was attacked by a great number of others until the clang of swords deafened the ears and paper bullets fell on him like hail. Defending himself courageously, one person drove off and dispersed all his assailants. Another fell, overcome by wounds. I observed here a cruelty unusual elsewhere. They spared neither the wounded nor the dead, but mercilessly hacked and lashed at them all the more, each more gladly proving his valor against one who did not defend himself. Some behaved more moderately, though they were not free from disputes and misunderstandings. For no sooner did someone utter a word than someone else immediately contradicted him. There were even arguments about whether snow was white or black, or whether fire was hot or cold.

Great confusion among them

11. Then some began to intervene in these quarrels and to counsel peace. This sight gladdened me. A rumor also arose that all quarrels were to be settled. The question remained as to who would bring about this reconciliation. The reply was that by the permission of Queen Wisdom, the most judicious people of all estates should be chosen and given authority, after hearing the opposing sides, to make a decision on each case and to declare which was the truer argument. Many of those who were chosen or who wished to be judges gathered together. There also assembled a great multitude of those who disputed among themselves over different views. Among them I saw Aristotle with Plato,[27] Cicero with Sallust,[28] Scotus with Aquinas,[29] Bartolus with Bardus,[30] Erasmus with the Sorbonnists,[31] Ramus and Campanella with the Peripatetics,[32] Copernicus with Ptolemy,[33] Theophrastus with Galen,[34] Hus, Luther, and others with the pope and the Jesuits,[35] Brenz with Beza,[36] Bodin with Wier,[37] Sleidanus with Surius,[38] Schmiedlein with the Calvinists,[39] Gomarus with Arminius,[40] the Rosicrucians with the philosophasters,[41] and countless others. When the *conciliatores* ordered them to present their charges, complaints, arguments, and inferences in the shortest possible written form, they piled up such heaps of books that six thousand years would not suffice to survey them. They desired that this outline of their opinions be accepted at the moment. Later, as need arose, each should be given complete freedom to explain and defend their views more fully. Then they began to look at these books; and whatever book one scanned immediately intoxicated him, and he began to defend its ideas. So there arose among the arbiters and mediators great dissensions; for one defended one view, another something else. Consequently, they solved nothing and dispersed. The learned returned to their quarrels, and I was brought to tears.

Chapter 11
The Pilgrim Among the Philosophers

In general

1. The interpreter said to me, "Now I will lead you among the philosophers, whose task it is to discover the means of correcting human deficiencies and to show where true wisdom lies."

"God grant that I may learn something certain," I said.

"Of course you will," he replied, "for these are people who know the truth of everything, without whose knowledge neither does heaven reveal anything nor hell conceal anything. They nobly guide human life toward virtue, they enlighten communities and countries, they have God for a friend, and their wisdom penetrates his mysteries."

"Let us go then," I urged. "Let us go among them as soon as possible." But when he led me there and I observed the multitude of old men and their strange behavior and trivial antics, I stiffened. Indeed here Bion sat quietly; Anacharsis walked about; Thales flew; Hesiod plowed; Plato hunted in the air for ideas; Homer sang; Aristotle disputed; Pythagoras kept silent; Epimenides slept; Archimedes pushed back the earth; Solon wrote laws and Galen prescriptions; Euclid measured the hall; Cleobulus searched the future; Periander measured out duties; Pittacus waged war; Bias begged; Epictetus served; Seneca praised poverty while sitting amidst tons of gold; Socrates told everyone that he knew nothing; Xenophon, on the contrary, promised to teach everyone everything; Diogenes found fault with every passerby while peering out of a barrel; Timon cursed everybody. Democritus laughed at all this; Heraclitus, on the other hand, cried; Zeno fasted; Epicurus feasted; Anaxarchus proclaimed that all this was really nothing, but only seemed to be something real. There were many similar philosophers, and each one promulgated something special, which I neither remember nor wish to recall.[42] "Are these then the wise men, the light of the world?" I exclaimed, observing this spectacle. "Alas, I had hoped for something else. These people are like peasants in a tavern. Each one howls his own song."

"You stupid fellow," said my interpreter, "you do not understand such mysteries." Hearing that these were mysteries, I began to reflect on them carefully, and the interpreter started to explain them to me.

Just then a certain man, dressed in the garb of a philosopher (he was called Paul of Tarsus), approached me and whispered in my ear: "If any one considers himself wise in this world, let him be a fool, that he may be made wise. Indeed the wisdom of this world is foolishness with God. For it is written, 'The Lord knows the thoughts of the wise, that they are futile.'"[43]

Since what my eyes saw and ears heard agreed with these words, I willingly acquiesced and said, "Let us go elsewhere." My interpreter then berated me for being a fool, for though I had something to learn from the wise, I fled them. But I proceeded in silence.

He came among the grammarians

2. Then we came to an auditorium full of young and old who were drawing letters, lines, and points with writing implements. Whenever one wrote or said anything different from another, they either laughed at him or quarreled with him. Moreover, they hung words on the walls and disputed as to what belonged to which. Then they composed, separated, and rearranged them in different ways. Looking at this and seeing nothing in it, I said, "These are children's games; let us go elsewhere."

Among the rhetoricians

3. We entered another hall where many people stood with brushes discussing how words, either written or released from the mouth into the air, could be colored green, red, black, white, or whatever shade one desired. I asked why this was so.

"So that the listeners' brain may be colored in this fashion or another," my interpreter replied.

"Are these colors used for the portrayal of truth or lies?" I asked.

"Either one," he answered.

"Then there is as much falsehood and vanity here as truth and benefit," I concluded, and I went out from there.

Among the poets

4. We entered another place where a crowd of nimble youths were weighing syllables on scales and measuring them with rulers while frolicking and jumping about. I wondered what this was, and the interpreter said to me, "Of all the literary arts, none is more skillful and merry than this one."

"But what is it?" I asked.

"Whatever cannot be said by the simple coloring of words is expressed by this process of folding them," he explained.

Seeing that those who were learning this technique of folding words referred to certain books, I also looked at them and saw their titles: *De Culice, De Passere, De Lesbia, De Priapo, De arte amandi, Metamorphoses, Encomia, Satirae;* in sum, farces, poems, amorous adventures, and all kinds of frivolities.[44] This whole process disgusted me, especially when I saw that whenever one flattered these measurers of syllables, they expended all their art on his adulation; but when one did not suit them, they cast all manner of ridicule at him. This art was used only for praise or scorn. Having seen how passionate these people were, I gladly hurried away from them.

Among the dialecticians

5. Going further, we entered another building where they made and sold eyeglasses. When I asked what they were, he replied that they were *Notiones secundae.* Whoever possessed them saw not only the surface but to the inner core. One could especially observe another's brain and examine his mind. Many people came and bought these glasses; and masters taught them how to put them on and, when necessary, to adjust them. The masters who made these glasses were specialists, and they had their workshops in remote corners. However, they did not make the glasses uniformly. One made them large, another small; one round, another square. Each one praised his own goods and tried to attract buyers. Meanwhile, they argued implacably and threw things at each other. Some bought glasses from each dealer and set them all on their noses; others chose and put on only one pair. Some said that they could not see as deeply as had

been promised; others affirmed that they could, and claimed to penetrate even the depths of the brain and intellect [literally, pointed to each other beyond the brain and even beyond all intellect]. But among this latter group I saw several people who, when they began to step forward, immediately fell over stones and logs and into pits. (As I have already said, the place was full of such obstructions.) "How is it that though everything can be seen through these glasses, yet they do not avoid these obstacles?" I inquired. He answered that not the glasses, but those who do not know how to use them are at fault.

The masters also said that it was not sufficient to have the glasses of dialecticians, but that one's vision must be cleaned with the clear eye salve of physics and mathematics. Therefore they should go to other halls and have their vision improved. So they went, one here, another there. And I said to my guide, "Let us go as well." However, I did not succeed in this until, at the instigation of Searchall, I too had secured and put on some of these glasses. It is true that it seemed I could see somewhat more, and that some things could be seen from several points of view. But I urged that we continue onward, wanting to try the eye salve about which they had spoken.

Among the natural scientists[45]

6. So we went, and they led me to a certain square in the middle of which I saw a large wide-spreading tree on which grew all manner of leaves and fruits (all in shells). They called it *nature*. Around it was a crowd of philosophers, examining it and telling each other what the branches, leaves, and fruits were called. "I hear that these people are learning the names of these objects," said I, "but I do not yet see that they understand nature."

"Not everyone can do that," the interpreter answered, "but watch these people."

I saw some break off branches and open the leaves and shell the fruit. When they came to the nuts, they gnawed at them until they cracked their teeth. But they claimed that they had cracked the shells, and picking through them, they boasted that they had discovered the kernel. Only rarely did they show them secretly to one another. However, carefully surveying the process, I saw clearly that they had broken and crushed the outer rind and husk, but that the hardest shell, which contained the kernel, was still whole. Seeing, then, their vain pretensions and futile striving (indeed I saw how some of them lost their sight and broke their teeth), I urged that we go elsewhere.

Among the metaphysicians

7. Thus, we entered another hall, where philosophers had before them cows, asses, wolves, snakes, and various other beasts; birds and reptiles, as well as wood, stone, water, fire, clouds, stars, and planets—indeed, even angels. They disputed over how each of these creatures could be deprived of the features that distinguished it from others so that all would become alike. They first divested them of form, then of substance, and finally of all accidents, until only the being remained.

Unum, verum, bonum

Then they quarreled as to whether all these things were one and the same, whether all were good, and whether all things really were what they appear to be, and many other similar questions. Observing these discussions, some people began to express their amazement at how high human intellect had risen that it could grasp the essence of all being and divest all corporeal things of their corporeality. I too became fascinated by these subtleties. Just then, someone stepped forward and cried out that these were only fantasies and should be abandoned.[46] Indeed, he attracted a following. But others rose up and condemned them as heretics, claiming that they wanted to deprive philosophy of its status as the highest form of knowledge, in a sense decapitating the head of the arts. After listening to these squabbles, I left this place.

Among the arithmeticians

8. Next we came upon a group of people whose hall was full of numbers through which they were sorting. Some, taking a few from the pile, set them aside; others, scooping up handfuls, piled them into heaps. Some took a portion from these piles and placed them separately; while another group gathered these portions

into one pile again. Still others divided and distributed them until I was amazed at their work. Meanwhile they recounted how in all of philosophy there was no more certain knowledge than theirs, for here there could be no error, no loss, no excess.[47]

"What, then, is the purpose of this knowledge?" I asked.

Amazed at my stupidity, they began one after another to recount marvels to me. One told me without counting them how many geese were flying in a flock. Another told me how long it would take a cistern with five pipes to empty itself. A third told me how many pennies I had in my purse without looking into it. One even undertook to count the grains of sand of the sea and immediately wrote a book about it (Archimedes). Another, following his example (but wanting to show more subtleties), devoted himself to counting the dust flying in the sunlight (Euclid). I stood amazed. Wanting to help me understand, they showed me their rules: *trium, societatis, alligationis, falsi,* which I vaguely understood.[48] But when they wanted to lead me to the deepest knowledge of all, which is *algebra* or *cossa,* I saw there piles of such wild-looking zigzags and hooks that I was nearly overcome with giddiness. Closing my eyes, I begged to be led away.

Among the geometricians

9. We came to another auditorium, above which was written *Udeis ageametretos eisito.*[49] Stopping, I inquired, "Can we go there, since only geometricians are permitted?"

"Just go straight in," replied Ubiquitous. So we entered.

There were many in this place drawing lines, angles, crosses, circles, squares, and points, each one quietly and by himself. Then one approached another, and they showed each other their work. One said that it should be done otherwise, another that it was done well. And so they quarreled. If one discovered some new line or hook, he cried out with joy and called others to show them. They envied him, pointed their fingers, and turned their heads. Each ran to his own corner and tried to do likewise. One succeeded, another did not. In time, the entire hall, the floor, the walls, and the ceiling were full of lines; and they allowed no one to tread on them or touch them.

Praecipua apud geometras controversia, de quadrando circulo[50]

10. The most learned among them assembled in the middle and strove with great effort at a certain task, and I saw all the others waiting with open mouths. There was much talk about this, how it would be more amazing than any subtlety in the whole world, and how, should it be discovered, nothing else would be impossible. Curious about what this might be, I approached and observed that they had a circle between them and were questioning how it could be made into a square. When they had examined it with an immense expenditure of labor, they separated once again, advising each other to reflect on the problem on their own. Shortly thereafter, one of them suddenly jumped up and cried out,

(J. Scaliger)

"I have it! I have it! I have uncovered the secret!" They all gathered around him, hurrying to see and to marvel. And he, bringing forth a large folio volume, showed them. There arose shouts and cries such as is customary following a victory.

(J. Clavius)

However, another man soon put an end to this jubilation, shouting at the top of his lungs that they should not be deceived, that it was not a square. And having brought forth an even larger book, he converted all of the alleged squares into circles again, powerfully affirming that what had been attempted was not humanly possible. They all hung their heads and returned to their lines and hooks.[51]

Among the land surveyors

11. From there we went on to another hall where they sold fingers, spans, ells, fathoms, scales, measures, levers, windlasses, pulleys, and similar tools and which was full of people measuring and weighing. Some were measuring the hall itself, and almost everyone measured differently. Then they quarrelled and measured once again. Some measured the length, width, and depth of a shadow; others weighed it on a scale. In sum, they said that there was nothing in or out of the world that they could not measure. After observing their trade for some time, I recognized

that there was more boasting than practicality in all this activity. Shaking my head, I left.

Among the musicians

12. Then we came to another room that was full of music, singing, and the clanging and strumming of various instruments. Some people were standing around them, observing them from above, from below, and from the sides. They bent their ears in their desire to grasp what the sound was, where it came from, where it was going, and how and why it either did or did not make noise. Some claimed that they already knew and rejoiced, saying that this was something divine and a mystery above all mysteries. Therefore, with great zest and frolicking, they took apart, put together, and transposed the sounds. But not one in a thousand succeeded in this endeavor; the others only watched. Whenever someone wanted to try out an instrument, it creaked and squeaked. This happened to me as well. So seeing a sufficient number of prominent people who considered this a childish game and a waste of time, I went away.[52]

Among the astronomers

13. Then Ubiquitous led me upstairs to a kind of gallery where I saw a crowd of people making ladders and setting them against the sky. Then they climbed up and caught stars; and stretching out strings, rulers, weights, and compasses, they measured their orbits. Some sat and wrote rules determining when, where, and how they should meet or diverge. I marveled at this human audacity, daring to raise itself to the skies and give orders to the stars. Having a desire myself for such a glorious science, I also began to study it eagerly. I tried my hand at it, but clearly observed that the stars danced to a different tune than that of the astronomers. They themselves perceived this and complained of "the anomaly of the sky." They were always striving to place them in order, constantly changing their locations, bringing some down to earth or raising up the earth among them.[53] In general, they contrived various hypotheses, but none of them agreed perfectly with the facts.

Among the astrologers

14. Therefore, some no longer climbed up to the sky. Rather, merely observing the stars from below, they studied the direction of a star. Arranging their trines, quartiles, sextiles, conjunctions, oppositions, and other aspects, they predicted the fortunes or misfortunes of the future, either publicly to the world or privately to a specific individual. They wrote horoscopes and prognostics and distributed them among the people. Sometimes these caused dread and fear among the people, sometimes merriment. Some paid no attention to them, threw them into a corner, and called them astro-liars,[54] saying that even without the prognostications they could eat, drink, and sleep well enough. It seemed to me that this criticism should not be heeded if in fact the science itself were reliable. However, the more I examined the matter, the less certain it appeared to me. If one prediction should hit the target, five others would miss. Realizing, then, that it was easy to predict even without the stars when guessing correctly is praised and failure is excused, I considered it useless to delay myself any longer with such affairs.[55]

Among the historians

15. Then we came to another square where I observed something new. Not a few people stood here with certain crooked and curved pipes, one end of which they pressed to their eyes, and the other they placed over their shoulders facing backwards. When I inquired as to what this might be, the interpreter explained to me that they were telescopes with which one could see behind one's back. For whoever wishes to be human must not only see what lies before his feet, but must also look at what has passed and lies behind his back. This will enable him to learn lessons from the past for the present and the future. Assuming that this was something new (for I did not know before that such crooked telescopes were possible), I begged one of them to lend me his for a short while so that I could look through it. They handed me several of them, and oh, what a frightful sight! Through each one I saw things differently. Through one an object seemed far away, while through another the same thing seemed nearer. Through one tele-

scope something appeared one color, through another, a different color; and through a third, it disappeared altogether. Thus I determined that one could not be certain that things were as they appeared; rather the color a thing appeared depended on how the telescope was positioned. From this I perceived that each one believed his own perspective. Consequently, they argued bitterly about some issues. This displeased me.[56]

Among the moralists and politicians

16. When they began to lead me elsewhere, I asked, "Will there soon be an end to this learned profession? For it is wearisome to wander among them."

"The best is yet to come," Ubiquitous replied.

Then we entered a hall that was full of pictures. On one side they were exceedingly beautiful and pleasant. On the other side they were hideous and monstrous. Philosophers were walking around them, not only looking at them, but also adding what they could with colors to the beauty or ugliness of each one. I asked what this was, and the interpreter said to me, "What, don't you see the inscriptions above the pictures?" Then leading me onward, he showed me these inscriptions: Fortitude, Temperance, Justice, Concord, Government, etc., and on the other side, Pride, Gluttony, Lust, Discord, Tyranny, etc.

The philosophers begged and exhorted all the passers-by to love the beautiful and to hate the ugly, praising the former and denouncing and abusing the latter as much as they could. This pleased me greatly, and I said, "At last I have found people who are doing something good for their generation." Meanwhile, I noticed that those fine exhorters were no more partial to the beautiful than to the ugly pictures, nor did they refrain from the ugly any more than from the beautiful. In fact, not a few bustled very eagerly around the ugly ones. This sight attracted others also, and they dallied and amused themselves with these monstrosities. Then I said angrily, "Here I see that people say one thing and do another (as Aesop's wolf commented); for what their mouths praise, their mind rejects; and what their tongue claims to abhor, to that their heart inclines."

"I presume you are seeking angels among people!" the interpreter railed. "Will anything ever please you? You find fault everywhere." So I was quiet and hung my head, especially when I saw that all the others, aware that I was watching them, were looking at me disfavorably. So I left them and went out.

Chapter 12
The Pilgrim Examines Alchemy[57]

1. "Come along now," urged Ubiquitous, "I will lead you to a place where you will see the height of human ingenuity and such delightful work that whoever once turns to it can never again abandon it because of the noble pleasures it brings to the mind." I begged him not to delay showing me this place. Then he led me down to certain cellars where there were several rows of fireplaces, small ovens, cauldrons, and glass instruments, which were all shining. People tending fires gathered and piled on brushwood. They blew on it, then extinguished it again, alternately pouring things out and filling things up.

"Who are these people, and what are they doing?" I asked.

"They are the shrewdest philosophers," he replied, "who do what the sun with its heat cannot do in the bowels of the earth in many years, transforming all kinds of metals into their highest state, that is, into gold."

"But for what purpose" I asked, "for are not iron and other metals used more than gold?"

"What a fool you are," said he, "for gold is the rarest metal, and whoever has it need not fear poverty."

Lapis philosophicus[58]

2. "Moreover, that which changes metals into gold also has other amazing powers. For example, it preserves human health in its wholeness until death and wards off death for two or three hundred years. In fact, whoever learns to use it could make himself immortal. Indeed, this stone is none other than the seed of

life, the kernel and essence of the whole world, from which animals, plants, metals, and even the elements derive their being."

Upon hearing these amazing claims, I was shocked. "Are these people, then, immortal?" I asked.

"Not all succeed in finding the stone," he answered. "And those who do find it do not always know how to use it effectively."

"If I had the stone," I said, "I would take pains to use it to keep death away and would want to have enough gold for myself and others. But where is this stone found?"

"It is prepared here," he replied.

"In these cauldrons?" I asked.

"Yes."

The fortunes of the alchemists

3. Curious, I walked about, looking at everything to see what and how matters were conducted here. I saw that not everyone fared equally well. One kept the fire too cool, and the mixture did not boil. Another had too hot a fire, his implements exploded, and something evaporated. He said that his nitrogen had escaped, and he wept. Another spilled while pouring or mixed wrongly. Another burned his eyes and was unable to observe the calcination and the fixation, or, getting smoke in his eyes before he could rub it out, his nitrogen escaped. Some also died of asphyxiation from the smoke. The majority of them did not have enough coal in their bags and had to run to others to borrow it. Meanwhile, the cauldron cooled and everything came to naught. This was a very frequent and almost continual occurrence. Although they did not allow any among them except those with full bags, these were quickly emptied so that nothing remained in them. They had to either abandon their operations or run elsewhere to borrow.

4. Looking at them I said, "I see a good number of people here who work in vain, but I do not see anyone who has obtained the stone. I see that boiling and burning both gold and their lives, these people squander and ruin both. So where are those with heaps of gold and immortality?"

"Of course they do not reveal themselves to you," he answered, "nor would I advise them to do so. Such priceless knowledge must be kept secret. For if one of the rulers should learn about such a person, he would want to seize him and make him a virtual prisoner for life. Therefore they must keep silent."

5. Then I observed that some of the people who had been burned gathered together. Inclining my ear, I heard that they sought among themselves the causes of their failure. One blamed the philosophers for describing their art in too complicated a fashion; another lamented the fragility of their glassware; a third pointed to the untimely and inauspicious aspect of the planets; a fourth was angered by the earthly impurities in the mercury mixture; a fifth complained of lack of capital. In sum, I saw there were so many reasons for failure that they did not know how to repair their art. Thus, when they left one after another, I also departed.

Chapter 13
The Pilgrim Observes the Rosicrucians[59]

Fama Fraternitatis, anno 1612 latinè ac germanicè edita[60]

1. Then I heard on the square the sound of a trumpet, and I turned and saw a rider on horseback summoning the philosophers. When they crowded around him from all sides like herds, he began to recount to them the deficiencies of the liberal arts and of all philosophy. He explained that some famous men, called forth by God, had ascertained and corrected these deficiencies and had brought human wisdom up to that level which it had in Paradise before the Fall. Making gold, he said, is the least among hundreds of their accomplishments. Indeed, all nature stands naked and uncovered before them, and they can give to or take from a creature any form according to their pleasure. They can speak the languages of all nations and know all that is happening everywhere in the world, including the New World. They are able to converse with one another even when a thousand miles apart. They have the philosophers' stone with which they can perfectly heal all kinds of diseases and confer longevity. For

their president, Hugo Alverda, is 562 years old, and his colleagues are not much younger.[61] Though they have concealed themselves for so many centuries, working alone (only seven of them) for the reform of philosophy, they have brought it all to perfection. Since the reformation of the whole world is coming, they do not want to remain silent any longer. Rather, announcing themselves publicly, they are ready to share their precious secrets with whomever they deem worthy. Should anyone make himself known to them, be he of whatever language or nation, he will learn all of their secrets, and no one will be left without a friendly answer. However, should any unworthy person be curious to obtain them out of sheer avarice or inquisitiveness, such a person will learn nothing.

Varia de Fama judicia[62]

2. Having finished his speech, the messenger disappeared. Looking at these learned people, I saw that they almost all panicked at the news. Gradually they began to put their heads together and come to a judgment about the matter, some in whispers, others aloud. Drawing near to various groups, I listened. Indeed, some rejoiced exceedingly, unable to contain their happiness. They pitied their ancestors, who obtained nothing comparable in their generation. They congratulated themselves that a perfect philosophy had been fully offered to them. Whoever so desired could know all without error, have everything without lack, and live several hundred years without sickness or grey hair. They kept repeating the refrain: "Happy, truly happy, is our age." Hearing these words, I myself was glad. I was hopeful that, God willing, I too might receive what others were expecting.

But I saw others in deep thought, very puzzled as to what to think about this. Should what was announced be true, they would be glad, but the matter seemed obscure to them and surpassing human reason. Others openly rejected it, claiming that it was deception and fraud. If they are hundreds of years old, they questioned, why had they not revealed themselves earlier? If they are sure of what they affirm, why do they not step out boldly into the light instead of only squeaking like bats out of some dark corner? Philosophy is well established and does not need reformation. If it should be snatched out of our hands, we would have nothing. Others cursed and railed at them horribly, denouncing them as diviners, sorcerers, and incarnate devils.

Fraternitatem ambientes[63]

3. In short, noise filled the whole square, and each one burned with desire to get to them. Therefore, not a few people wrote petitions (some secretly, others openly), and sent them off, rejoicing that they too would be accepted into the fraternity. But I saw that after having been sent to all corners, each petition was returned without answer, and their joyful hope was turned into depression. They also had to contend with the ridicule of the skeptics. Some wrote again, even two, three, or more times. They begged and even implored as eloquently as possible, through the aid of the Muses, that minds curious for knowledge be not held off. Some, impatient because of the delay, ran from one end of the world to the other, lamenting their misfortune in not being able to find these happy people. Some attributed this failure to their own unworthiness, others to the ill-will of the fraternity. Consequently, one despaired, while another looked about seeking new paths in an effort to discover their whereabouts, only to be vexed once again, until I myself grew weary waiting for the end to come.

Continuatio Famae Rosaeorum[64]

4. Then a trumpet began to blow again. Many, including myself, ran toward this sound. I saw a certain man setting up shop. He was soliciting people to examine and purchase his wonderful mysteries which, he said, were taken from the treasures of the new philosophy and would bring satisfaction to all who were eager for the secret wisdom. There was great joy that the holy Brotherhood of the Rose openly and generously shared their treasures. Many approached and bought the wares. All the goods that were sold were enclosed in painted boxes with various beautiful inscriptions: The Gates of Wisdom, The Fortress of Science, The Universal College, The Good Guide to the Large and Small

Cosmos, The Harmony of Both Worlds, Christian Cabala, The Cave of Nature, The Castle of Primordial Matter, The Divine Magic, The General Tri-Trinity, The Triumphal Pyramid, Hallelujah, etc. Those who bought the boxes were forbidden to open them. For such is the power of this secret wisdom that it works by means of osmosis, but if the box were opened it would evaporate. Nevertheless, some of the more inquisitive ones did not restrain themselves from opening them. Finding their boxes completely empty, they showed them to others. These others also opened their boxes, and no one found anything. They cried out "Fraud, fraud!" and shouted furiously at the dealer. He pacified them, explaining that these were the most secret mysteries and were invisible save to the sons of science. Since only one in a thousand could see them, he, the dealer, was not to blame.

Eventus Famae[65]

5. The majority of the buyers were pacified by this. Meanwhile, the dealer removed his wares. The onlookers dispersed, one here, one there, in different moods. But whether or not any of them learned these new mysteries, I have hitherto been unable to ascertain. I know only this, that everything then quieted down, and those whom I first saw running and rushing about the most, I now saw sitting in corners with their mouths locked shut. Either they had been admitted to the mystery (as some thought) and had been compelled to take an oath of silence, or they were ashamed of their vain hopes and misspent labor (as it seemed to me looking under my glasses).

Thus everything passed and quieted down as clouds disperse after a storm without rain. I said to my companion, "Is all this, then, for nothing? Alas, my hopes! Having such high expectations, I looked forward to finding a pleasant pasture for my mind!" "Who knows but that it might yet be found," my interpreter responded. "Perhaps they know their hour, when and to whom they should reveal themselves."

"Should I wait for this," I asked, "since I have not seen a single example of success among so many thousands of people more learned than I? I do not want to gawk at this any longer. Let us leave this place."

Chapter 14
The Pilgrim Examines the Medical Profession

Anatomy[66]

1. Leading me through some alleys between the physics and chemistry auditorium, they placed me on another square where I saw a horrible spectacle. They stretched a man out, cut one limb after another and examined all his internal organs, showing with keen interest what they found there. "But what cruelty to treat a human being as a beast," I said.

"This must be so," the interpreter rejoined, "for this is their school."

Botany

2. Meanwhile, leaving this activity, they ran about in gardens, meadows, fields, and mountains. They plucked whatever they found growing there and piled it into such heaps that many years would not suffice for sifting and examining it. Each one grabbing from the pile whatever he liked or happened to come across, he ran to examine the corpse. Spreading it out over the limbs, he measured the length, width, and thickness of them together. One said that this fitted that; another that it did not. Thus they argued and shouted about the matter. There was a great to-do about the very names of the herbs. Knitting together a wreath of these herbs, they crowned the one who knew the most herbs and was able to measure and weigh them and proclaimed that he be called the doctor of this science.

Praxis medendi[67]

3. Then I saw that they brought or conducted to them those with various internal and external wounds that were rotten and putrid. The doctors approached them, examined the rotten stuff, sniffed the stenches coming from them, and studied the

putrid matter coming out of them from above and below until the sight was disgusting. They called this an examination. Then they cooked, steamed, roasted, broiled, cauterized, cooled, burned, chopped, cut, stabbed, sewed again, bound up, anointed, hardened, softened, wrapped, wet, and I know not what more. Meanwhile patients were dying in their arms. Not a few people accused the doctors, claiming that the victims had met their end through the doctors' ignorance or neglect. In short, I saw that although their art brought some profit to these fine healers, it also brought (if they wished to do justice to their calling) a great deal of very difficult and, in part, very disgusting labor. In the end, it brought them as much disfavor as acclaim. This did not please me.

Chapter 15
The Pilgrim Observes the Legal Profession

Finis juris[68]

1. Finally, they led me to yet another spacious auditorium in which I saw an even greater number of distinguished people than elsewhere. All along the sides there were painted walls, blockhouses, fences, ramparts, bars, rails, and partitions. Through these there were gaps and holes, doors and gates, bolts and locks, and together with them, various larger and smaller keys and hooks. Pointing all this out to one another, the people measured where and how one could or could not pass through. "What are these people doing?" I asked. It was explained to me that they were seeking the means by which each person in the world would be able to retain his property or peacefully take over some part of the property of another while maintaining order and concord. "This is a fine thing," I said. But after watching for awhile, I became disgusted with it.

Jus circa quid versetur[69]

2. In the first place, I noticed that neither the soul, nor the mind, nor the human body were enclosed in these barriers, but

119

only property, which is an incidental matter for humankind. It did not seem to me to merit as much arduous toil as I saw it received.

Fundamentum juris[70]

3. I also saw that this entire science was based merely on the whim of a few, inasmuch as it seemed to one or another that some particular thing ought to be made law, which others then observed.

Perplexitas juris[71]

Moreover (as I noticed here), one either built up or tore down the walls or gaps as the thought occurred to each. As a result, there was much outright contradiction here. Others had to knock their heads together in curious and ingenious ways to rectify and settle the differences. I was amazed that they toiled and sweated so much over insignificant matters, some of which occur hardly once in a thousand years and amount to very little; and they showed considerable pride in the process. For the more a person could break through a barrier or make an opening and close it up again, the more pleased he was with himself and the more others envied him. Some, however, (also wishing to demonstrate their intelligence) stepped forward in opposition, claiming that one should set up a barrier or make an opening in some other manner. So dissensions and quarrels arose. Separating from each other, this one painted the situation in one way, that one in another fashion, each drawing spectators to himself.

Observing this trifling for some time, I shook my head and said, "Let us hurry away, for I already feel distressed here."

"Then what in this world will please you?" the interpreter snapped at me angrily. "You find fault even with the noblest callings, you fickle fellow."

"His mind smells of religiosity," Ubiquitous added. "Let us lead him to another place. Perhaps there he will find some attraction."

Chapter 16
The Pilgrim Observes the Promotion of
Masters and Doctors

1. But behold, a trumpet sounded as if calling people to a celebration. Understanding what was about to happen, Searchall said, "Let us go back for a moment. Here there will be something worth seeing."

"And what will this be?" I asked.

Searchall explained, "The Academy is going to crown those who, having been more diligent than others, have attained the summit of learning. These, I say, will be crowned as an example for others."

Curious to behold such a scene and seeing a crowd rushing in that direction, I too followed after them. Here, under the philosophical sky[72] stood a certain man holding a paper scepter to whom some from among the crowd stepped forward wanting an attestation of their high learning. Having approved their request as fitting, he ordered that they submit in writing what they know and what accreditation they desire. One brought forth a summary of philosophy, another of medicine, another of law. Moreover, to make the process go more smoothly, they greased palms with their purses.

2. Taking the candidates one after another, he pasted a title on each of their foreheads: this is a Master of Liberal Arts; this is a Doctor of Medicine; this is a Licentiate of Civil and Canon Laws,[73] etc. He confirmed these titles with his seal, commanding all present or absent, on pain of the disfavor of the goddess Pallas Athena, not to address them otherwise upon meeting. With these words he dismissed them and the crowd.

"Will there be anything more?" I asked.

"Isn't this enough for you?" the interpreter replied. "Or don't you see how everyone steps aside for them?" Indeed, they did give way.

3. Nonetheless, since I still wanted to see what would become of them afterwards, I watched one of those masters of arts. They asked him to calculate something, and he could not; to measure

something, he could not; to name the stars, he could not; to make syllogisms, he could not; to speak foreign languages, he could not; to deliver an oration in his own language, he could not; finally to read and write, but he could not. "What a shame," I said, "to call oneself a master of seven arts but not to know any of them."

The interpreter responded, "If this one does not know it, the second, third or fourth one does. All cannot be proficient in everything."

"Am I to understand," I inquired, "that after spending an eternity in schools, expending a fortune on education, amassing titles and seals, it is still necessary to ask whether he has learned anything? May God save us from such a process!"

"You won't stop with your wisecracks," he said, "until you meet with some unpleasant experience. Only chatter further, and I swear you will pay for it."

"Well, then," I replied, "even if they are masters and doctors of seventy-seven arts, and know all or none of them, I will not say anything more. Only let us go from here."

Chapter 17
The Pilgrim Observes the Religious Profession

The pagans

1. They led me through certain passages until we came to a square where there were many churches and chapels constructed in various styles. Crowds were going in and coming out of them. We entered the nearest of these, where there were engravings and statues of men and women on all sides, as well as all kinds of animals, birds, reptiles, trees, and plants; also the sun, moon, and stars; and even an abundance of horrible demons. Each of those entering chose whatever pleased him and kneeled, kissed, burned incense, and offered a sacrifice before it. I was amazed by all the concord there, for almost everyone performed his devotion differently, yet tolerated all and peacefully allowed the others to hold their own opinions (which I have not seen elsewhere).

A certain horrible stench overcame me, and I was seized with terror, so I hurried away.

The Jews[74]

2. Then we entered another temple, white and clean, in which there were none but living images.[75] Shaking their heads, they either mumbled something quietly, or arising and stopping up their ears, they opened their mouths wide and let out sounds not unlike the howling of wolves.

Talmudi figmenta[76]

Then gathering together, they examined certain books. Approaching them, I saw strange illustrations, for example, feathered and winged beasts, unfeathered and wingless birds, beasts with human and humans with beastlike limbs, one body with many heads and one head with many bodies. Some monsters had a head in place of a tail or a tail in place of a head. Some had eyes below their belly and feet on their back. Some had eyes, ears, mouths, and feet without number, while others had none of these at all. All this was strangely displaced, twisted, bent, and crooked and in great disproportion. One limb was a foot long, another a rod in length; one was the width of a finger, another the width of a barrel. In short, everything was monstrous beyond belief. Nevertheless, they claimed that these illustrations were historically accurate. Praising them as noble, the older people showed them to the younger as a mystery.

"Who would have expected that there would be people who could like such disgusting things?" I remarked. "Let us leave them and go elsewhere." While leaving, I saw these people walking among the others. However, they were disliked by all and merely became the target of laughter and pranks. This caused me to despise them.

The Muslims

3. Next we entered another temple, which was round and no less beautiful inside than the other. It was without decoration, except for some lettering on the walls and carpets on the floors.

The people within were quiet and behaved religiously. They were dressed in white and were great lovers of cleanliness, for they were always washing themselves and giving alms. Thus, because of their fine appearance, I began to be favorably disposed toward them. "What kind of foundation do they have for these practices?" I asked.

"They carry it hidden under their clothes," Searchall answered.

I approached, wanting to see what he meant. They explained that it was not fitting for any except their interpreters to see it. I persisted nonetheless, basing my request on the permission I had received from Lord Fate.

Summary of the Koran

4. Then they obtained and showed me a chart on which there was a tree with its roots rising up into the sky and its branches buried in the ground. Many moles were digging around it, and one big mole was walking about, calling the others and directing their labor. They explained to me that the underground branches of this tree bore all kinds of pleasant fruit, which the quiet and industrious little creatures procured. "And this is the sum of their religion," said Searchall. I understood that their foundation rested on the wind of supposition and that its goal and fruit was to burrow in the ground, to take comfort in invisible delights that did not exist, and to seek blindly what they did not know.

Islam is based on force

5. Leaving this place, I said to my guide, "How, then, do they prove that this is a sure and true foundation of religion?"

"Come and see," he replied. And we passed behind the church to a square. There we saw those white-clad and well-washed people with rolled-up sleeves and sparkling eyes, biting their lips and roaring frightfully, running about, putting to the sword whomever they encountered, and wading in human blood.

I was frightened and ran back, asking, "What are they doing?"

"They are disputing about religion and proving that the Koran is a true book," he answered.

Quarreling between the Persians and Turks about the Koran

6. We entered the temple once again and saw an argument between those who carried the chart concerning, as far as I could understand, the chief mole. Some claimed that he alone directed the smaller moles; others said that he had two assistants. They quarreled so implacably about this matter that finally they contended with iron and fire as much among themselves as with those outside until it was terrible to behold.[77]

Chapter 18
He Examines the Christian Religion

1. Seeing that I was terrified, my guide said to me, "Let us move on now. I will show you the Christian religion, which, being founded upon the certain revelations of God, satisfies both the simplest and the most learned. It brings clearly to light the heavenly truth, while it also defeats opposing errors. Its ornament is concord and love, and it has hitherto stood and still remains unconquered in the face of countless adversities. From this you can easily understand that its origin must be from God, and thus you will be able to find in it true comfort." I rejoiced in this speech, and we went on.

Baptism

2. When we arrived, I saw that they have a gate through which one must pass. This gate stood in water through which each one must wade and wash himself and then receive his badge, white and red in color. He must also take an oath to heed their laws and rules, believe as they do, pray as they do, and observe their ordinances. This pleased me, for it seemed like the beginning of a noble order.

Preaching the word

3. Proceeding through the gate, I observed a great crowd of people among whom some were distinguished from others by

their vestments. They were standing here and there on plat-forms, displaying a picture that was so skillfully painted that the more one looked at it, the more one found in it to admire. Since it was adorned neither with gold nor with brilliant colors, it was not clearly visible from a distance. Therefore, I saw that those who stood far off were not attracted by its beauty, while those who stood nearer could not tire of looking at it.

The image of Christ

4. Those who carried this image praised it exceedingly, calling it the Son of God and saying that all manner of virtues are depicted in it. They said that it had been sent from heaven to earth in order that people might practice virtue in their own lives by following its example. There was great joy and celebration. Falling on their knees, the crowd raised their hands to heaven and praised God. Seeing this, I too joined my voice to theirs and praised God that he had led me to this place.

Spiritual feasts of the Christians

5. Meanwhile, I heard many and various admonitions that everyone should conform to this image. I also observed that they gathered together in different places, and those to whom the image had been entrusted made little likenesses of it and distributed them to all in a kind of wrapping. The people, in turn, brought it piously to their mouths. I asked what this meant. They explained to me that it was not sufficient merely to look at this much-hailed image outwardly, but one must receive it inwardly to be transformed into its beauty. For it is said that sins must yield to this heavenly medicine. I was satisfied with this explanation, and I praised Christians within myself as blessed people who had such means and aids to drive off evil.

Lawlessness of Christians

6. In the meantime, however, I observed some who had a little while earlier received God into themselves (as they said). One after another they gave themselves up to drink, quarrels, sexual impurity, robbing, and stealing. Not believing my eyes, I looked more

closely and saw that in very truth they drank and vomited, quarreled and fought, defrauded and stole from one another with cunning and violence, neighed and leaped in wantonness, whooped and shrieked, committed fornication and adultery worse than any others I had seen. In short, they did everything contrary to the admonitions they had received and the promises they had made. Grieved by this sight, I said sorrowfully, "For God's sake, what is happening here? I expected something different."

"Do not be overly amazed," my interpreter rejoined. "What is presented to people for imitation is a level of perfection that human weakness does not allow everyone to reach. Those who lead the others are more perfect, but the ordinary person stands behind, beset with cares and unable to equal them."

"Then let us go among these leaders," I suggested, "that I may observe them."

Barrenness of preachers

7. Then they led me to those standing on the platforms. They were admonishing people to love the image, but it seemed to me that they did this quite feebly. For if anyone obeyed and followed them, it was good; if not, however, it was just as well. Some jangled certain keys, claiming they had the power to lock the gate to God to those who disobeyed, while at the same time refusing entry to no one; or if they did bar access, they did it as if in jest. Indeed, I saw that they dared not do this openly. For if someone wished to speak a bit more sharply, they railed at him for preaching against individuals. Therefore some denounced sins in writing, not daring to do so orally. But they berated these preachers also for spreading lampoons. People either turned away from them so as not to hear their message, or they threw them down from the platforms, appointing more moderate preachers in their stead.

When I saw this, I exclaimed, "What a folly that they wish to have followers and flatterers as their leaders and counselors!"

"Such is the way of the world," said the interpreter, "and it does no harm. If those loudmouths were given complete liberty, who knows what they would not dare. They too must be shown where the limits are."

Carnality of the clergy

8. "Let us go, then," I said, "that I may see how they order their affairs at home, away from their pulpits. I know that at least there no one interferes or hinders them." We entered a place where only priests live. I expected to find them praying and searching the mysteries of the faith. Unfortunately, I found them snoring and lounging on feather beds, seated behind tables and feasting, drinking and gorging themselves to speechlessness. Some were dancing and jumping about; others were stuffing their purses, trunks, and treasure chambers. Some indulged in lechery and wantonness; others spent their time putting on spurs, daggers, rapiers, and muskets; yet others in hunting hares with dogs. They spent the least time with the Bible, some hardly even picking it up, yet calling themselves teachers of the Word. Observing this, I said, "Oh what a tragedy. Are these supposed to be guides to heaven and examples of virtue? Will I ever find anything in the world without fraud and deception?"

Hearing my words and realizing that I was lamenting their irregular life, some began to look askance at me and to grumble. If I were looking for hypocrites and some kind of superficial saints, they said, I should look elsewhere; for they knew how to perform their duty both in church and at home, and to behave in a worldly way among people of the world. Thus I was compelled to keep silent, seeing clearly, however, that it was a monstrosity to wear a coat of mail over a cassock and a helmet over a biretta; to have the Law in one hand and a sword in the other; to carry Peter's keys in front and Judas's purse behind; the mind trained in Scripture, the heart exercised in cunning; the tongue full of piety, the eyes full of wantonness.

With heavenly gifts they help others but not themselves

9. In particular, I noticed some who preached very eloquent and pious sermons and were regarded by themselves and others as no less than angels fallen from heaven. Yet their lives were as

dissolute as the rest. I could not restrain myself from saying, "Behold, pipes through which good things flow, while they themselves retain none of it!"

"To be able to speak eloquently about divine matters is also a gift of God," said the interpreter.

"It is indeed a gift of God," I rejoined, "but should one stop with words?"

Disorder among the bishops

10. Meanwhile, I saw that all these priests had elders above them (called bishops, archbishops, abbots, priors, deans, superintendents, inspectors, etc.), important and distinguished men to whom all rendered honor. "Why then do they not keep these lower ranks in order?" I thought. Wishing to understand the reason, I followed one back to his room, then a second, third, and fourth. I saw that they were so fearfully busy that they had no time to oversee anyone. Their occupation (besides those things that they had in common with the others) was keeping records of revenues and ecclesiastical treasures (as they called them). "I suspect it is by mistake that they are called spiritual fathers; they should be called fathers of revenue,"[78] I said.

"Care must be taken so that the church does not squander that which the Lord God has bestowed and pious forebears have given to her," the interpreter responded.

Acts 6

Then one of them (called Peter), who had two keys hanging on his belt, stepped up and said, "Men and brothers, it is not right that we should neglect the Word of God and serve tables and coffers. Let us choose men of good repute and assign this work to them; but let us be diligent in prayer and the ministry of the Word."[79] I rejoiced upon hearing this, for in my opinion, it was good advice. None of them wished to heed it, however. They themselves continued counting, receiving, and disbursing. They assigned others the tasks of prayer and the ministry of the Word or performed these duties hastily.

11. Whenever one of them died and the cares of leadership

had to be passed on to another, I observed not a little strutting about, striving, and gathering recommendations. Each one tried to elbow his way into office before the seat grew cold. The one responsible to fill the empty position received recommendations from and about the candidates. These differed greatly. One claimed to be a blood relative; another related on the wife's side; a third hoped for a reward, having long served as an elder; a fourth that he had a promise on which he relied; a fifth expected an honorable office because he was of honorable parents; a sixth submitted a laudatory reference from some other place; a seventh offered gifts under the table; an eighth, being a person of deep, high, and broad thoughts, desired a position where he could develop further; and I know not what more. Observing this scene, I remarked, "Surely it is inappropriate to thrust oneself forward into such a position; rather, one should wait to be called."

"Should they call those who are unwilling?" the interpreter retorted. "Let him who aspires to this office make himself known."

"I really thought that one must wait on the call of God," said I.

"And do you imagine that God will call someone out of heaven?" he said in return. "God's call is the favor of the elders, and whoever prepares himself for this calling is free to attain it."

"I see," I said, "that it is not necessary to search for someone or to drive someone to this service of the church, but rather to drive him away. Moreover, if one must always seek favor, one should endear oneself to the church through humility, quietness, and industry, and not in the way I have seen and heard here. Say what you will, but such things are disorderly."[80]

The trust of Christians in faith without works

12. When my interpreter saw my determined stand, he said, "It is true that in the life of Christians, and even of theologians, there are more incongruities than elsewhere. It is also true, however, that though Christians live wickedly, they die well. For human salvation is based not on deeds, but on faith. If this faith is true, then one cannot fail to attain salvation. So do not be sur-

prised that the lives of Christians are irregular. It is sufficient if only their faith is sure."

Disputes about faith also

13. "Do they at least all agree about the faith, then?" I asked.

"There are some trivial differences," he answered, "but what does that matter? They all have the same foundation." Then they led me behind some bars into the center of the great church where I saw a large, round stone hanging from a chain.

Holy Scripture is the touchstone

They said this was the touchstone. The foremost people approached it, each one carrying something in his hand, for example, a piece of gold, silver, iron, lead, a handful of sand or chaff. Then each one rubbed what he had brought on the stone and praised it for standing the test. Others who were watching maintained that it did not. They began to shout at each other, for no one allowed insults to be hurled at his object, while none wished to acknowledge the goods of another. They denounced and cursed each other, grabbing and pulling at each other by the hood, the ears, or wherever else they could. Several argued about the stone itself as to its color. Some averred that it was blue; others that it was green; others, white; still others, black. A few were found who even maintained that it changed color, assuming the hue of whatever it touched. Some advised that the stone should be broken and ground into powder so that its true appearance could be seen. Others advised against this. Still others went further, saying that the stone was only a cause of dissension and that it should be taken down and removed so that they might be more easily reconciled. A large number of them, among whom were the most prominent ones, agreed. Another group opposed the proposition, saying that they would rather lay down their lives than permit it. In fact, some were killed when the quarreling and fracas increased. The stone, however, remained; for it was round and very smooth. Whoever grasped it could not hold on to it. It immediately slipped out of his hands and continued to turn behind the railing.

The division of Christians into sects

14. Leaving this enclosure, I saw that this church had many chapels surrounding it into which those who could not agree concerning the touchstone dispersed. Each drew a certain group of people after him. They gave them rules regarding how they should differ from others. Some were to mark themselves with water and fire; others were to have the sign of the cross always ready in their hands and their pockets; others, for greater perfection, were to carry with them, besides that main portrait at which all had to gaze, as many other smaller ones as possible; others maintained that it was a pharisaical practice to kneel in prayer; some regarded music as a wanton thing that ought not to be tolerated among them; others claimed they did not need to be taught, for they had an inner revelation of the Spirit. In short, as I examined these chapels, I saw some kind of special regulations everywhere.

The most splendid among the chapels

15. One of these chapels was the biggest and most ornate, glittering with gold and precious stones and resounding with the music of merry instruments. I was led to this one in particular and invited to seek there a religion more pleasing than anywhere else. Here the walls were filled with pictures showing how one could reach heaven. Some were depicted making ladders for themselves, setting them against the sky, and climbing up on them. Some piled up mountains and hills by which they could ascend; others prepared wings and fastened them on; others captured winged creatures and, tying them together and binding themselves to them, they even dared to fly heavenward beside them. There were also many priests in different vestments who were showing and praising the pictures to the people. They then instructed them how to distinguish themselves from others by means of various ceremonies. One of them, clad in gold and silver, sat on a high throne and distributed gifts to subordinates and those counselors intimately associated with him.

This seemed to be a fine order and merrier than anywhere else. But when I saw other sects rushing upon them, attacking them, denouncing all their affairs and condemning them, I became suspicious, especially when I heard their diffident replies and self-defense. On the one hand, they resorted to stoning, drowning, fire, and the sword; on the other, to enticing deceitful people to themselves with bribes of gold. I also observed among them much discord, quarreling and envy, shoving each other from their places, and other similar disorders. Therefore, I left that place to look at another group, which called itself reformed.[81]

Others negotiate in vain for unification

16. There I saw that several of these chapels (two or three that were close to each other) were negotiating how they might become one. However, they could in no way find a compromise between themselves. Each one held to whatever was in his own head, forcing the others to accept it as well. Some who were more stupid held to whatever came their way. Those who were more clever approached or withdrew depending on the opportunity for profit, until I was shocked by the wretched confusion and vacillation of these dear Christians.[82]

The true Christians

17. Meanwhile, there were some who claimed to have nothing to do with these arguments. They walked silently, as if in deep thought, looking often to heaven and conducting themselves kindly toward all. They were unprepossessing in appearance, ragged, and emaciated by fasting and thirst. Others only laughed at them, jeered and whistled at them, scratched and plucked at them, tripped them up, and cursed them. However, bearing everything, they walked among the others as if blind, deaf, and dumb. When I saw them going in and out behind a certain curtain in the choir, I wanted to go in and see what they had there. But the interpreter pulled me back.

The pilgrim does not recognize them

"What do you want to do there?" he asked. "Or do you also want to be laughed at? There is little else to aspire to there!" Thus I complied. But alas, here I erred, having been deceived by my unhappy companion, Delusion. I missed the center of heaven and earth and the path leading to the fullness of joy. I was led again to the maze of the world's labyrinth until my God rescued me from it and led me back to that spot where I had taken the wrong path. When and how this occurred, I will recount later. At the time, however, I did not judge rightly. Rather, seeking only external peace and comfort, I hurried away to gape at other things.

His adventure among the clergy

18. I will not pass over in silence what else happened to me in this street. Ubiquitous kept on urging me to join the clergy, assuring me that I was destined to belong to this profession. I confess that I too was so inclined, although I did not approve of all their customs. I allowed myself to be persuaded, assumed cap and cowl, and stepped onto a platform beside others until my own was allotted to me. But looking about me, I saw some turning their backs on me. A second group shook their heads, a third glowered at me, a fourth threatened with their fists, a fifth pointed their fingers. Finally, some attacked me, drove me off, and put someone else in my place, threatening that there was more to come. I became alarmed and ran away, saying to my guides, "Oh, this miserable world! Everything at once is giving way."

"Doubtless," the interpreter replied, "why do you not take care to avoid irritating people? Whoever wants to live with other people must accommodate himself to them, and not, like you, chisel away foolishly without regard to others."

"I do not know," said I, "but it might be better to abandon all."

"Not yet, not yet!" Ubiquitous replied. "We ought not despair. If this is not right for you, something else will be. Only come, let us look further." Then taking me by the hand, he led me on.

Chapter 19
The Pilgrim Observes the Ruling Class

Different levels of magistrates

1. We then entered another street where I saw on all sides many higher and lower seats, which were occupied by men called

the honorable constable, the honorable burgomaster, the honorable magistrate, the honorable regent, the honorable burgrave, the honorable chancellor, the honorable governor, the honorable judges, his grace the king, prince, lord, and so forth. The interpreter explained to me, "Here you have people who pass judgments and sentences in lawsuits, punishing evil-doers, defending the good, and preserving order in the world."

"This is indeed a fine thing," I remarked, "and one that is indispensable for humanity. Where do such people come from?"

"Some are born into their office. Others are either chosen by the former or by the community, being acknowledged as the wisest, the most experienced of all, and the most knowledgeable in justice and law."

"This too is fine," I said.

2. Just then I was able to see clearly, and I saw that some obtained their seats by bribery, others by begging, flattery, or force. "Look, look at the corruption!" I cried.

"Be quiet, you meddler," warned the interpreter. "If they hear you, you will pay dearly for it."

"But why do they not wait until they are elected?" I asked.

"Well, they are doubtless confident of their ability for this work," he answered. "And if others accept them, what is it to you?"

3. So I remained silent. Adjusting my glasses, I looked diligently at them and saw an astounding thing. Scarcely any of them had all their limbs, and almost all of them lacked some necessary part. Some did not have ears with which to hear the complaints of their subjects; others lacked eyes to notice the disorders around them; others lacked noses to sniff out the illegal schemes of crooks; others lacked a tongue to defend the mute and oppressed masses; others lacked hands with which they could administer the decrees of justice; many even lacked the heart to dare to execute what justice demanded.

4. However, I saw that those who had all their bodily parts were greatly harassed. People constantly overwhelmed them with petitions, so that they could neither eat nor sleep in peace. Meanwhile, these others spent more than half their life in idleness.

"But why is justice and law entrusted to such people as these who do not have the necessary organs for the task?" I asked.

My interpreter insisted that this was not the case, but that it only seemed that way to me. "For," he explained, *"qui nescit simulare, nescit regnare."*[83] Whoever rules others must often fail to see, hear, and understand, though in fact he sees, hears, and understands all. But you, being inexperienced in political affairs, do not understand this."

"Nevertheless," I asserted, "I see in truth that they lack what they ought to have."

"I advise you to keep silent," he replied. "I swear that if you do not stop making wisecracks, you will find yourself where you do not wish to be. Don't you know that contempt of court is a capital offense?"

Thus, I kept silent and quietly observed everything. However, it does not seem necessary to me to recount all that I saw concerning each particular seat. I will touch upon two incidents only.

Frequent injustices and corruption among the judges

5. I stopped and observed very carefully what was happening in the senatorial court, where I saw the names of the lord judges: Atheist, Lovestrife, Hearsay, Partisan, Personrespecter, Lovegold, Bribetake, Inexperienced, Knowlittle, Heednot, Hasty, and Negligent. The president of them all and the highest judge or primate was Lord SoIwillit. From their names I immediately began to figure out what kind of judges they were, and soon in my presence an example confirmed my suspicions. Sincerity was charged by Accuser of maligning some good people, having called usurers misers, tipplers souses, and I know not what else. The witnesses brought forward were Gossip, Lie, and Suspicion. The counsel for the prosecution was Flattery; the counsel for the accused was Babbler, whom, however, Sincerity claimed she did not need. When asked whether she pleaded guilty to the accusation, she affirmed, "I do, your honors," and added, "Here I stand; I cannot speak otherwise, so help me God!"[84]

The judges, having gathered together, collected the votes. Atheist commented, "What that hussy says is indeed so, but what business did she have prattling about it? If we let it pass, perhaps she will try to blather about us as well. I advocate her punishment."

"Certainly," Lovestrife agreed, "for if this were to be passed over once, then others also would want to be excused."

"I really do not know what happened," said Hearsay, "but since Accuser places so much weight on the affair, I conclude that it has really injured him. Therefore, let her be punished."

"I knew beforehand that Gossip blabbers everything she knows," Partisan said. "Her mouth must be shut."

"The injured party is a good friend of mine," said Personrespecter. "For my sake at least, she ought to have spared him and not taunted him so. She is worthy of punishment."

Lovegold said, "You know how generous Accuser has shown himself to be. He is worthy of defense."

"I agree," said Bribetake. "We would be ungrateful if we did not take notice of his case."

"I do not know a similar case," Inexperienced added. "Let her suffer what she has earned."

Knowlittle said, "I do not understand the matter. However you decide, I give my consent."

Negligence said, "I agree to everything, either way."

Heednot asked, "Do we not want to delay? Perhaps it will clear itself up later."

"No," Hasty insisted, "Let judgment be passed quickly."

"Of course," the lord judge agreed. "Why should we consider anybody else? What the law demands must be executed." Then rising, he pronounced the sentence. "Since that chattering woman has given herself to such indecent behavior as to malign decent people, in order to tame her licentious tongue and to serve as an example to others, let her sentence be forty slaps in the face save one."

Then bowing, Accuser with the prosecuting attorney and the witnesses thanked them for this just decision. Sincerity was told to do likewise, but she broke out in tears and wrung her hands. Since she did not honor the court, they decreed that her sentence be made more severe, and apprehending her, they led her to her punishment.

Seeing that she had been wronged, I could not restrain myself, and cried aloud, "If all the courts in the world are like these, help me, Almighty God, neither to become a judge nor to pursue a lawsuit with anyone."

"Be quiet, you lunatic," my interpreter warned, putting his hand over my mouth, "or I swear that you will talk yourself into this same punishment, if not something worse." Indeed, Accuser and Flatterer began to gather witnesses against me. Noticing this, I was frightened, and somehow flew from the place, breathless.

Perversity of lawyers

6. Catching my breath before the courthouse, I rubbed my eyes and saw many coming to the court with their lawsuits. I also saw that lawyers (whose names were Babbler, Flattery, Leadwrong, Procrastination, and the like) were scurrying up to these people, offering each one their services. They took no account of their clients' complaints, but rather examined their purses. Each lawyer diligently carried his own lawbook (which I had not noticed among the theologians) and often examined the contents. I saw the title on some of the copies: "Rapacious Gnawing of the Land"; on others, "Voracious Defrauding of the Land."[85] Not wanting to look at this any longer, however, I went away sighing.

The unlimited power of princes and the schemes of their officials

7. "The best is yet to come," Searchall said to me. "Come and look at the estate of kings, princes, and others who rule over their subjects by hereditary right. Perhaps this will please you." Then we entered another room and saw them sitting on thrones so high and wide that one could scarcely approach or reach them except by means of strange contrivances. Instead of ears, each one had long tubes on both sides, and whoever wanted to speak to them had to whisper into these. But the tubes were so twisted and filled with holes that many words escaped before they reached the listeners. Those words that did arrive were for the

greater part changed. For this reason, I noticed that an answer was not always given to those who spoke, for even when someone shouted, he was unable to reach the ruler's brain. Sometimes an answer was given, but it was not to the point in question. Likewise, in the place of eyes and tongues, there were tubes through which things often appeared other than they really were, and answers were given that differed from what the ruler intended. Comprehending this arrangement, I said, "But why do they not remove these tubes and simply look, listen, and answer with their own eyes, ears, and tongues like other people?"

"Because of personal honor and the dignity of their position, such ceremonies must be maintained," my interpreter responded. "Or do you regard them as peasants that anyone might simply touch their eyes, ears, and tongues?"

How inconvenient is the need for counselors

8. Then I saw some moving about the thrones who blew directly into the ruler's ears, not using the tubes. Others placed variously colored glasses on the ruler's eyes, or burned incense under his nose, or opened and closed his hands, or bound and loosened his feet; still others repaired and strengthened the seat beneath him, and so on. Witnessing this strange scene, I asked, "Who are these people and what are they doing?"

"They are the privy counselors who advise the king and the great lords," the interpreter answered.

"I would not tolerate these people if I were in the ruler's place," I said. "Rather I would want my limbs to be free and my actions unhindered."

"A single person ought not to depend on himself alone," the interpreter responded, "nor should this be permitted."

"Then these great lords are more wretched than peasants," I added, "for they are so bound that they cannot even move except according to the will of others."

"But in this way they are more certain of themselves," he rejoined. "Just look at these!"

Without counselors the situation is even worse

9. I turned back and observed that some sitting on these thrones did not allow themselves to be advised, but drove their counselors away from them. This I liked. But immediately I perceived other difficulties here. In place of the few who had been driven away, many others came who blew into the rulers' ears, nose, and mouth, covered and uncovered their eyes in different ways and tried to stretch apart their hands and feet in different directions. Each one who came had his own intentions and sought to persuade and pull the ruler over to his side, until the unfortunate ruler did not know what to do, whose petition to grant and whose to deny, and how to protect himself against them all.

"I see now," I said, "that it is better to entrust oneself to a chosen few than to fall prey to an unruly mob. But is there no other way in which to manage affairs?"

"How, then, should it be managed otherwise?" the interpreter asked. "This calling carries with it the responsibility to receive the complaints, accusations, requests, petitions, arguments, and counterarguments of all and to deal with everyone justly. These here, however, are quite different."

Indifferent rulers

10. Then he showed me some who did not permit any to approach them except those who labored for and attended to their comforts. All around them I saw people skipping about, patting them, laying pillows beneath them, placing mirrors before their eyes, fanning them, cleaning up feathers and dust, kissing their robes and slippers. Some even licked the ruler's spittle and mucus, praising its sweetness. But again this greatly displeased me, especially when I saw that the seats of almost each of these rulers shook and, when he did not expect it, collapsed due to a lack of more faithful supporters.

The pilgrim's dangerous adventure

11. It happened in my presence that a throne suddenly began to shake. It broke apart, and the prince fell to the ground. Then a

crowd of people gathered. Turning to look at them, I observed that they led forth another prince and placed him on the throne, rejoicing that affairs would now be better than they had been. Dancing around the throne, whoever could, steadied and strengthened it. Considering that it was fitting to help support the common welfare (as they called it), I approached and drove in a wedge or two. Some praised me for this, while others scowled.

Just then the fallen prince, having gathered his retainers, fell upon us with clubs and attacked the crowd until everyone dispersed. Some even lost their heads. I was so gripped by fear that I was unable to think clearly, until Searchall, hearing that they were asking who else had helped to install and support the new prince, pulled me away so that I also could flee. Delusion said this was not necessary. Wondering whom I should obey, I brushed against a club that was swinging near me. I gathered my wits together and ran into a corner. Thus I came to understand that it is dangerous to sit on these seats, to be around them, or even to support them in any manner. I gladly left this place and resolved never to return. Then I said to my guides, "Let anyone who will, approach these mountains, but not I."[86]

Lawlessness of people everywhere

12. I was strengthened in my resolve when I found out that although all these people wanted to be called the rulers of the world, yet lawlessness was rampant everywhere. For whether the ruler admitted his subjects directly into his presence or only allowed them to communicate with him by means of the tubes, whether he issued decrees by himself or with the advice of others, I saw as much wrongdoing as justice. I also heard as much sighing and groaning as joy, and observed that equity was mixed with lawlessness and that abuse of power was commingled with justice. Town halls, law courts, and offices were as often workshops of injustice as of justice, and those who were called defenders of order in the world were as much (or even more) defenders of disorder. Amazed that this estate should conceal in itself so much vanity and glittering misery, I took my leave of these people and this place.

141

Chapter 20
The Military Profession

Human cruelty

1. Then we entered the last street, where several people were dressed in red. Approaching them, I heard them discussing how to give wings to death so that it could instantly penetrate from far off as well as from nearby. They also discussed how to destroy in an hour what had been constructed in the course of many years. I was alarmed at these words, for I had hitherto observed that human words and actions were directed to the upbuilding and expanding of humanity and the comforts of life. But these men were discussing the destruction of human lives and comforts. "The goals of these people are the same, but they pursue them somewhat differently," the interpreter explained. "They work by clearing away obstacles. You will understand later."

Enlistment

2. When we approached the gate, we saw several drummers instead of gatekeepers. Each one who wanted to enter was asked whether he had a purse. When each showed it and opened it, they filled it with money and said, "This skin is paid for." Then they led him to a certain cellar, conducted him out again encased in iron and fire, and ordered him to proceed to the square.

The arsenal or armory

3. Curious to see what was in the cellar, I also went into it. There I saw piles of weapons lying on the ground in endless masses, covering all the walls as far as the eye could see. There were so many that thousands of wagons would not be sufficient to carry them away. There were all kinds of ghastly weapons for stabbing, hacking, slashing, jabbing, felling, chopping, severing, tearing, burning—in sum, for the destruction of life. These weapons were made of iron, lead, wood, and stone. Seized with terror, I exclaimed,

"For what wild beast were such weapons designed?"

"For people," my interpreter replied.

"For people?" I queried. "I imagined they were intended for

142

ferocious beasts and wild animals. But, for God's sake, what cruelty that people should invent such horrible things to use against other people!"

"How squeamish you are!" he said, laughing at me.

The profligate life of the soldier

4. Coming out of that place, we went further and came to a square where I saw those men clad in iron with horns and claws and bound to one another in masses like herds. They were lying in front of troughs and pails into which their food and drink had been dumped and poured. One on top of another, they gobbled and slurped. "Are these hogs being fattened for the slaughter?" I asked. "Admittedly I see human appearance but swinish deeds."

"Such are the comforts of this profession," the interpreter replied. Just then they got up from the troughs and began hopping, skipping, dancing, and shouting. "Look at the delights of this life," said the interpreter. "What cares do they have? Is it not merry here?"

"I will wait to see what is to come," I responded. Meanwhile, they gave themselves to hunting and robbing civilians whom they encountered. Then wallowing on the ground, they committed sodomy and disgraceful acts without any shame or fear of God, until I blushed and said, "This should not be tolerated."

"But it must be tolerated," said the interpreter, "for this estate demands all sorts of liberties." Then they sat down and began to gobble again, gorging and guzzling themselves to stupefaction until they fell down and snored. Then they were led to the square where they were exposed to rain, snow, hail, frost, sleet, thirst, hunger, and various other discomforts. As a result, many shook, trembled, languished, and perished, becoming food for dogs and crows. But others took no notice of their plight and continued their revelling.

Description of the battle

5. Then drums sounded, trumpets blared, and a great hue and cry arose. Each one got up and seized daggers, knives, bayonets,

or whatever else he had. They stabbed each other mercilessly until blood spurted, and hacked and chopped at each other more fiercely than the most savage beasts. Then the noise increased on all sides. One heard the stamping of horses, the clanging of armor, the clash of swords, the boom of the artillery, the whiz of shots and bullets past one's ears, the sound of trumpets, the beating of drums, the cries urging men to battle, the shouts of victors, the groans of the wounded and dying. In one place I saw a horrible hail of lead; in another place I saw frightful, fiery lightning and heard the noise of thunder. Here a soldier's hand, head, or leg was blown off; elsewhere one fell upon another, and everything was bathed in blood. "Almighty God, what is happening here?" I cried. "Must the whole world perish?" Barely regaining my senses, I fled from that square, how and wither I have no idea. Catching my breath, but still trembling, I asked my guide, "Where have you led me?"

"What a sissy you are!" my interpreter replied. "To be a man is to be unafraid to attack others."

"But what have they done to each other?" I inquired.

"Their masters argued, so the matter had to be settled," he explained.

"And this is how they settle it?" I asked.

"Of course," he answered. "For how else would great lords, kings, and kingdoms who have no judge over them settle disputes? They must resolve such matters among themselves by the sword. Whoever brandishes iron and directs fire more effectively triumphs."

"Oh what barbarity and beastliness!" I exclaimed. "Are there not other paths to peace? Settling disputes in this way befits wild beasts and not people."

Survivors of the battle

6. Then I observed many being led or carried from the battlefield with chopped off arms, legs, head, or nose, or with riddled body and lacerated skin, all mangled and bloody. I could hardly look at them for pity.

"Everything will heal. A soldier must be calloused," the interpreter said to me.

"But what about those who lost their lives there?" I asked.

"Their skin had already been paid for," he answered.

"How so?" I queried.

"Did you not see what comforts were granted to them earlier?"

"Yes, but also what discomforts they had to endure," I replied. "Even if they had formerly led lives of pure pleasure, it is a wretched thing to fatten a man only to lead him immediately to the slaughterhouse. All things considered, this profession is disgusting, and I want nothing to do with it. Let us go from here."[87]

Chapter 21
The Knightly Order

Why titles of nobility and coats of arms are given

1. "At least look at what honor is rendered to those who act heroically and fight their way through swords, spears, arrows, and bullets," said the interpreter. Then they led me to a palace where I saw a man sitting under a majestic canopy and summoning to himself those who had acted with greater courage. Many came forward, bearing skulls, limbs, ribs, hands, and the plundered and pillaged purses and pouches of their enemies for which they were praised. For this, the man under the canopy gave them a painted emblem and granted them certain special privileges above those of other people. Sticking the emblem on a pole, they carried it on display for all to see.

Others also crowd into this class

2. Seeing this, others, not only from the fighting class as in former times, but also many from the trades and learned professions, stepped forward. Having neither scars nor plunder taken from their enemies that they could exhibit, they brought out and presented their purses and the writings that they had made into books. They were then given such things as were given to others,

though their emblems were usually more magnificent, and they were admitted to an upper hall.

Splendor of knights

3. Following after these people, I saw groups of them strutting about with feathers on their heads, spurs on their heels, and steel at their sides. I did not dare to approach them closely, and it was well that I did not. For I soon saw that others who mixed with them did not fare well. Indeed, some who came too close to them or who did not steer sufficiently clear of them or bend their knee low enough or know how to pronounce their titles correctly met with fists. Fearing this fate, I begged to leave this place.

"First observe them more closely," said Searchall, "but be careful."

Knightly deeds

4. Then I observed their deeds from a distance. I saw that their work (according to the privileges of their estate, as they said) consisted in pounding the pavement; hanging two legs over a horse; hunting greyhounds, hares, and wolves; driving the peasants to hard labor, placing them in dungeons, and setting them free again; enjoying the dishes set before them at long tables and stretching their legs out below them for as long as possible; bowing and kissing hands; skillfully playing checkers and dice; prattling shamelessly about lewd and obscene subjects; and the like. They claimed that their privileges certified that whatever they did should be called noble, and no one but a virtuous person should associate with them. Some measured their shields, comparing them one with another. The more ancient and worn it was, the more highly a shield was esteemed. Others shook their heads in reproach at those who bore a new shield. I also saw here many other things that seemed strange and absurd, but I dare not speak of them all. I will say only this, that having sufficiently observed all the vanities of these people, I once again begged my guides to leave, and my request was granted.

The road to the castle of fortune

5. As we proceeded, the interpreter said to me, "You have already examined the labors and occupations of humankind, and nothing has pleased you. Perhaps this is because you suppose that these people have nothing besides work. You must realize, however, that all their toil is the path to rest, to which all who have not spared themselves finally attain; that when they gain estates and riches, or fame and honors, or comfort and pleasure, their minds have much in which to delight. Therefore, let us lead you to the Castle of Pleasure that you may see the goal of human labors." I rejoiced at this suggestion, promising myself rest and consolation for my mind.

Chapter 22
The Pilgrim Finds Himself Among the Newsmen

Newsmen are amazed at many things

1. When we approached the gate, I saw on the left side of the square a crowd of people. "We must not pass these people by," Ubiquitous exclaimed.

"What are they doing?" I asked.

"Come and see!" he replied.

As we walked into their midst, they were standing in groups of two or three, gesticulating with their fingers, shaking their heads, clapping their hands, and scratching themselves behind their ears. Finally, some of them jumped for joy, while others burst out crying. "What is going on here?" I inquired. "Are they performing some comedy?"

"No, don't mistake this for a play," said the interpreter. "They are occupied with real affairs, at which they are amazed, amused, or angered, as the case may be."

"I would like to know what amazes, amuses, or angers them," said I. Watching them, I observed that they were busy with whistles. Leaning toward each other, they blew into one another's ears. When the sound of the whistle was pleasant, they rejoiced, but when it was shrill, they were sad.

Whistles have diverse sounds

2. Something seemed strange to me, however. The very same sound of the whistle was so very pleasant to one group of people that they could not refrain from jumping for joy, whereas another group found it so painful that they stopped up their ears and ran to the side or began to wail and cry bitterly. "What a monstrous thing this is," I said, "that the same whistle sounds so sweet to some and so bitter to others."

"The difference is not in the sound but in the hearing," the interpreter explained. "For as one and the same medicine works differently on patients depending on their disease, so it is here. The way one is inwardly disposed or inclined to a thing determines the way he hears the external sound, whether sweet or bitter."

The limping messenger

3. "But where are these whistles obtained?" I asked.

"They are brought from everywhere," he answered. "Don't you see the dealers?" Then I looked and saw people walking or riding who had been charged to distribute the whistles. Many of them rode swift horses, and a great number of people bought from them. Other dealers walked on foot, and some even hobbled on crutches. Wise people bought more readily from these, saying that they were more reliable.[88]

The delight of news

4. Not only did I watch them, but stopping here and there, I also listened to them. I admit that there was indeed a certain pleasure in hearing different voices coming from everywhere. But it displeased me that some acted immoderately, buying all the whistles that they could possibly get, blowing them awhile and then throwing each of them away. There were people of various classes who rarely sat at home but were always on the watch in the square keeping their ears open for the sound of a whistle.

The vanity of gathering news

5. I was not at all pleased, however, when I recognized the vanity of this activity. For often a sad noise went forth, and all grieved; but shortly thereafter another sound was heard, and the fear turned to laughter. Again, the sound of a particular whistle was so pleasant that everyone exulted and rejoiced; but then it suddenly changed, either subsiding or turning into a shrill noise. Thus, those who were guided by these sounds hoped or feared in vain, for all went up in smoke. It was amusing to see that people allowed themselves to be deceived by every gust of wind. Therefore, I praised those who paid no attention to these follies but concentrated on their own tasks.

Discomforts both with and without news

6. But I also observed another drawback. When someone paid no attention to what was being whistled, some evil might well befall him. Finally, I also saw that dealing with these whistles was dangerous in many ways. For since noises sounded differently to different ears, quarrels and brawls often arose. I myself met with such an experience. Having come upon a clear-sounding whistle, I passed it on to my friend. But others seized it, threw it to the ground, and stamped on it, threatening me for having divulged such things. Seeing them so inflamed with anger, I was forced to flee. Meanwhile, since my guides were constantly encouraging me with thoughts of the Castle of Fortune, we proceeded toward it.

Chapter 23
The Pilgrim Examines the Castle of Fortune: First of All, the Entrance

Virtue, a forgotten gate to fame

1. When we came to that fine castle, I saw, first of all, a crowd of people converging from all the streets of the city. They milled about, trying to determine how they could get to the top. There was only one steep and narrow gate leading to the castle, but it was in ruins, covered with debris and overgrown with thorns. I

think it was called Virtue. I was told that in former times it had been built as the only entrance to the castle, but soon afterward it had been destroyed by some accident. Therefore, other smaller gates were built; and this one was abandoned since it was very steep, almost inaccessible, and too difficult to enter.

The side entrances

2. So the walls had been broken through, and some smaller gates had been built at both sides. Looking at these, I noticed the names inscribed over them: Hypocrisy, Lie, Flattery, Unrighteousness, Guile, Violence, and so forth. When I called the gates by name, however, those who were entering heard me, were enraged at me, grumbled, and wanted to throw me down the hill. So I had to keep my mouth closed. Looking again, I observed that some were still trying to climb up by the old gate through debris and thorns. Some managed to get through; others did not. These latter returned again to the lower gates and entered through them.

Fortune promotes whomever she seizes by chance

3. I entered also and perceived that this was not yet the castle, but only a courtyard in which a crowd of people stood looking up toward the higher palaces and sighing. When I asked what they were doing, I was told that they were candidates for admission, waiting for a glance from gracious Lady Fortune and permission to enter the castle. "But do not all these people finally gain admission?" I asked. "For they have all labored faithfully toward this end."

"Each one can strive according to his knowledge and ability," he answered. "In the end, however, it lies with Lady Fortune to admit or reject whom she wishes. You can see for yourself how this works."

I observed that there were neither stairs nor gates, but rather a wheel that was constantly turning. By grasping it, one would be lifted up to the floor above, where he would be received by Lady Fortune and allowed to proceed further. Not everyone below was able to grasp the wheel, however, but only those who had been led to it or placed upon it by an official of Lady Fortune named

Chance. All the others lost their grasp on it. This regent, Chance, walked among the crowd and grabbed and seated on the wheel whomever she happened to come upon, although others pressed themselves before her eyes, stretched out their hands and begged, alleging sweat, callouses, scars, and other hardships they had endured. But I maintain that she must have been totally deaf and blind, for she neither looked at anyone nor heeded anyone's entreaties.

The lonely fate of those who seek fortune

4. There were many people of various classes here. As I had seen earlier, they spared no toil or sweat in their occupation and passed either through the gate of virtue or through a side entrance, yet they were unable to attain happiness. Another, who perhaps had not even been thinking about it, was taken by the hand and lifted up. Many of those who were waiting became very depressed that their turn did not come, and not a few of them turned grey waiting. Some despaired, abandoning all hope of happiness, and returned to their drudgery. Some, pining wistfully, climbed to the castle once again, turning their eyes and stretching out their hands to Lady Fortune. Thus I saw that in both cases, the state of those waiting was miserable and lonely.

Chapter 24
The Pilgrim Observes the Lifestyle of the Rich

1. Then I said to my guide, "Now I would like to examine also what is above, how Lady Fortune honors her guests."

"Good," said he, and before I knew it I was taken up with him. There Lady Fortune was standing on a globe, distributing crowns, scepters, offices, chains, necklaces, purses, titles and names, honey and sweets. Only those who received them were allowed to proceed further up. I looked at the design of the castle, which consisted of three floors, and observed that some people were being led to the lower, some to the middle, and some to the upper rooms. The interpreter explained, "Here on the lower story dwell those whom Lady Fortune has honored with money and possessions; in the middle rooms are those whom she fattens with delights; in the upper palaces are those clad with fame in order to be seen, praised, and honored by the others. Some are favored with two or all three endowments. These people can go wherever they wish. You see what a happy thing it is for those who reach this place."

The fetters and burdens of wealth

2. "Then let us go first among those who live on the first floor," I proposed. Thus, we entered the lower rooms. It was dark and gloomy there, so that at first I could hardly see anything, but only heard some kind of jingling sound. A fetid stench coming from all sides checked my progress. When my vision cleared a little, I saw people of all classes walking, standing, sitting, or lying, and each one had feet bound with fetters and hands tied with chains. Some even had a chain around their necks and some kind of burden on their backs. I was alarmed and said, "What is this, for goodness sake? Have we come to some kind of prison?"

"How foolish you are!" my interpreter answered laughing. "These are the gifts of Lady Fortune with which she endows her dear sons." Looking at one, then another and then a third, I saw steel fetters, iron chains, and baskets of lead and earth. "What strange gifts these are," I said. "I certainly would not be eager for them."

"You fool! You look at these things wrongly," my interpreter responded, "for this is all pure gold." Then I examined them again more carefully, but told him that I saw nothing there but iron and clay.

"Well, then, don't philosophize so much," said he. "Believe others rather than yourself. Look at how they value these things!"

Delusions of the wealthy

3. Then I looked and saw a wonder. Those people actually delighted in their chains. One counted the links of his chain; another took them apart and put them together again, or

weighed the chain in his hand, or measured it in inches, or brought it to his mouth and kissed it, or protected it from frost, heat, and injury by wrapping it in a handkerchief. Some gathered in groups of two or three and compared their measurements and weights. The one who had the lighter chain was grieved and envied his neighbor; whoever had the larger and heavier chain strutted about puffed up with pride, exulting and boasting. But there were also some among them who sat quietly in corners, secretly delighting in the great size of their chains and fetters, not wanting others to see them. I assume they feared envy and theft. Others had chests full of lumps of earth and stones that they carried here and there and kept locking and unlocking. They neither dared nor wished to go anywhere, lest they lose something. Still others did not trust the chests but bound and tied so many of their possessions onto themselves that they could neither walk nor stand but could only lie panting and groaning. Seeing this, I said, "But in the name of all the saints, are these people supposed to be happy? In all the work and human striving I observed below, I have never seen anything more miserable than such happiness."

"It is certainly true. (What is there to hide?)" said Searchall. "Merely to have these gifts of Lady Fortune and not to use them is greater trouble than delight."

"But Lady Fortune is not to blame that some do not know how to use their gifts," the interpreter interjected. "She is not stingy with them. Rather, some of these misers do not know how to turn them into comforts for themselves or others. After all, make what you will of it, but it is certainly great happiness to have riches."

"I care nothing for such happiness as I see here," I concluded.

Chapter 25
The Ways of the Hedonists

Spoiled hedonists

1. "Let us go upstairs, where I promise you will find nothing but pure delights," said Searchall. So we went upstairs to the first

153

hall. There I saw several rows of couches with soft downy cushions hanging in the air and rocking back and forth. People lounged on them and had a multitude of servants with fly-swatters, fans, and other devices ever ready for all kinds of service. Whenever one of them arose, hands immediately stretched out to him from all sides; if he wished to get dressed, he was handed nothing but soft, silk garments; if he needed to go somewhere, they carried him on chairs strewn with pillows. "Behold, here you have the comfort you have been seeking," said the interpreter. "What more could you want? To possess such an abundance of every good thing that one need not worry about anything or touch anything, to have all that the heart desires and not even to allow any evil wind to blow on you—is this not a blessed state?"

"Of course it is happier here than in those torture chambers below," I answered. "Nevertheless, not even here is everything to my liking."

"What, is something wrong again?" he asked.

"I see these lazy men with bulging eyes, swollen faces, bloated bellies, and untouchable limbs like a painful, festering boil," I replied. "If they brush against something, or if anyone rubs against them, or if a strong wind blows on them, they immediately get sick. Stagnant water putrefies and stinks, I have heard, and here I see examples of this. These people also do not enjoy anything of life, because they sleep through it and spend their waking hours in idleness. This is not for me."

"You are a strange philosopher," the interpreter responded.

Games and amusements

2. They led me to a second hall, charming to the eyes and ears. There I saw delightful gardens, fish ponds, and game preserves with game, fowl, and fish. I heard the pleasing sound of music and observed a merry company who jumped about, chased each other, danced, hunted, fenced, played games, and I know not what more. "This is not stagnant water," said the interpreter.

"That is true," I replied, "but allow me to look closer at this spectacle." After examining them, I said, "I see that none of these people are able to drink and eat their fill of these amusements. Rather, they grow tired, and each one runs to the side looking for other forms of entertainment. This seems to me to be little pleasure."

"If you seek pleasures in eating and drinking," he said, "let us go on!"

The gluttons

3. Then we entered a third hall. There I saw people feasting at tables loaded with food. They had an abundance of everything before them and were making merry. I approached and observed how some people were continually stuffing and pouring down food and drink until their stomachs could not hold it all, and they had to loosen their belts. In some cases the food overflowed both from the top and from the bottom. Others chose only delicacies, smacking their lips and wishing that they had necks as long as cranes (that they might be able to savor the taste longer). Some boasted that they had not seen the sun rise or set for ten or twenty years, because at sunset they were never sober, and at sunrise they were still drunk. They did not sit in gloomy silence but had to be entertained by all kinds of music, to which each of them joined his own voice, so that the songs heard were like that of various birds and beasts. One howled, another roared, quacked, barked, whistled, twittered, or croaked, at the same time making strange gestures.

What kind of feast the pilgrim had among the gluttons

4. Then the interpreter asked me how I liked this harmony.

"Not at all," I replied; to which he retorted, "Will you ever find anything you like? Are you a stump, that not even this merriment can enliven you?"

Then some of them sitting at the tables saw me, and one drank to my health. Another winked at me, indicating that I should sit down with them. A third began to interrogate me, questioning who I was and what I wanted there. A fourth demanded threateningly why I did not say "May God bless you." I was incensed at this and exclaimed, "What, do you really think that God would bless such swinish feasts?" But before I had finished speaking, such a hailstorm of plates, platters, cups, and glasses fell upon me that I was hardly able to dodge them, pull myself together, and dash out. But it was easier for me, a sober man, to flee than for those drunkards to hit me.

"Just look," said the interpreter. "Did I not tell you long ago, 'Keep your tongue behind your teeth, and don't be a smart ass'? Seek to conduct yourself like other people, and don't assume that others ought to heed your ideas."

He went back again

5. Ubiquitous burst out laughing, and taking me by the hand, he said, "Let's go there once again." But I did not want to. "There is still much to see there, things you could have observed had you kept quiet. Let us go back. Only be careful and stand at a distance." I allowed myself to be persuaded and entered again. Why should I deny it? I was persuaded to sit among them, allowed them to drink toasts to my health, and began to empty my glass. Finally, wanting to discover what kind of pleasure there was in this activity, I began to join with them in singing, shouting, and frolicking. In short, whatever the others did, I did as well. But I did all this somewhat timidly, for such behavior seemed out of character for me. Seeing that I was unable to fit in, some laughed at me, while others railed against me for not drinking enough. Meanwhile, something began to gnaw under my coat, to sting under my cap, to force itself out of my throat; my legs began to stagger, my tongue to stutter, my head to spin. I began to get angry at myself and at my guides and frankly declared that this was bestiality and not worthy of humanity, especially when I examined the delights of these hedonists a little more closely.

The wretched way of the hedonists

6. Then I heard some complaining that they had no desire for food or drink, nor could they force it down their throat. Others pitied them, and in order to help them, compelled merchants to search the world over to find what appealed to their appetites. Cooks had to examine samples of all their various seasonings in an effort to impart to the delicacies a special aroma, color, or taste so

that they could be acceptable to the stomach. In order to make more room, doctors had to use funnels to fill the stomach from above and empty the bowels from below. Thus, with great toil and effort, what was needed to cram and pour down their throats was gathered; with great cleverness and ingenuity, it was conveyed into them; and with great pain and cramping in their bellies, they either endured it or threw it up. Furthermore they constantly suffered from lack of appetite, hiccupping, belching, and retching. They slept poorly, coughed and sniffled, salivated, and had runny noses. Their tables and all the corners of the hall were full of vomit and excrement. They walked or wallowed about with putrid bellies, gouty legs, trembling hands, and festering eyes. "Are these supposed to be their delights?" I asked. "Let us leave this place before I say something more and meet with maltreatment again." Thus, turning away my eyes and holding my nose, I left.

Veneris regnum[89]

7. Then we entered another hall in that same section of rooms where I saw crowds of people of both sexes walking hand in hand, embracing and kissing each other, not to mention what else. Of all I saw, I will say only this as a warning to myself.

Libidinis aestus[90]

All these people locked up by Lady Fortune had a burning, scabby skin disease that caused them such incessant itching that they could have no peace. Wherever they went, they scratched themselves against whatever they could until they drew blood. Nevertheless, this scratching could not relieve the itch but only intensified it. They were truly embarrassed by it, but secretly in corners they did nothing but scratch themselves.

Morbus Gallicus[91]

Clearly this was an insidious and incurable disease. In not a few cases, this abomination broke out externally as well. As a result, they hated one another and were mutually repulsive and abhorrent. It was unbearable for healthy eyes and minds to look at them or to endure the stench coming from them.

Libido desperationis praecipitium[92]

Finally, I saw that this was the last of those palaces of delight, from which one could neither go forward nor back. There were, however, holes in the back through which many who had wholeheartedly embraced this life of sensual pleasures fell alive and found themselves in the darkness surrounding the world.

Chapter 26
Life of the World's Elites

Discomforts of the exalted

1. From there we went to the highest palace, which was open, having no other covering than the clouds. There we beheld many seats, some higher than others, placed all around the edges where they could be seen from the city below. On them were seated those whom Lady Fortune had set in higher or lower positions. All passersby rendered them honor (although only ostensibly), bending their knees or nodding their heads. The interpreter said to me, "Look, is it not a fine thing to be so exalted that you can be seen from everywhere and all must look at you?"

"And to be exposed so that the rain, snow, hail, heat, and cold can assail you!" I added.

"What does it matter?" he answered. "For it is a fine thing to be in such a position that everyone must pay attention to you and watch you."

"It is true that they watch," said I, "but such observation is more of a burden than a comfort. For each one is watched by so many people, as I see already, that he is neither allowed nor able to move without all seeing and criticizing him. What kind of comfort is that?" I felt all the more certain in this regard when I saw that however much respect was shown them to their faces, there was just as much disrespect behind their backs and at their sides. Indeed, behind each one lounging in his seat, stood some who leered malignantly at him, scowled, and shook their heads contemptuously at him, mocked him, and fouled his back with spittle, mucus, or something else. Some even overturned the seats and contrived the downfall of their occupants. Not a few of them met with this or other accidents in my presence.

Perils of the exalted

2. For these seats, as I have said, stood at the edges, and a slight push sufficed to knock them over immediately. The one who had earlier been puffed up with pride now fell quickly down. The seats were set upon some kind of precarious swivel that the slightest touch overturned, and the one sitting on it fell to the ground. The higher a seat, the easier it was to knock over and fall from it. I also found here great jealousy and envious looks between the occupants of the seats. They expelled one another from their seats, usurped each other's rule, knocked down one another's crowns, and annulled each other's titles. Thus everything was constantly changing here. One climbed into a seat, while another climbed down or fell from it head over heels. Observing this, I said, "It is unjust that after such long and arduous toil that one must endure to attain this position the reward is so short. One has hardly begun to enjoy fame when immediately it comes to an end."

"Lady Fortune must distribute her honors in this way so that all whom she wishes to favor can share in them," the interpreter answered. "One must give way to another."

Chapter 27
The Glory of the Famous People in the World

1. "Moreover," continued the interpreter, "for those who behave well or otherwise deserve it, Lady Fortune has another means by which to honor them, that is, by immortality."

"How, then, does this happen?" I asked. "It is indeed a glorious thing to be made immortal. Now show me this."

Fama fermè vulgi opinione constat[93]

Then Searchall turned me around and showed me a still higher place or balcony on the western side of the palace. It was also under the open sky and reached by a lower staircase. At the bottom of these steps was a small door at which sat a certain monstrous man (whom they called *Censor vulgi,* or *Judgeall*) who had eyes and ears all over his body. Each one who wished to enter the Hall of Fame had not only to report to him but also to show and surrender for examination all the evidence that he believed would validate his claim to be worthy of immortality. If his deeds were extraordinary or unusual, whether good or bad, he was allowed to go above; if not, he was left below. Most of the people who attained entry, as I noticed, were from the class of rulers, soldiers, and scholars. There were fewer from the religious, artisan, and domestic classes.

Indignis quoque confertur[94]

2. It annoyed me greatly that as many evil people (robbers, tyrants, adulterers, murderers, arsonists, etc.) as good were allowed to enter. For I realized that this would only reinforce perverse people in their vices.

Herostratus

Indeed, it happened that one came requesting immortality, and having been asked what deed he had done worthy of immortal memory, he replied that he had purposely destroyed the most glorious thing he knew in the world, a temple on which the toil and treasures of seventeen kingdoms had been expended during the course of three hundred years. He had burned it down and reduced it to ruins in a single day.[95] Even the judge was horrified by such shameful audacity and did not want to grant him entry, considering him unworthy. But Lady Fortune came and ordered that he be admitted. By this example, others were encouraged to recount the horrible deeds they had committed: one, that he had spilled as much human blood as he could;[96] another, that he had invented a new blasphemy with which one could curse God;[97] another, that he had sentenced God to death;[98] still another, that pulling the sun from the sky, he had sunk it in the abyss;[99] and yet another, that he had begun a new association of arsonists and murderers through which he would purge the human race, and so forth.[100] All of these, without exception, were allowed to enter. As I have said, this displeased me greatly.

Vanity of fame

3. I followed them in, however, and beheld there a certain official of Lady Fortune who was receiving them. This official, named *Fama*, or Fame, consisted of nothing but mouths. Indeed, as the official below was full of eyes and ears, so this one was covered with mouths and tongues on all sides from which came forth no little noise and sound. Thereby the dear candidate for immortality derived this benefit, that his name was spread far and wide by means of these cries. But when I examined this more closely, I noticed that the cry made on behalf of each candidate gradually subsided until all was silent, and the name of another candidate began to sound forth. "What kind of immortality is this?" I questioned. "Each one is remembered for only a moment and then immediately disappears from people's eyes, mouths, and minds."

"All is trivial to you," the interpreter responded. "Now, then, at least look at these people."

Is it not futile to make one's way into history?

4. Then, looking around, I saw artists sitting and looking at these people and painting them. I asked why they were doing this. "So that their names might not gradually fade and disappear like the sound of a voice," the interpreter explained. "The memory of these people endures."

I looked and saw that each one who had been painted was thrown into the abyss just like all the others. They left only their image, placing it on a pole so that it could be seen by all. "What kind of immortality is this!" I exclaimed. "For all that remains is the paper bearing their image and the ink with which their name is decoratively written, while they themselves perish miserably like the others. This is a delusion, dear God, nothing but a delusion! For what is it to me if someone scrawls my name on a piece of paper when who knows what has happened to me afterwards? I care nothing for this." Hearing my words, the interpreter scolded me for being a madman and asked me what purpose there was in the world for someone with such ideas that ran contrary to all others.

In history also there is much falsehood

5. I became quiet, but then I beheld another falsehood. The image of one whom I had seen handsome and graceful in life now appeared monstrous. Conversely, they painted the most beautiful pictures of those who were in actuality ugly. For some of them they made two, three, or four portraits, and each one of them was different. I was angered partly by the negligence and partly by the untrustworthiness of these painters. I also saw the vanity of this work; for examining these pictures, I observed that many of them were so dusty, moldy, decayed, and dark with age, that little or nothing could be recognized in them. There were such piles of them that they could not be distinguished from others, so that some of these paintings were never examined at all. Such then was fame!

Erected memorials also pass away

6. Meanwhile, Lady Fortune appeared and ordered that not only were some of the old and decaying paintings to be thrown away, but some of the new and fresh ones as well. I understood that precious immortality is nothing in itself and that it depended on the fickleness of capricious Fortune (on the one hand accepting paintings, on the other hand, throwing them out); one could be certain of nothing. This made her and her gifts all the more loathsome to me. For she dealt with all her sons in the same manner as she walked about the castle, sometimes adding to and sometimes taking away the delights of the hedonists or the wealth of the rich, and likewise suddenly taking everything from them and throwing them out of the castle.

Death at last destroys all

7. The appearance of Death at the castle increased my terror, when I saw her removing them one after another although not in the same manner. She shot at the rich with her usual arrows, or

kneeling, she strangled and suffocated them with their chains; she poured poison into the delicacies of the hedonists; she threw down the famous so that their skulls cracked or dispatched them with swords, muskets, or daggers, sending almost each one out of the world in some unusual manner.

Chapter 28
The Pilgrim Begins to Despair and Quarrels with His Guides

1. I began to fear that the satisfaction that the mind can embrace surely, confidently, and wholly was to be found neither in the world nor in the castle itself. The more I dwelt on these thoughts, the more grievous they became to me. Nor could my interpreter, Delusion, break me away from them (although he tried in every which way).

Sapientiae apex, desperatio de rebus mundi[101]

Finally I cried out, "Oh, woe is me! Will I ever find satisfaction in this wretched world? For everything is full of futility and anxiety!"

"And who is to blame but yourself, you sourpuss, if you are disgusted by all that should please you?" my interpreter retorted. "Look at others, how happy and cheerful they are in their estate, finding sufficient pleasure in their affairs."

"Either they are all completely crazy, or they are liars," I exclaimed, "for it is not possible that they have enjoyed true satisfaction."

"Be crazy yourself," said Ubiquitous, "that you might ease your anxiety."

"I don't know how to manage this," I answered. "You know how many times I have tried, but seeing the violent changes and the miserable end of all things has always driven me away."

In the world, the human mind does not find what it seeks

2. "What else but your own fantasies causes this?" said the interpreter. "If you did not sort through human affairs in this way

and toss them about everywhere like a swine with a wisp of straw, you would enjoy a peaceful mind, satisfaction, joy, and happiness, just as others do."

"That is to say, if I, like you, were impressed by external appearances and took casual, tasteless laughter for joy, the perusal of a few useless books for wisdom, and some bit of fortuitous happiness for the height of satisfaction. But what about the sweat, tears, groans, confusion, shortcomings, accidents, and other misfortunes without number, extent, and end that I have observed in all classes? Alas, alas, what a miserable life! You have led me through everything, and to what avail? Time and again you have shown me and promised me riches and knowledge, comfort and security. But what do I possess? Nothing. What have I learned? Nothing. Where am I? I myself don't know. I only know this, that after so much confusion, so many labors, and after having been exposed to so much danger and having thoroughly wearied and exhausted my mind, I have finally found nothing but pain in myself and hatred toward me in others."

By what means people are misled and deceived

3. "It serves you right!" my interpreter retorted. "Why did you not heed my advice from the start: 'Do not be suspicious, but believe all; test nothing, but accept all; criticize nothing, but be pleased with everything.' Had you taken that path, you would have travelled peacefully and found favor with people and contentment in yourself."

"No doubt, having been quite nicely deceived by you," I responded. "I would have raved like others, foolishly rejoiced while wandering about, frolicked while groaning under a yoke, shouted for joy though sick and dying. I have seen, observed, and acknowledged that neither I nor anyone else is anything, knows anything, or possesses anything. We only imagine that we do. We grasp at shadows while the truth everywhere eludes us. Woe to us!"

Whoever sees through the world cannot but grieve

4. "What I have said before, I say again," the interpreter rejoined. "You alone are guilty because you seek something great and extraordinary that no one can attain."

"For this reason I grieve all the more, since not only I, but my whole generation is miserable," I responded. "What is more, it is so blind to this that it does not recognize its own miseries."

"I do not know how or by what means to satisfy your confused mind," said the interpreter. "Since not a single thing pleases you—not the world, nor people, nor work, nor idleness, nor learning, nor ignorance, I do not know what to do with you or what in the world to recommend to you."

5. "Let us escort him to the castle of our queen there in the center," Ubiquitous suggested. "Perhaps there he will come to his senses."

Chapter 29
The Pilgrim Examines the Castle of Wisdom, the Queen of the World

1. So taking me along, they led me onward. On the outside, this castle gleamed with various beautiful paintings. Its gate was guarded by sentinels so that none were admitted except certain officials and rulers of the world. Indeed, only the queen's servants and executors of her commands entered and exited freely. Others who wished to see the castle could only gawk at it from the outside. (For it is not considered proper to spy out the secrets by which the world is ruled.) In fact, I saw there many gaping loiterers who looked more with their mouths than with their eyes. I was glad that they led me to the gate, since I was eager to understand the secrets of the wisdom of the world.

2. But even here I did not pass without an incident. Blocking my way, the guards started to examine me, asking what I wanted there. Then they began to drive and push me back, threatening me with outstretched arms. But Ubiquitous, who was acquainted with them, answered I know not what on my behalf, grabbed me by the hand, and led me to the first courtyard.

3. Looking at the building of the castle itself, I saw its gleaming white walls, which they told me were of alabaster. But examining them more carefully and touching them with my hands, I saw that

they were made of nothing but paper, the cracks revealing occasional patches of tow. From this I judged that the walls were partly hollow and filled with stuffing. I was amazed at this deception and laughed aloud. We came to stairs leading up somewhere, but I did not want to ascend for fear of falling off (and I suspect my heart sensed what I was going to encounter there). "What fantastic notion is this, dear fellow?" said my interpreter. "You might just as well fear that the sky will fall on you. Or do you not see the crowds of people going up and down?" So, seeing the example of others, I went up the spiral staircase, which was so high and winding that one could well become dizzy.

Chapter 30
The Pilgrim Is Accused at the Palace of Wisdom

The pilgrim is placed before the Queen of Worldly Wisdom

1. They led me into a certain large hall where at first an extraordinary light streamed toward me, not only through the many windows, but also (as I was told) from the precious stones that were embedded all over the walls. The floor was covered with expensive rugs, sparkling with gold. In place of the ceiling, there was a kind of cloud or mist. I could not examine it closely, however, since my eyes were immediately turned to the glorious Queen herself, who was sitting on a high throne under a canopy. Surrounding her on both sides were her advisors and servants, a grand and splendid retinue. I was awestruck by such splendor, especially when they began one after another to look at me. "Fear nothing, but step closer," Ubiquitous said to me, "so that Her Majesty the Queen can see you. Be of good courage, but do not forget modesty and courtesy." Then he led me to the center of the hall and ordered me to bow low. Though I did not know how to do this, I obeyed.

Here he is accused

2. Then my interpreter, who had made himself my spokesman without my consent, began his speech with these words: "Most illustrious Queen of the world, most brilliant beam of God, sublime

wisdom! We have brought this young man before your worthy countenance, having by good fortune received permission from Fate (Your Majesty's regent) to pass through and examine all the classes and estates of this most glorious kingdom of the world. The most high God has placed you in his stead so that by your providence you may rule it from one end to the other. This young man has been conducted through all the classes of the world by us who, according to your providence, have been appointed guides for such people. But (we confess with humility and sorrow before you) despite all our sincere and faithful efforts, we have been unable to persuade him to take a liking to a particular occupation in which he might settle peacefully and become one of the faithful, obedient, and permanent inhabitants of our common homeland. Rather, he has been constantly anxious and displeased with everything and is eager for something extraordinary. Therefore, since we have been unable to understand or satisfy his wild desire, we have brought him before your serene Majesty and commend him to your providence to do with him what seems best."

He is alarmed

3. One can well imagine my state of mind upon hearing this unexpected speech. For I saw clearly that I had been brought here for judgment.

The adversary

Therefore I was alarmed, especially when I saw lying near the Queen's throne, a cruel beast looking at me with brightly shining eyes. (Whether it was a dog or lynx or some kind of dragon, I do not rightly know.) I realized that it needed but little instigation to attack me. Two men in armor, the Queen's guards, also stood there. They were attired in women's clothing, but were, nevertheless, terrible to behold, particularly the one on the left.

Power

For he wore a suit of armor studded with iron spikes like a hedgehog (which, I saw, was dangerous even to touch). He had steel claws on his feet and hands, a spear and sword in one hand, and a bow and firearm in the other.

Craftiness

The other guard appeared more ludicrous than terrifying, for instead of armor, he wore a fox fur turned inside out; in place of a halberd, he held a foxtail in his right hand and rattled a branch with nuts in his left.

The Queen's words to him

4. When my interpreter (or shall I rather say, my betrayer) finished speaking, the Queen (whose face was covered by the finest linen veil) delivered the following weighty and lengthy speech: "Worthy young man, I am not displeased with your intention to search out eagerly everything in the world. (This I gladly desire for each one of my dear subjects and willingly aid them through these my faithful servants and serving maids.) But it does not please me that you are so fastidious, and though having much to learn as a recent guest in the world, you give yourself over to carping and criticism. For this reason I could punish you as an example for others, but since I would rather be known by examples of tolerance and goodness than severity, I will bear with you a little longer and grant you a residence near me in my castle where you may better understand yourself and my rule. Value this my graciousness, and know that not everyone receives permission to enter these secret places where the decrees and policies of the world are determined." When she had finished speaking, she motioned with her hand, and I accordingly stepped aside, eager to observe what was to come.

The royal counselors

5. Meanwhile, having stepped aside, I asked the interpreter what these counselors were called, what was their rank, and what were their duties. "Those closest to Her Majesty the Queen are her privy counselors," he explained. "On her right hand are Purity, Watchfulness, Prudence, Discretion, Affability, and Moderation; on her left hand are Truth, Zeal, Veracity, Bravery,

Patience, and Constancy. These counselors always stand near the royal throne.

The Queen's female officials

6. Those women standing at the lower levels are her officials and governors in the world. The one in the grey skirt, veiled, is the governor of the lower region and is called Industry. The one in the golden headdress, wearing the ruffled collar and crowned with a wreath, is the governor of the castle of blessings and is called Lady Fortune (but I presume that you have already seen her). Both of these, along with their assistants, are sometimes there at their posts, sometimes here, where they render service and receive judgments and commands. They each have their own under-regents. Lady Industry has placed Love over the married state, Diligence over trades and crafts, Sagacity over the scholars, Piety over the clergy, Justice over the governing class, Courage over the soldiers, and so forth."

The rule of women in the world

7. Hearing these lofty names while seeing that everything in the world was in disarray, I would have liked to say something, but I did not dare. Rather, I only thought to myself, "What a peculiar order of government in this world! The ruler is a woman, the counselors are women, the officials are women, the whole government is female! How could anyone fear it?"[102]

The guards

8. I asked about the two guards, who they were and what were their duties. The interpreter explained that even Her Majesty the Queen has enemies and foes against whom she must defend herself. The one in the fox fur bears the name Craftiness, while the other, clothed in iron and fire, is called Power. When the one is unable to guard, the other defends. They replace each other in turn. The dog also serves as a guard, warning against and driving off with his bark anyone suspicious who approaches. In the court, he is known by the name Speedy Messenger, but those who dislike his duties have nicknamed him Adversary. "You, however, should

stop your gawking and listen and pay attention to what is about to take place here."

"Very well," I replied, "I will gladly do so."

Chapter 31
Solomon, with His Great Retinue, Comes to the Palace of Wisdom[103]

Solomon approaches, seeking Wisdom as a spouse

1. As I was getting ready to listen to what was about to happen, a great noise and din arose, and when all looked around, I followed suit. I saw someone entering the palace in radiant splendor, wearing a crown, bearing a golden scepter, and followed by such a large retinue that all were overwhelmed by the spectacle. All eyes turned toward him, including my own. After stepping forward, he announced that he was honored by the highest God of Gods so that he could survey the world with greater freedom than anyone who had come before him or would come after him. Above all, he was to take Wisdom, who is the ruler of the world, as his wife. Therefore, he had come to seek her. (His name was Solomon, the king of Israel, the most glorious nation under heaven.)

The answer and his reply
(Eccl. 1:17)

2. He was informed through the Chancelloress Prudence that Wisdom was the wife of God himself and could not give herself to another; but if it pleased him to enjoy her favor, it would not be refused him. "Allow me to sit here where I might see the difference between wisdom and folly," Solomon proposed, "for nothing that takes place under the sun pleases me."

The pilgrim rejoiced

3. Oh, how I rejoiced upon hearing this, that at last, God willing, I should receive a guide and counselor other than the one I had had until now. With him, I would be safer and could more

accurately examine everything. Finally, wherever he went, I would follow. And I began to praise the Lord God within myself.

Solomon's company

4. Solomon was accompanied by a large retinue of his servants and friends who had come with him to examine Wisdom, the Queen of the World. Among them, at his side, were men of honor and serious deportment, who (when I asked about them) were called patriarchs, prophets, apostles, disciples, and so forth. In the back of this crowd, I was shown some of the philosophers: Socrates, Plato, Epictetus, Seneca, and others. All these people sat along the sides. I also sat down in eager expectation of what was to come.

Chapter 32
The Pilgrim Observes the Secret Judgments and Government of the World

1. I soon understood that they administered here only public matters touching all the estates. Particular business was trans-acted in its own place: in town halls, court houses, consistories, and so forth. What happened here in my presence I will relate as succinctly as possible.

Complaints of the world's disorders

2. At first the world's two officials, Industry and Fortune, stepped forward. They reported the disorders that took place in all the classes. These were caused by mutual perfidy, craftiness, trickery, and all kinds of deceptions. They requested that this be somehow rectified. I rejoiced when I saw that the officials them-selves had come to acknowledge what I myself had found, namely, that there is no order in this world. Perceiving this, the interpreter said, "Look, you assumed that you alone had eyes and that no one besides you saw anything. Now you see how carefully those entrusted with oversight attend to this business."

"I am glad to hear this," I replied. "May God only grant that the right path be found."

Search for the causes

3. I saw that the counselors assembled, and after consulting with each other, they asked through the Chancelloress Prudence whether it would be possible to ascertain who was the cause of this chaos. After an extensive investigation, it was reported that certain conspirators and rebels had sneaked in and were spreading disorders both secretly and publicly. The greatest blame was ascribed to Drunkenness, Greed, Usury, Lechery, Pride, Cruelty, Laziness, Idleness, and several others. (All were mentioned by name.)

A decree against those who cause disorders

4. After another consultation about these individuals, a decree was finally composed and read. It was to be announced through public proclamations (which should be hung in public places and displayed and sent out throughout the land) that Her Majesty, Queen Wisdom, having perceived that many disorders had been brought into the land by cunning foreigners who had furtively entered, decreed that the perpetrators—particularly Drunkenness, Greed, Usury, and Lechery—were forever banished from all communities of the kingdom. From this hour they were not to be seen anymore under pain of death. When this decree was made public, an incredible shout of joy rose from the people everywhere. Each one, including myself, hoped that a golden age had begun.

New complaints and new decrees

5. After a little while, however, when the situation in the world was no better, many rushed forward to complain that the decree was not being enforced. Then, after the counselors had consulted again, the Queen appointed as commissioners Carenot and Overlook. To them, because of the great peculiarity of the case, Moderation was added from among the Queen's counselors. They were ordered to investigate carefully whether those infamous exiles had remained in the land despite the decree, or whether they had had the audacity to return again. The commissioners went away, and after a short while they returned and reported that they had indeed discovered some suspicious characters. These suspects did not consider themselves among the banished, however, and they also bore

different names. One resembled Drunkenness, but he was called Intoxication or Merriment; the second resembled Greed, but was called Economy; the third resembled Usury, but was called Interest; the fourth was like Lechery, but they called him Graciousness; the fifth was similar to Pride, but was called Dignity; the sixth resembled Cruelty, but was called Severity; the seventh was like Laziness, but bore the name Good-naturedness; and so forth.

The decree is explained

6. When this report had been considered in council, it was again announced that Merriment is not Drunkenness, nor ought Economy be called Greed, etc. Therefore, the persons named were to be set free, for the decree did not relate to them. When this edict was proclaimed, they departed freely, followed by a crowd of common people who associated and fraternized with them. I glanced at Solomon and his colleagues and saw that they were shaking their heads. Nevertheless, since they kept silent, I did likewise, although I did hear one of them whisper to another: "The names have been proscribed, but the traitors and destroyers have changed their names and have free access. Nothing good will come of this."

The estates of the world demand greater liberties

7. Then emissaries from all the estates of the world came and sought an audience. Having been admitted, they presented with strange gestures a humble petition on behalf of all the faithful subjects. They asked that Her Majesty, the most illustrious Queen, would graciously deign to remember how faithfully and obediently all the loyal estates had upheld the scepter of her reign until now, remaining true to her laws, her decrees, and her whole rule, and having no other intention for the future. They humbly requested that as a reward for the past and an encouragement to faithfulness for the future, Her Majesty the Queen grant an increase of their privileges and freedoms in keeping with her good pleasure. For this act of kindness, they promised to prove their thankfulness by constant obedience. Once finished speaking, they bowed deeply and withdrew. Rubbing my eyes, I asked, "What will happen now? Does not the world

already have enough liberties that it seeks still more? A bridle for you, a bridle and a whip, along with a little bit of hellebore!"[104] But I only thought this to myself since I had determined to say nothing, for it was not fitting that I should speak in the presence of these sages and greybeards who had also observed the scene.

The distribution of new privileges

8. Then they gathered together in council once again, and after a long deliberation, the Queen made it known that she had always endeavored to improve and adorn her kingdom, for she had always been so disposed. Indeed, having heard the petition of her dear and faithful subjects, she did not wish to turn a deaf ear to their request. Thus, in order to augment the honor of her subjects, she decided to increase the titles of all the estates. In this way, one would be distinguished from others with greater distinction and approbation. Toward this end, she ordered and decreed that artisans should be addressed as renowned; students as illustrious and most learned; masters of arts and doctors as most renowned; priests as reverend, venerable, and worthy of all honor; bishops as most holy; the richer townspeople as noble; squires as noble and valiant knights; lords as twice lords;[105] counts as very noble lords and lords; princes as most powerful; kings as most illustrious and invincible. "In order to establish this law more firmly, we decree that no one be compelled to receive communication if anything is omitted from the appropriate title or if it is worded incorrectly." Having expressed their gratitude, the emissaries departed. I thought to myself, "What a great prize for you—a few lines on a piece of paper."

Supplication of the poor

9. Then a supplication from the poor of all classes was presented, in which they decried the great inequality in the world. Others had an abundance of possessions, while they lived in abject poverty. They begged that this situation be rectified. After considering this matter, it was ordered to answer the poor that although Her Majesty the Queen desired for everyone as much comfort as each one desires for himself, nevertheless the glory of

174

the kingdom required that some be more exalted than others. In keeping with the established order in the world, it could not be otherwise. Just as Fortune must fill her castle, so Industry must fill her workshops. This, however, was permitted, that all who were not idle might freely raise themselves from poverty by whatever means they could.

Supplication of the industrious

10. When this answer given to the supplicants was announced, a short while later others approached bearing petitions from the industrious. They requested that those who had not been idle in their respective estates and enterprises should be assured of obtaining that for which they had worked and aspired without it being left for blind luck. The counselors held a long consultation concerning this petition, from which I judged that it was not an easy matter to resolve. It was finally announced that although the power and authority once entrusted to Fortune and her faithful servant Chance (for she was not known to be other than faithful) could not be taken from their hands, nevertheless their petition would be remembered. Moreover, an order would be given that the industrious should be attended to before the idlers (as far as possible) and that they should direct themselves in accordance with this decree. Then they left.

Supplication of the learned and famous

11. Immediately afterwards Theophrastus[106] and Aristotle, sent by some distinguished people, came seeking two things: first, that they should not be subject to such accidents as are other people; second, that since by God's goodness they were honored with superior intellect, learning, and riches (and the death of such people would be a great public loss), they desired to possess the privilege of immortality, which would set them apart from the common people. When their first desire had been considered, they were told that this request was fitting. Therefore, they were permitted to defend themselves as best they could: the learned by their learning, the cautious by their caution, the powerful by their power and the rich by their riches.

175

Regarding the second petition, Queen Wisdom ordered that all the most eminent alchemists should gather and with all diligence should search for the means by which immortality could be attained. Having received this order, they dispersed.

When no one returned for a long time, and the delegates pressed for an answer, a resolution was given them for the interim. Her Majesty the Queen did not wish that such distinguished people should perish along with ordinary mortals, but for the present she knew no way to avoid this. They were, however, granted this privilege: that while the common people were immediately buried as soon as possible after death, they would be kept among the living as long as possible; and that while others were buried only under green turf, they would be covered with stones. This privilege, and whatever else they could invent, was granted to them so that they could distinguish themselves from the riffraff.

Supplication of the rulers

12. After they departed, some came forward in the name of the ruling class. They presented the hardships of this estate and requested relief. They were permitted to enjoy themselves and direct their affairs through governors and officials. They agreed to this concession, expressed their thanks, and departed.

And of the subjects

13. Not long after this, emissaries of the subjects came, peasants and craftsmen, complaining that those who were over them wished only to drink their sweat. They even ordered them to be hunted and chased until they sweated blood. Moreover, those whom the masters employed for this task were all the more cruel to them in order to gain greater profit. As proof, they immediately dumped piles of callouses, bruises, scars, and fresh wounds (which they had brought as samples), seeking the Queen's favor. This seemed to be an obvious injustice that ought to be stopped. However, since the rulers were permitted to govern through their servants, these deputies were judged to be the guilty ones. They were, therefore, summoned to appear. Subpoenas were

sent out to all royal, princely, and manorial counselors, regents, officials, revenue agents, collectors, clerks, magistrates, etc., ordering them to appear without excuse.

No sooner was it ordered than executed. Nevertheless, against one accusation of the subjects, ten countercharges were presented: the laziness of the peasants, disobedience, insubordination, conceit, all kinds of mischief when the reins were but slightly loosened, and many and various similar complaints as well. After hearing these charges, the matter was again deliberated in council. It was proclaimed to the subjects that since they neither wanted nor were able to appreciate the love and favor of their superiors, they must get used to their severity; for in the world, there must be some who rule and others who serve. But otherwise, they could gain and enjoy as much favor as possible from their masters and regents by compliance, acquiescence, and genuine submission.

Grievances of jurists and attorneys

14. After the subjects were dismissed, the jurists (counselors of kings and lords, doctors of law, attorneys, magistrates, etc.) remained. They complained of the imperfection of written law, which, they claimed, was unable to decide all disputes that arose between people (although they had precedents for a hundred thousand cases). For this reason, they were unable to keep perfect order among people. If they added something of their own for the purpose of explanation or settling disputes, it was considered by the unreasonable as stretching the law or subverting the case. As a result, the jurists were held in disfavor, and mutual disputes increased all the more. Therefore, they desired either advice or protection against critical judgments of others. They were ordered to step out, and a consultation began. It would take too long to recount what opinion each of the queen's counselors expressed. Therefore I will only relate what decision was announced to the jurists after they were recalled. They were told that Her Majesty the Queen did not see a way that new laws perfectly fitting all cases could be written. Therefore the former laws and customs should stand.

Ratio status is given to them as a rule

However, Her Majesty the Queen was pleased to give them this rule and key to all the laws: that in all their interpretations and enactments, they should be guided by their own or the common good. This principle would be called *ratio status*.[107] With this they could defend themselves as with a shield against the libelous invectives of the masses, for one might claim that the present case (which not everyone understood) required such and such, and therefore it must be thus and so. The jurists accepted this principle, promised to abide by it, and departed.

Complaints of women against men and of men against women

15. A little later, a group of women came forward, complaining that they were compelled to live under the authority of men as if they were slaves. At the same time, men were also lamenting the disobedience of the women. The Queen gathered together with her counselors for two consultations. After this the Chancelloress announced this decision: "Since nature has given superiority to men, it should remain with them, with these important stipulations: First, since women constitute half the human race, men should do nothing without their advice. Second, since nature often pours out her gifts more liberally on women than on men, any woman who has greater intellect and power than her husband should be called an amazon,[108] and her husband can not take away her superiority."

This was the first pronouncement, though it did not seem to satisfy either the men or the women. Indeed, the women demanded either that the men share the rule with them or that they alternate, such that the rule would be held now by men and then by women. Some were even found who wanted nothing but exclusive rule, pointing to their greater agility of body and dexterity of mind. Likewise, since men had had priority for so many thousands of years, it was time that they should cede authority to the women.[109] A perfect example of this was seen a few years ago in the English kingdom during the reign of Queen Elizabeth. In her honor, men offered their right arm to women, and this praiseworthy custom is still practiced. Also, since Her

178

Majesty Wisdom, Queen of the World, and all her counselors had been created by God female and yet were placed in authority over the world, it was therefore fitting *(Regis ad exemplum totus componitur orbis)*[110] that the principle of the world should apply to the management of households and communities. They assumed that this speech would easily move the Queen to their point of view. But men, in order not to lose the case by their silence, defended themselves. They said that although God had entrusted rule of the world to Queen Wisdom, ultimately he himself held it in his own hands, fully and eternally. Therefore they sought the same right.

An agreement between men and women

16. Then there were several more consultations, from which I judged that such a difficult matter had rarely been brought to them. But when we all awaited a final decision, we waited in vain, for Prudence and Affability were ordered to negotiate with each party secretly. Mediating in the affair, they found a compromise. For the sake of peace and concord in the home, men should at least tacitly cede priority to the women and accept their advice. Women, however, should be satisfied with this concession and outwardly show obedience to men. Affairs would thus run according to the ancient customs, and the domestic power of women would be strengthened. Otherwise, the great secret of communal government would be revealed: men rule the community, the community rules women, and women rule men. Her Majesty the Queen begged both sides to prevent this from happening. Both parties assented to this request. Seeing this, one from Solomon's retinue said,

(Sir. 26:29)[111]

(Eph. 5:23)

"A women who honors her husband is considered wise." A second added, "Man is the head of woman as Christ is the head of the church." But that friendly agreement was maintained, and the men and women went their way.

Chapter 33
Solomon Reveals the Vanities and Deceptions of the World

(Eccl. 12:15)[112]

The mask of worldly wisdom is uncovered

1. Then Solomon, who up to this point had been sitting quietly observing the proceedings, could restrain himself no longer and cried out in a loud voice: "Vanity of vanities, all is vanity! Cannot what is crooked be made straight, and cannot what is lacking be counted?" Then he arose along with his whole company, and with a great din he proceeded directly to the throne of the Queen (for neither the fierce Messenger nor the two guards on her sides were able to prevent this; they were intimidated by his cry and his splendor, as was the Queen herself and her counselors). Extending his hand, he pulled the veil from her face. Although it had seemed at first to be something costly and brilliant, it was discovered to be nothing but a spider's web. And behold, her face was shown to be pale and bloated, and though there was some redness on her cheeks, it was painted (as was evident since it was peeling off in places). Her hands appeared scabby, her whole body unappealing, and her breath stank. I was so terrified, along with all present, that we stood as if paralyzed.

And that of her counselors as well

2. Having turned to the counselors of the supposed Queen, Solomon ripped off their masks and said, "I see that in place of Justice, Injustice reigns, and instead of Holiness, Abomination. Your Watchfulness is Suspicion; your Prudence is Cunning; your Affability is Flattery; your Truth is mere Appearance; your Zeal is Fury; your Bravery is Audacity; your Love is Lust; your Diligence is Slavery; your Sagacity is Presumption; your Piety is Hypocrisy. Ought you, then, to rule the world in place of Almighty God?

(Eccl. 12:14)

God will bring every deed and every secret thing to judgment, whether it be good or evil. But I will go and announce to the whole world that it should not allow itself to be led astray and deceived."

Solomon proclaims the vanities of the world throughout the whole world

3. Turning away, he left in anger, and his retinue followed. When he began to cry out in the streets, "Vanity of vanities, all is vanity," people of all nations and languages and kings and queens from faraway lands converged on him from all sides.[113] Pouring forth eloquence, he taught them. For his words were like spikes and firmly embedded nails.[114]

The counsel against Solomon in order to outwit him

4. I did not follow him, however, but remained standing there at the palace with my still terrified guides and observed what was yet to take place. The queen, recovering from her astonishment, began to consult with her counselors about what to do. Then Zeal, Veracity, and Bravery proposed that all the forces should be mobilized and sent after Solomon that he might be overcome. Prudence, however, advised against this, saying that nothing would come from the use of force, since not only was Solomon himself powerful, but he had drawn almost the entire world to his cause (as messengers, returning one after another, reported). Rather, Affability and Craftiness should be sent after him, taking with them Delight from the Castle of Fortune. Wherever he was, they should ensnare him by flattery pointing to and praising the beauty, glory, and attraction of this kingdom. In this way he might perhaps be caught, but she knew no other means. This counsel was praised, and the three were ordered to set out immediately.

Chapter 34
Solomon Deceived and Seduced

Solomon pours forth wisdom

1. Observing this scene, I begged my guides to let me watch what was going to happen. Ubiquitous permitted this immediately,

and we set out along with the interpreter. We found Solomon on the street of the learned where, to the amazement of all, he was explaining the nature of plants and trees, from the cedars of Lebanon to the moss growing on the wall.[115] Likewise, he spoke about beasts, birds, reptiles, and fish and about the substance of the world, the power of the elements, the positioning of the stars, the nature of human reflection, and so forth. People of all nations came to listen to his wisdom. Excessively exalted by this attention, he began to feel well pleased with himself, especially when Affability and Craftiness, carefully worming their way into his company, began to sing his praises before all people.

He invents craftsmanship

2. Rising up, he went to examine other parts of the world. Having entered the street of the craftsmen, he observed their various arts and delighted in them. With his own great ingenuity, he himself invented extraordinary methods for the skillful maintenance of gardens, orchards, and fishponds, for the construction of houses and cities, and for the furtherance of all human delights.

He becomes entangled in the state of matrimony

3. Then, when he finally entered the matrimonial street, cunning Delight presented to him the most beautiful young women, wearing gorgeous apparel and accompanied by sweet-sounding music. She had some of the most exquisite women welcome him with great solemnity, calling him the light of the human race, the crown of the nation of Israel, the ornament of the world. Moreover, they continued, as the learned class and the artisans had attained great knowledge and enlightenment from the radiance of his presence, so did the married state hope to gain an increase of its glory from his presence. After thanking them courteously, Solomon announced that he intended to honor that state by participating in it. Therefore, choosing from the whole company of young women one who seemed most suitable for him (they called her Pharaoh's daughter), he allowed himself to be weighed and fettered with her. Abiding with her and being overcome by her beauty, he spent more time gazing at her and seeking pleasure than in pursuing his wis-

dom. Moreover (something I would have never expected), he allowed his eyes to run over the crowd of frolicking maidens (more and more of whom cunning Delight displayed before him). Captivated by the beauty and charm of one after another, he called to himself only the most exquisite whom he came upon, even dispensing with the process of weighing. In a short while, seven hundred of them were seen around him. Besides these, he surrounded himself with three hundred who were not married.[116] For he considered it glorious to surpass in all fashion those who came before him or were to come after him. Nothing other than all kinds of flirtation were to be seen in his presence. Even his own followers grieved and sighed over the state of these affairs.

In the religious class he sinks completely

4. Then, crossing the street, he proceeded on with his entourage and entered the street of the religious class. He allowed himself to be drawn wherever the miserable company to which he was fettered happened to pull him. Among beasts, reptiles, dragons, and poisonous worms he began to find sad amusement.

Chapter 35
Solomon's Company Is Dispersed, Captured, and Put to Hideous Death

Solomon's companions are enraged

1. Seeing him so deluded, the most eminent ones in his company, Moses, Elijah, Isaiah, and Jeremiah, became greatly enraged. They protested before heaven and earth that they would not allow themselves to take part in these abominations, and they admonished the whole company to abandon such vanity and folly. Since not a few still followed Solomon's example, they were all the more ignited in their ardor and railed against him more furiously, especially Isaiah, Jeremiah, Baruch,[117] Stephen, and Paul. Moses began to gird his sword,[118] Elijah called down fire from heaven,[119] and Hezekiah ordered that all the idols be destroyed.[120]

They pay no heed to flattering speech

2. When those who had been sent to seduce Solomon—Affability, Craftiness, and Delight—saw this, they took along some philosophers, such as Mammon and others, and addressing the denouncers, they advised them to collect themselves and to act more moderately. Since Solomon, the wisest man of all, had yielded his mind and accommodated to the customs of the world, as everyone could see, why should they stand apart and philosophize? But they paid no attention, and the more they noticed that Solomon's example was seducing and deceiving many, the more they increased in ardor, ran about, cried out, and screamed. This provoked a great tumult.

Popular uprising against them

3. The Queen, having been apprised by her emissaries, sent out proclamations by which she stirred up the populace. Installing her bodyguard, Power, as general, she ordered that those rebels be apprehended and punished as an example for all. The alarm was sounded, and a multitude gathered ready for battle. They came not only from the class of mercenaries but also from among the rulers, officials, magistrates, judges, artisans, philosophers, doctors, jurists, and even priests; indeed, even women, dressed and armed in various fashions (for they said that against such public enemies of the world all must give aid, whether young or old). Seeing the army mobilizing, I asked my guides what was going to happen. "Now you will learn what happens to those who instigate riots and storms in the world by their philosophizing," said my interpreter.

Battle, seizure, murder, burning, and other tortures

4. Launching an attack, the army fell on one, then a second, a third, a tenth, and so forth. They struck, hacked, felled, trampled, seized, and bound, according to the fury of each assailant, and led them off to prison. It is surprising that my heart did not break from sorrow from this sight. Fearing this cruelty and shaking all over, I did not dare to move. I saw that some of those who had been captured and knocked down wrung their hands and

asked pardon for their deeds; while others, the more harshly they were treated, the more resolutely they held their ground. Some were cast into fire right before my eyes; others were thrown into water; still others were hanged, beheaded, stretched on a cross, torn with pincers, sawed, pierced, chopped, or roasted on gridirons. Nor can I enumerate all the cruel forms of death they endured while the crowds rejoiced and exulted over them.[121]

Chapter 36
The Pilgrim Wants to Flee from the World[122]

The pilgrim flees from the world

1. Unable to watch this or to bear any longer the pain in my heart, I fled. I wanted to go to a desert, or if possible, to escape the world entirely. But my guides set out after me, overtook me, and asked me where I wanted to go. Hoping to turn them away by my silence, I answered nothing at all. But when they continued to pursue me, not wanting to let me go, I cried, "I already see that it will be no better in this world. My hopes are dashed. Woe is me!"

"Won't you ever come to your senses," they retorted, "even after seeing such examples as you have observed?"

"I would rather die a thousand deaths," I replied, "than to be here where such things happen and to behold vice, fraud, prevarication, guile, and cruelty. Therefore, I prefer death to life. I will go that I might see the fate of the dead whom I see being carried out."

Delusion disappears

2. Ubiquitous immediately assented, saying that it was good to observe and understand this as well. The other guide advised against this, vigorously opposing the idea. Paying no attention to him, I tore myself away from him and went on, while he remained behind and left me.

The pilgrim observes the dying and dead

3. Looking around, I observed the manner of the dying, many of whom surrounded me. I saw a sad spectacle, for each one gave

up his spirit with terror, cries, fear, and trembling, not knowing what would become of him or where he would end up after leaving the world. Although I was afraid, I wanted to understand something more of this. I walked between the rows of coffins until I came to the end of the world and the light. There people closed their eyes and blindly threw their dead into the abyss. Throwing off the glasses of delusion and rubbing my eyes, I proceeded as far as I was able.

Bottomless abyss beyond the world

Leaning out, I beheld fearful darkness and gloom of which neither the bottom nor the end could be fathomed by human reason, and in which there was nothing but worms, frogs, snakes, scorpions, pus and stench, and the smell of brimstone and pitch overwhelming body and soul. In sum, unspeakable horror!

The pilgrim faints from fear

4. All my inner parts were paralyzed, and my whole body trembled. I was terrified and fell swooning to the ground. "Oh, most miserable, wretched, unhappy people," I cried out dolefully, "is this your ultimate glory? Is this the conclusion of your many splendid deeds? Is this the goal of your learning and great wisdom with which you are so puffed up? Is this that peace and rest you so desired after so much work and countless labors? Is this the immortality that you always promise yourselves? Oh, that I had never been born! That I had never passed through the gate of life, if after all the vanities of the world I should have as my portion only this darkness and horror! Oh God, God, God! God, if you are God, have mercy on me, a wretched man!"

Chapter 37
The Pilgrim Finds His Way Home

The first conversion is the work of God

1. When I stopped speaking but was still trembling all over with horror, I heard behind me a soft voice saying, "Return!" I

lifted my head, and I looked around to see who was calling me and where he was commanding me to return. But I saw nothing, not even my guide Searchall, for he too had already left me.

2. Then the voice sounded again: "Return!" Not knowing where to return or how to get out of the darkness, I began to grieve. But then the voice called out a third time: "Return whence you came, to the home of your heart, and shut the door behind you!"

The second conversion requires our own endeavors also

3. I obeyed this counsel as far as I understood it, and I did well to obey God who was counseling me; but even that was his gift. Then, collecting my thoughts as well as I could and closing my eyes, ears, mouth, nostrils, and all external passages, I entered into my heart and found that it was dark. But when with blinking eyes I looked about a little, I could see a faint light coming through the cracks, and I distinguished up above, in the vault of this little chamber, a large, round, glass window. But it was so dirty and smeared with grime that hardly any light could penetrate.[123]

Description of corrupt human nature

4. Looking about here and there by this dark, meager light, I perceived some pictures on the walls, which seemed once to have been beautiful, but now the colors were faded and the limbs of some of the people were severed or broken. Approaching them more closely, I noticed the inscriptions: Prudence, Humility, Justice, Purity, Temperance, and so forth. In the middle of the chamber, I saw some broken and damaged ladders strewn about; likewise, broken pulleys and ropes and large wings with broken feathers. Finally, clock wheels with broken or bent cylinders, teeth, and rods were all scattered randomly here and there.

Worldly wisdom cannot reform it

5. I wondered what was the purpose of these instruments, how and by whom they had been damaged, and how they could be repaired. But looking and thinking about this, I could imagine nothing. However, the hope began to rise in me that he who had led me into this chamber by his call, whoever he might be, would

make himself heard again and direct me further. For the beginnings of what I saw here began to please me. This chamber did not stink like those other places through which I had walked in the world. Also, I did not find here the rustle and clatter, the blare and clang, the commotion and whirl, the contention and violence (of which the world was full), for all was quiet.

Chapter 38
He Receives Christ as His Guest

Our illumination comes from above

1. I pondered these things within myself and awaited what was to follow. Then behold, a bright light burst forth from above. Raising my eyes toward it, I saw the upper window full of brilliance, out of which a man came down to me. In form, indeed, he was similar to us people, but in his splendor he was truly God. Although his face shone greatly, yet it could be looked upon with human eyes; nor did it inspire terror, but radiated a loveliness such as I have never seen anywhere in the world. Then he, the epitome of kindness and good will, addressed me in these most gracious words:

The source of all light and all joy

2. "Welcome, welcome, my dear son and brother." Having said this, he embraced me cheerfully and kissed me. Such an exquisite fragrance proceeded from him that I was overcome by ineffable joy, and tears flowed from my eyes. Nor did I know how to respond to such an unexpected welcome, so I sighed deeply and gazed humbly at him. Seeing me so overwhelmed with joy, he spoke further to me: "Where have you been, my son? Where have you tarried so long? Where have you travelled? What have you been seeking in the world? Happiness? And where should you have sought it but in God? And where should you have sought God but in his temple? And what is the temple of the living God but the living temple that he has prepared for himself, your own heart? I have watched, my son, while you wandered, but I did not want to see you stray any longer. I have led you to myself by leading

you into yourself, for here I have chosen a palace for my dwelling. If you wish to dwell here with me, you will find here what you sought in vain in the world—rest, happiness, glory, and an abundance of everything. I promise you, my son, that here you will not be disappointed as you were there."

He commits himself fully to the Lord Jesus

3. Hearing this speech and realizing that this was my Savior, Jesus Christ, of whom I had heard some mention even in the world, I clasped my hands, not with fear and doubt as in the world, but with full joy and complete trust. Reaching out to him, I said, "Here I am, my Lord Jesus, take me to yourself. I wish to be yours and to remain yours forever. Speak to your servant, and grant that I may obey. Say what you wish, and grant that I may find pleasure in it. Impose on me what you please, and grant that I may bear it. Use me for whatever you desire, and grant that I may be equal to the task. Command what you wish, and grant what you command.[124] May I be nothing that you alone may be everything."

Chapter 39
Their Betrothal

God's wisdom directs our foolishness as well

1. "I receive that from you, my son," he said. "Stand firm in this: be mine, call yourself mine, and remain my own. Indeed, from eternity you were and are mine, but you did not know this before. Already long ago I prepared for you that happiness to which I will now lead you, but you did not understand this. I have led you to myself along strange paths, through circuitous and winding ways that you did not know. You did not perceive what I, the guide of all my chosen ones, intended by this; neither did you recognize my work within you. But I was with you everywhere, and that is why I led you through these roundabout ways, that in the end I might bring you closer to myself. Neither the world, nor your guides, nor Solomon could teach you anything; they could in

no way enrich you, fulfill you, or satisfy the desires of your heart, for they did not have within them that which you sought. But I will teach you everything. I will enrich you. I will satisfy you.

All worldly striving should be transferred to God

2. This only I ask of you, that you transfer and turn over to me whatever you have seen in the world, whatever human efforts you have witnessed for the sake of earthly goods. As long as you live, let this be your task and occupation. I will give you in abundance that which people in the world seek and do not find: peace and joy.[125]

The pilgrim should be joined only with Christ, the eternal bridegroom

3. You have seen in the married state how those who fall in love abandon all to belong to each other. Do likewise: forsake everything, even your own self, and give yourself over fully to me. Then you will be mine, and all will be well. As long as you fail to do this, you will surely find no peace of mind; for in the world everything changes, all that your mind and desire pursues apart from me. All else will bring toil and discontent. Finally, all will forsake you, and the happiness that you found in the world will turn to sadness. Therefore, my son, I advise you faithfully: leave everything and take hold of me. Be mine and I [will be] yours. Let us close ourselves together in this chamber, and you will experience truer pleasures than can be found in earthly marriage. Seek to please me alone, to have me as counselor, guide, witness, comrade, and companion in all things. And whenever you speak to me, say, 'I only and you my Lord,' for there is no need to concern ourselves with a third. Cling only to me, gaze only on me, converse sweetly with me, embrace me, kiss me; and in turn, expect all these things from me.

Christ himself should be his only gain

4. You have seen in the second group with what kind of endless tasks people who seek profit occupy themselves, what kind of tricks they use, what kind of dangers they risk. Consider all this activity futile, for one thing alone is necessary, the favor of God. Keep in mind that one calling that I have entrusted to you.

Committing to me the end and goal of all, conduct your work faithfully, uprightly, and quietly.

He should learn how to know Christ himself

5. Among the scholars, you have seen how they struggle to understand everything. Let the highest point of your learning be to search for me in my deeds, to see how wonderfully I guide you and all things. Here you will find more matter for reflection than those scholars and that with inexpressible delight.[126] To read is endless work, little use, often even harm, always weariness and trouble.

(The Bible)

In place of all libraries, I give you this book in which you will find contained all the liberal arts.[127] Your grammar will be the contemplation of my words; your dialectics, faith in them; your rhetoric, prayers and sighs; your science, examination of my works; your metaphysics, delight in me and in eternal things; your mathematics, calculating, weighing and measuring my blessings on the one hand, and the ingratitude of the world on the other. Your ethics will be my love, which will provide you with the rule for all your conduct toward me and toward your neighbors. You will pursue all this learning not in order to be seen [by others] but rather that you might draw nearer to me. And in all of this, the simpler you become, the more learned you will be. For my light illumines simple hearts.

Recognizing Christ as the best physician

6. Among the physicians, you have seen the search for various means for the preservation and prolongation of life. But why should you worry about the length of your life? For is this in your control? You did not come into the world when you wanted, nor will you depart from it when you wish, for my providence determines this. Consider, therefore, how to live well, and I will determine how long you should live. Live simply and uprightly according to my will, and I will be your physician. Indeed, I will be your life and the length of your days. Truly, without me even medicine is poison; and when I so decree, even poison must

become a cure. Therefore commit your life and your health to me alone, and be in perfect peace about these things.

And as counselor, guide and advocate

7. In the legal profession, you observed strange and complicated human schemes, and you saw how people are taught to quarrel over their various affairs. Let these be your legal principles: envy nothing of others or of your own, but leave to each one whatever he has; do not refuse anyone in need of your own possessions; pay each one what you owe, and if you are able to give beyond your debt, consider it your obligation to do so. For the sake of the peace of all, give up even yourself. If anyone should take your coat, give your cloak as well. If someone should strike you on the cheek, turn the other to that person also.[128] These are my laws, and if you observe them, you will preserve peace.

What the religion of Christ is

8. You have seen in the world how people perform religious ceremonies and stir up disputes over them. Let your religion be to serve me in quietness and to be free from bondage to ceremonies, for I do not require them of you. When you serve me as I teach you, in spirit and in truth, then quarrel no longer with anyone about these matters, even if they call you a hypocrite, a heretic, or anything else. Rather cling quietly to me, and continue in my service.

And what the government in his kingdom is

9. Among the authorities and the rulers of human communities, you have observed how people eagerly contend for the highest positions and strive to rule over others. But you, my son, as long as you live, seek always the lower places and desire to obey rather than to command. For truly it is easier, safer, and more comfortable to stand behind others than to be at the head. If you still want to rule and command, then rule your own self. In place of a kingdom, I give to you body and soul. You will have as many subjects as there are members of the body and different stirrings

of the soul. Seek to govern such that all may be well. And if in my providence it pleases me to entrust you with something more besides, go obediently and do it faithfully, not for your own sake, but because of my call.

And what the wars are

10. In the military class, you observed that heroism is based on the destruction and plundering of fellow creatures. But I tell you of other enemies against whom you must henceforth prove your valor: the devil, the world, and your own carnal desires. Defend yourself against these as well you as you can. Drive the first two away from yourself; then strike and kill the last. When you have courageously done this, I promise that you will obtain a more glorious crown than that which the world possesses.

In Christ alone there is sufficiency of all things

11. You have also seen what the people in the castle of pretended fortune are seeking and in what they revel: in riches, pleasure, and glory. But do not care for these things. They do not give peace but rather trouble, and they are the path to sorrows. Why should you care for an abundance of riches? Why should you desire this? Life requires little, and it is my business to provide for each one who serves me. Therefore endeavor to collect inner riches, piety, and illumination, and I will give you everything else. Be sure of this: heaven as well as earth will be yours by hereditary right. These riches will neither oppress nor burden you but give unspeakable joy.

And the most dear companionship

12. People in the world eagerly seek companionship. But as for you, avoid tumult and love solitude. Companionship is but an aid to sin, promoting uselessness, idleness, and waste of time. But you are not alone. Do not fear, even if you should be alone. I am with you along with a multitude of angels, and you may have fellowship with us. But if at times you should desire visible companionship, seek out those of like spirit so that your interaction would be a mutual support in God.

And delights

13. These others base their happiness in an abundance of feasts, eating, drinking, and laughter. Let it be your pleasure, when necessary, to hunger, thirst, cry, and endure blows and similar trials with me and for my sake. If I grant you a life of comfort, you may rejoice not on its own account but in me and for my sake.

And glory

14. You have seen how these people yearn for glory and honor. Pay no attention to human opinions. If people speak good or ill of you, it need not concern you if I am satisfied with you. When you know that you are pleasing to me, do not rely on the approval of people. Their favor is inconstant, imperfect, and perverse. They often love what is worthy of hatred, and they hate what is worthy of love. Nor is it possible to please all; seeking to appeal to one, you become distasteful to others. Thus you would do best to abandon all these and cling to me alone. If we are in mutual agreement, what people say can neither add anything to you or me nor take anything away. Do not seek to be known by many, my son. Let it be your glory to be humble so that if possible the world may know nothing about you. This is best and safest. Be sure of this, however: my angels will know about you, speak about you, seek to serve you, and should it be necessary, proclaim your deeds on earth as well as in heaven. Indeed, when the time of the amendment of all things comes, all you who have devoted yourselves to me will be led to unspeakable glory before the angels and the whole world. Compared with this, all the glory of this world is less than a shadow.

Here is the summit of all

15. Therefore, my son, to sum up I say that if you possess riches, learning, beauty, wit, favor among the people, and whatever is considered successful in the world, by no means exalt yourself on this account. If you do not have these things, do not be concerned about it; but leaving all these things, whether they belong to you or others, commune inwardly with me here alone. Thus ridding yourself of all created beings and denying and

renouncing even your own self, I promise that you will find me, and in me the fullness of peace."

To surrender oneself fully to Christ is the most blessed thing

16. Then I said, "Lord, my God, I understand that you alone are everything. Whoever has you can easily dispense with the whole world, because in possessing you there is more than one can desire. Now I understand that I erred, wandering through the world and seeking rest in created things.[129] But from this hour I desire no delight apart from you. Now, at this moment, I submit myself wholly to you. Only strengthen me, that I might not again fall away from you to created things, committing once more those follies of which the world is full. May your grace preserve me, for I depend on it alone."

Chapter 40
How the Pilgrim Was Transformed

Description of the new birth

1. While I was speaking, a still greater light began to shine around me. Those pictures that I had first seen scratched and broken now appeared to be completely whole, clear, and beautiful. They began to move before my eyes. The scattered and broken wheels were joined together to form a marvelous instrument similar to a clock that illustrated the course of the world and God's wonderful guidance.[130] Ladders were repaired and set against the window that let in the light of heaven. Thus, I perceived that it was possible to look out.

The wings that I had first seen plucked now received new and large feathers. He who spoke to me, my Lord, took the wings and attached them to me. "Son," he said, "I live in two places, in my glory in heaven and in the penitent heart on earth. So from this time forward, I want you also to have two dwellings: one here at home, where I have promised to dwell with you; the other with me in heaven. I give you these wings (which are the desire for eternal things and prayer) so that you might reach heaven.

Whenever you wish, you will be able to raise yourself up to me so that we may experience delight in one another."

Chapter 41
The Pilgrim Is Sent to the Invisible Church

1. "Meanwhile, for your strengthening and for true understanding of this comfort to which I have called you, I am sending you among my other servants who have already abandoned the world and committed themselves to me, so that you may observe their way of life."

"And where do they dwell, my Lord?" I asked. "Where should I seek them?"

"They live in the world, scattered among others, but the world does not know them.

A new bridle and spectacles

But in order that you may recognize them and so that you may be safe from the world's deceptions, since you will still be in the world until I take you out of it, in place of the spectacles and bridle that you previously received, I place on you my yoke (which is obedience to me) so that henceforth you will follow no one but me. I also give you these glasses. Through them you will be able to discern still more clearly the vanities of the world, if you should want to look at them, and the comforts of my chosen ones." (The exterior frame of these glasses was the Word of God, and the glass within was the Holy Spirit.) "Go, then," he said, "and return to the place that you passed over earlier. You will see things that you were not able to perceive at that time without these aids."

True Christians among the pretenders and how they differ

2. Remembering where it was that I went astray, I arose and hurried back eagerly.[131] Although surrounded by the turmoil of the world, I paid no attention to it. Entering the temple called Christianity and seeing in its innermost part, which is the choir, a curtain or screen, I went directly toward it not even looking at

196

the sects quarreling on the sides. Only then did I understand what that corner was, namely *Praxis christianismi,* or the 'truth of Christianity.' The curtain had two parts. The exterior, which could be seen from the outside, was dark-colored and was called *Contemptus mundi,* 'contempt of the world.' The interior was brilliant and was called *Amor christi,* the 'love of Christ.' I saw that this place was enclosed and separated from the others by these two curtains. The inner curtain was not visible from the outside. Whoever went behind this veil became immediately different from other people, full of bliss, joy, and peace.

There are few true Christians and the reason why

3. Still standing outside and observing, I saw something strange and amazing taking place. Although many thousands of people were constantly walking around the enclosure, they did not enter it. I do not know whether they simply did not notice it or whether it seemed unattractive to them from the outside. I saw those learned in the Scriptures, as well as priests, bishops, and many others who pretended to be holy walking around it. Some even stopped to look at it, but they did not enter. This made me sad. I saw that when someone stepped closer, a ray of light flashed through a crevice or a fragrance wafted out and attracted him, so that he wanted to find its source. But even some of these people, while beginning to look for the door, turned back. The brilliance of the world dazzled them once more, and they went away again.

Necessity of new birth

4. When I approached the door of the enclosure, however, I saw the real reason why so few people arrived there; namely, because of the very rigorous examination that was held there. Those who wished to enter had to surrender all their possessions and even their eyes, ears, minds, and hearts; for, they said, whoever wants to be wise in God's sight must become simple in his own; whoever wishes to know God must forget all else; whoever wants to possess God must forsake all else. Therefore, some who did not want to relinquish their possessions or their learning, contending that these were aids to heaven, remained outside and did not enter. I

saw that those who were admitted not only had their clothing examined, lest some remnant of worldly vanity be concealed there, but also (which is unusual elsewhere) had their inner parts, heads, and hearts disassembled so that nothing unclean to God would defile his dwelling. Although this treatment was not undergone without some pain, yet it was executed so skillfully with the aid of a heavenly medicine that it increased rather than diminished the patient's life. For in place of the blood that had been shed by the piercing and cutting, a kind of fire was kindled in his limbs. This transformed the person so completely that he was himself amazed that he had hitherto bothered to carry such useless burdens as the world calls wisdom, glory, pleasure, and wealth (for, indeed, they are nothing but burdens). Here I saw the lame leap, the stutterers speak eloquently, the simple shame the philosophers, and those who had nothing claim to possess everything.

The church is the world turned upside down

5. Having observed this at the door, I went further beyond the screen to look at these things (first what was common to all, then what pertained to particular callings). With unspeakable delight, I observed that everything here was in opposition to the world. In the world I had seen blindness and darkness everywhere, but here bright light; in the world deception, here truth; the world was full of disorder, here was marvelous order; in the world was striving, here peace; in the world were cares and concerns, here joy; in the world was want, here abundance; in the world were slavery and bondage, here freedom; in the world all was toilsome and difficult, here all was easy; there tragic accidents everywhere, here perfect safety. I will now relate all this more fully.

Chapter 42
The Light of True Christians

The twofold light of true Christians

1. The world and those who grope about in it are guided almost exclusively by supposition. Imitating one another in their

actions, like blind men they do everything by touch, stumbling here and there and colliding. But in Christians a bright, twofold inner light shines, the light of reason and the light of faith, both of which are guided by the Holy Spirit.

The light of reason

2. For although upon entering, [Christians] must lay aside and relinquish reason, yet it is returned to them again by the Holy Spirit, refined and polished. Thus, they are as if full of eyes; wherever they go in the world, whatever they see, hear, smell, or taste above them, below them, or around them, they see everywhere the footprints of God and know well how to turn everything into the fear of God. Therefore, they are wiser than all the philosophers of the world, whom God blinds by his righteous judgment so that while supposing they know everything, they know nothing. They know neither what they have, nor what they do not have; neither what they should do, nor what they should not do; neither where nor to what goal they should aim or strive. Their learning is fixed only on the outer shell, that is, a survey of the exterior; it does not penetrate to the inner kernel where God's glory pervades all. But in everything that he sees, hears, touches, smells, or tastes, a Christian sees, hears, touches, smells, and tastes God, having the certainty within that this is not mere supposition but the real truth.

The light of faith

3. Of course, the light of faith also shines brightly in the Christian, so that he sees and knows not only what he sees, hears, and has before him, but also everything that is absent and invisible. For God has revealed in his Word what is above the heavens in the highest, what is beneath the earth in the abyss, what was before the world, and what will be afterward. Believing this, the Christian views everything as if it stood clearly before his eyes, whereas the world cannot understand it. The world wants nothing but tangible proofs, believing only what it holds in its grasp. The Christian, on the other hand, depends so confidently on what is invisible, absent, and future, that things that are present disgust him. The world seeks proofs, whereas the Christian finds sufficiency in the

words of God alone. The world demands assurances, guarantees, hostages, and seals; the Christian considers faith alone as sufficient for all certainty. The world suspects, examines, tests, and finds fault; the Christian relies wholly on God's truthfulness. Thus, whereas the world always has cause to stop, doubt, examine, and hesitate, the Christian always has a reason to trust completely, obey, and submit. For the light of faith shines in him, enabling him to see and know that these truths are unchangeable and that they cannot be otherwise, even though he cannot grasp them all by the light of reason.

The wonders of God are seen in this light; the course of the world

4. Looking around myself in this light, I saw a spectacle more astounding and wondrous than I am able to express. I will relate at least some of what I observed. Before me, I saw the world as a great clocklike machine, composed of visible and invisible parts. Transparent and fragile, it was fashioned completely from glass. It had thousands, nay, thousands and thousands of larger and smaller shafts, wheels, hooks, teeth, and notches that all moved and hummed together. Some moved quietly; others whirred or rattled. In the middle of everything was the largest and principal wheel, which was invisible, and from which the motion of all the others proceeded in some unfathomable manner. For the spirit of that wheel was diffused through them all and directed everything. Although it seemed to be impossible for me to comprehend fully, nevertheless I observed it clearly and distinctly. I was amazed and very pleased that although many of those wheels were constantly wobbling and slipping, for the teeth and notches and even the wheels and shafts themselves sometimes loosened and fell off, yet the general movement never stopped. It was maintained by some wondrous and mysterious means of direction that constantly replaced, restored, and renewed everything.[132]

How everything is directed by God's secret ordinance

5. Let me speak more clearly. I saw the glory of God, how the heavens, the earth, the abyss, and all that can be imagined beyond the world even to the limitless reaches of eternity were

filled with his power and his divinity. I saw, I say, how his omnipotence penetrated everything, for it was the foundation for all things. I saw that whatever occurs throughout the breadth of this world, everything from the greatest affair to the smallest detail, happens only by his will.

Especially among people

6. Let me speak particularly about people. I saw that all people, whether good or bad, live and move and have their being only in God and by God,[133] for their every motion and breath proceed from God and by his power. I saw how his seven eyes, each one a thousand times brighter than the sun, penetrate the whole world. They perceive everything that happens, in light or in darkness, in the open or in secret, even in the deepest depths; and they constantly look into the hearts of all people. I also beheld how his mercy is poured out through all his deeds, especially in his dealings with men and women. For I saw how he loves them all and seeks their good, shows forbearance to sinners, cleanses the guilty, recalls those who stray, receives those who return, waits for the lingerers, is patient with those who resist, bears with those who provoke him, forgives the penitent, embraces the humble. He teaches the simple, comforts the sorrowing, warns the falling, raises the fallen, gives to those who ask, renders aid even to those who ask not, opens to those who knock and seeks admittance of those who do not knock, allows himself to be found by seekers and reveals himself to those who seek him not.

Dreadful to the evil

7. I also observed his terrible and fearful wrath directed against the rebellious and the ungrateful. Everywhere they turned, they were pursued and followed by his fierce anger. It was impossible to escape from his hands and unbearable to fall into them. In short, all those who had devoted themselves to God witnessed how his terror and majesty ruled above all and that all things, from the greatest to the smallest, happened only through his will.

201

Chapter 43
The Freedom of Hearts Devoted to God

True Christians are not moved

1. Therefore Christians gain what the wisest of the world vainly seek in their own endeavors, namely, complete freedom of mind. Henceforth, they are subjected and bound to nothing but God nor constrained to do anything against their will. I saw that coercion reigned in the world. Each one's affairs went contrary to his desires, and each was inordinately bound either to himself or to others. Being driven by the force of his own will or that of someone else, he had constantly to struggle either with himself or with others. Here, however, all is quiet. For each one who has committed himself wholly to God cares for nothing else and acknowledges no one above himself save God. Therefore, they do not obey the commands of the world. They cast off its promises and laugh at its threats. They consider everything external of little worth since they are certain of the value of their inner treasure.

And are unyielding

2. Consequently, the Christian—otherwise so approachable, gracious, willing, and obliging—in the privilege of his heart is unyielding. The Christian is bound neither to friends nor foes, neither to lord nor king, neither to spouse nor children, nor finally to himself. He will not for their sake be deterred from his intention, namely, from the fear of God. Rather, he proceeds with a determined step. Whatever the world does, says, threatens, promises, commands, begs, advises, or compels, he does not allow himself to be moved.

The greatest freedom together with the greatest bondage[134]

3. The world is everywhere perverse; and in place of truth, it grasps at a shadow. It bases its liberty on the principle that the person who is free submits to no one but surrenders himself to idleness, pride, or passion. But the Christian behaves far differently. Carefully guarding his heart that it might preserve its freedom in God alone, he commits all else to the needs of his

neighbors. I have seen and recognized that there is no greater servitude in the world and no one is more enslaved, if I may say so, than the person devoted to God; for he gladly and willingly performs the lowliest services of which one intoxicated with the world is ashamed. Whenever he sees that he can be of help to a neighbor, he does not hesitate or delay in the least, does not pity himself, does not exaggerate the services he has rendered or reproachfully remind others of them, and he does not quit. Whether he receives gratitude or ingratitude, he continues serving quietly and joyfully.

And what a pleasure this is

4. Oh, the blessed servitude of the sons of God! Nothing freer than this can be imagined, that a person submits himself to God alone so that he may be free everywhere else! Oh, the unhappy freedom of the world! There can be nothing more slavish than this, that a person disregards God and permits himself to be miserably enslaved by other things! He serves creatures, over whom he ought to rule, and resists God, whom he ought to obey. Oh mortals, when will we understand that there is One and only One who is higher than we—the Lord, our Maker and future Judge! He alone, though having the authority to command us, does not command us as slaves but calls us as children to obey him, desiring that even when we obey, we may be free and not constrained. Indeed, to serve Christ is to rule. To be God's vassal is a greater glory than to be the monarch of all the world. What, then, will it mean to be a friend and child of God![135]

Chapter 44
The Code of True Christians

God's laws are brief

1. It is true that the Lord God wants his children to be free but not self-willed. Therefore, he hedges them in with clear rules better and more perfectly than anything similar that I could find in the world. There I saw that everything was full of chaos—partly because they had no clear order and partly because what order

they possessed was not observed. But those who dwell within the enclosure possess and heed a most excellent order. Indeed, God himself has given them laws full of justice. They are commanded that each one committed to God: I. must have and acknowledge him as the only God; II. must serve him in spirit and in truth, without imagining or creating any physical likenesses; III. should use his tongue, not for giving offense, but for praising his worthy name; IV. must spend the times and hours appointed for his service in nothing but his outward and inward worship; V. must be subject to his parents and others placed over him by God; VI. must do no harm to the life of his neighbor; VII. must preserve the purity of his body; VIII. must not seize the property of others; IX. must shun falsehood and deceit; X. finally, must restrain even his mind within the established limits and bounds.[136]

The sum of them in two words

2. The essence of the entire law is that he should love God above all that can be named and sincerely wish as much good to his neighbor as to himself.[137] I have heard the sum of God's law comprised in these two commands highly praised, and I myself have seen and tested that they are worth more than all the innumerable laws, rules, and decrees of the world. Indeed, they are a thousand times more perfect.

The true Christian does not need an abundance of laws

3. For the one who loves God sincerely and wholeheartedly, it is not necessary to prescribe when, where, how, and how many times to serve, worship, and honor him. True union with God and readiness to obey are themselves the best way to honor him. They lead persons to praise God always and everywhere in their very beings and to glorify him through all their deeds. Likewise, whoever loves his neighbor as himself does not need more detailed commands as to where, when, and in what circumstance he should attend to him, in what instance not to harm him, and how to return the debt that is due. Love will tell him and show him fully how he should behave toward his neighbor. It is the mark of an evil man always to seek rules and to want written laws

to dictate what he ought to do. For as the finger of God shows us in our hearts what we desire ourselves, we owe it to our neighbors to do likewise. But because the world does not heed the inner witness of its own conscience and only obeys external regulations, there is no true order in the world, but only suspicions, mistrust, misunderstandings, spite, quarrels, envy, hatreds, thefts, murders, and so forth. But those who are truly devoted to God pay attention only to their conscience, not doing what it has forbidden them to do. They do what it shows them ought to be done, not seeking profit, favor, or anything else.

There is unanimity among true Christians

4. There is a certain unanimity or likeness among them all as if they had been cast from one mold. All think the same, believe the same, like and dislike the same, because they have been taught by one and the same Spirit. What I witnessed here, and that with gladness, was astonishing. People who had never seen or heard each other and who were separated from each other geographically were nonetheless very similar to one another. As if they shared the same body, they talked, saw, and felt alike. Though they possess a diversity of gifts, there arises from them a pleasing harmony like a musical instrument whose strings or pipes emit various pitches, some softer and some louder. This is the reason for Christian unity and a foreshadowing of eternity when all will be done through one spirit.

And true sympathy

5. From this unanimity proceeds true sympathy. They rejoice with those who rejoice and mourn with those who mourn.[138] I had seen in the world a most evil thing that grieved me more than once. If misfortune befell a certain person, others would rejoice because of this. When one erred, others would laugh. When one suffered loss, others would seek advantage from it. For their own benefit, pleasure, and entertainment, they strove to bring about their neighbor's loss and downfall. Among the Christians, however, I found the situation quite different. For each one warded off unhappiness and calamity from his neighbor as earnestly and

diligently as from himself. If he was unable to avert misfortune, he grieved as if it had befallen him personally. It did affect him, in fact, for they were all of one heart and one soul. Just as the iron needles in compasses, when magnetized, all turn to one and the same side of the world, so the hearts of these people, anointed with the spirit of love, all turn to one and the same direction: in happiness to joy, in unhappiness to sorrow. Then I realized that those who carefully conduct their own affairs while disregarding their neighbors' are false Christians. Wherever the hand of God strikes, they shrewdly turn away from it. Guarding only their own nest, they leave others outside in the wind and rain. Here, however, I found things far different. When one suffered, the others did not rejoice; when one was hungry, the others did not feast; when one struggled, the others did not sleep. All things were done in common, and it was a joy to behold.

There is community in all good things

6. Regarding possessions, I saw that although for the most part they were poor, having little and caring little about what the world calls riches, yet almost everyone had something of his own. However, he did not conceal this or hide it from the others (as happens in the world), but held it as if in common, readily and willingly giving or loaning it to anyone who might be in need.[139] Thus, among themselves they all treated their possessions just as those sitting at a common table all use the provisions with equal right. Seeing their interaction, I was ashamed, for with us it is often just the opposite. Some fill and cram their houses with furnishings, clothing, food, gold, and silver as much as they can; meanwhile others, who are no less God's servants, hardly have enough to clothe and feed themselves. I understood, I must say, that this was not the will of God. It was the way of the world, the perverse world, that some should go about dressed in finery, while others are naked; some belch from having over-stuffed themselves, while others yawn with hunger; some earn laboriously, while others squander idly; some amuse themselves, while others wail. From such behavior comes pride and contempt of others on the part of the former, and self-pity, envy, and

other passions on the part of the latter. Here, however, there was none of this; for everything was common to all, even their souls.

And mutual friendship

7. As a result, there is mutual intimacy, openness, and holy companionship among them. However different their gifts and callings may be, they all consider and hold one another as brethren. For they say that we have all sprung from the same blood, are all redeemed and cleansed by one blood, and are all children of one Father, enjoying one common table and awaiting the same inheritance in heaven. No one had anything more than another, except as regards secondary matters. I saw how they surpassed one another in kindness and honor, willingly served one another, each one using his own position for the advancement of others. Whoever could give advice counselled; whoever possessed learning taught; whoever had strength defended the others; whoever had power maintained order among them. If anyone erred in some way, the others admonished him; if he sinned, they punished him. Moreover, each one submitted gladly to both admonition and punishment, being ready to amend anything in accordance with what was shown to him and even to give up his body if he were shown that it was not his own.

Chapter 45
All Things Are Light and Easy for Hearts Devoted to God

It is easy to obey God

1. Nor do true Christians resent submitting to such a rule; rather, it is their pleasure and delight. In the world, I saw that each one submitted only unwillingly, inasmuch as they were forced to do so. As for these people, God has truly removed their stony hearts and given them hearts of flesh,[140] pliant and fully yielding to the will of God. Although the devil by his crafty suggestions, the world by its scandalous examples, and the flesh by its natural disinclination toward the good have caused them many

difficulties, yet they pay no attention to these things. They drive away the devil by the artillery of their prayers, guard themselves against the world with the shield of resolute determination, and compel their bodies to obedience with the scourge of discipline. In this way they joyfully perform their duties, and the spirit of Christ dwelling in them gives them such strength that they lack neither in willingness nor in the actual performance of their affairs (in keeping with the limits of earthly perfection). Thus I found that truly to serve God with one's whole heart is not labor but delight, and I understood that those who so often excuse themselves on the grounds that they are only human do not realize the power and effect of the new birth and perhaps have not experienced it. Therefore let them take heed! I did not see any among the true Christians who justified their sins by virtue of the weakness of the flesh or excused a misdeed committed because of the frailty of human nature. Rather, I saw that if a person committed his whole heart to the One who had created it, redeemed it, and sanctified it as a temple, his other limbs followed after his heart, willingly and gradually inclining in whichever direction God desired. Oh Christian, whoever you are, free yourself from the fetters of the flesh! See, experience and know that the obstacles you imagine in your mind are too small to obstruct your will if it is earnest.

To suffer for Christ is a joy

2. I saw that it is easy not only to do what God desires but also to suffer what God imposes. For not a few of those here were slapped and spat upon by the world, yet they cried for joy, and lifting their hands to heaven, praised God that he had deemed them worthy to suffer for his name.[141] So they not only believed in the Crucified but also were crucified themselves in his honor.[142] Others, who had not endured such things, envied them with a holy envy, fearing God's wrath for lack of chastisement, and separation from Christ for bearing no cross. Therefore they kissed the scourge and the rod of God whenever it was inflicted and embraced every kind of cross.

The source of their willingness

3. All this comes from the complete devotion of their will to God, so that they desire to do nothing else and to be nothing other than what God wills. They are certain that whatever befalls them comes from God's providential direction. Nothing unexpected can happen to such people, for they count wounds, prisons, tortures, and death among God's good gifts. Whether they fare well or suffer evil, it is all the same to them, except that they consider the former more suspect and the latter safer. Thus they delight and boast in their discomforts, wounds, and scars. In sum, they are so steadfast in God that if they do not suffer, they assume that they are idling and wasting time. But do not lay hands on them! For the more willingly they expose their backs, the more difficult it is to beat them; the more they seem like fools, the more dangerous it is to mock them. For truly they are not their own, but God's; and what happens to them, God considers as done to himself.

Chapter 46
The Saints Have an Abundance of All

To be content with what one has is true riches[143]

1. The world is full of Marthas, hustling and bustling, striving to gather things from all sides, yet never having enough.[144] But these Christians have a different character. Each is content to sit quietly at the feet of his Lord and is satisfied with whatever befalls him there. They consider the grace of God dwelling in them to be their truest treasure, and comfort themselves with this alone. External things that the world calls riches they consider more as a burden than as profit, yet they use them for the necessities of life; I repeat, for the necessities. Therefore, whatever God has apportioned to them, whether it be little or much, each considers it sufficient. Indeed, they believe in and rely fully on God's care and judge it improper to desire anything more than what God has granted.

2. I saw here an amazing phenomenon. Some had a sufficiency of riches—silver, gold, crowns, scepters (for God has even such

among his own)—while others had almost nothing beyond their half-clad bodies, emaciated with hunger and parched with thirst. Yet the former claimed they had nothing, while the latter claimed they had everything; and both were equally cheerful. Here I understood that he is truly rich and lacks nothing who knows how to be content with what he has. Whether he has much, little, or no money; a large, small, or no dwelling; expensive, shabby, or no clothing; many, one, or no friends; high, low, or no position, office, honor, or reputation; in short, to be something or to be nothing, all is one and the same. Wherever God desires and leads, places, or seats them, there they should go, stand, or sit, believing all God's leading to be good and even better than they understand.

The godly lack nothing

3. Oh blessed and most desirable abundance! How happy are those who are wealthy in this manner! For some who seem wretched and miserable in the eyes of the world are truly a thousand times better cared for, even from the standpoint of daily needs, than the rich of the world. Indeed, the latter are their own guardians, and they, along with their possessions, are exposed to a thousand accidents, such as fire, water, rust, and thieves, for which they must prepare themselves. The former, on the other hand, have God as their protector, always having in him a living supply for all their needs. He feeds them daily from his provisions, clothes them from his chamber, gives them what they need for expenses from his treasury—if not in extreme abundance, yet always what is appropriate to their needs; if not in accordance with their reason, yet in accordance with his providence, on which they rely a thousand times more readily than on their own reason.

Chapter 47
The Security of People Committed to God

Angels as guardians

1. Although nothing seems more vulnerable and exposed to all manner of danger than the community of the godly, whom

the devil and the world threaten, pummel, and beat, I saw that nevertheless they were well guarded. Their community was visibly enclosed by a fiery wall, which I saw move when I approached it. For it was none other than a ring of thousands of thousands of angels that made it impossible for any enemy even to approach them. In addition, each one of these Christians had one angel given to him and appointed by God as his guardian, who was charged to watch over him and defend and protect him against all kinds of dangers and snares, pits and ambushes, traps and schemes. They are indeed (as I have learned and observed) lovers of people, their fellow-servants when they see them fulfill the duties for which they were created by God. They serve them gladly; guard them against the devil, evil people, and unfortunate accidents; and when necessary, even carry them in their arms to protect them from injury. Then I understood how much depends upon godliness, for these beautiful and clean spirits dwell only where they sense the fragrance of virtue and are driven off by the stench of sins and impurities.

Angels are our teachers

2. I also observed (something improper to conceal) another benefit of this holy, invisible company. They serve not only as guards but also as teachers of the elect. They often give them secret knowledge about all kinds of matters and teach them the deep hidden mysteries of God. For since they gaze constantly upon the face of omniscient God, none of those things that the pious person desires to know can be hidden from them. The angels, then, with God's permission, reveal to Christians what they themselves know that is in accordance with the needs of the elect. The heart of the godly often feels what happens elsewhere, experiencing sorrow in sad circumstances and joy on happy occasions. Through dreams, visions, or secret inspiration, Christians picture in their minds what has taken place in the past, occurs in the present, or will happen in the future.[145] From this source, there also proceeds an increase of other gifts from God within us, deep and beneficial meditations, and various wonderful insights by which one often surpasses one's own abilities without knowing

the origin of this power. Oh blessed school of the children of God! It is this that often brings all worldly wisdom to amazement when it sees some simple, insignificant person speak wondrous mysteries, foretell future changes in the world and in the church as if he saw them before his eyes, name kings and rulers of the world who have not yet been born, and predict and proclaim other matters that could not possibly be gleaned from any examination of the stars or by any other use of human ingenuity. All these matters are so marvelous that we cannot sufficiently thank God, our guardian, for them or sufficiently love our heavenly teachers. But let us return to the security of the godly.

God is a shield to his people

3. I saw that each of them was surrounded not only by an angelic guard but also by the awesome presence of God, which struck terror in those who desired to touch them in opposition to the will of God. I saw miracles performed by some who had been thrown into water or fire, or to lions and wild beasts, yet no harm came to them. Some had been shamefully attacked by human fury. Throngs of tyrants and hangmen along with their many henchmen surrounded them. Sometimes powerful kings and whole kingdoms labored to the point of exhaustion in their desire to destroy them. Yet nothing happened to them. They withstood the attacks and went on joyfully fulfilling their callings. Then I understood what it means to have God as one's shield. When he calls his servants to perform certain tasks in the world, and they fulfill them courageously, he who dwells in and around them guards them as the apple of his eye. As a result, they do not fall before accomplishing the task for which they were sent into the world.

The pious boasting of the godly

4. The godly know and joyfully depend on God's protection. I heard some of them boast that they did not fear even if the shadow of death should stand before them, or if thousands of thousands should fall beside them, or if the whole world should rise up, the earth be cast into the sea, or the world be full of dev-

ils. Oh, most happy security, unheard of in the world, when a person is so compassed and protected in the hand of God that he is safe from all other powers! Let us understand, all true servants of Christ, that we have a most watchful guardian, protector, and defender, the Almighty God himself! How blessed we are!

Chapter 48
The Godly Have Complete Peace

1. While I had previously observed in the world much confusion and toil, anxiety and care, horrors and fears among all classes everywhere, I found here much peace and good cheer in all who were devoted to God. For they neither dreaded God, being conscious of the kindly disposition of his heart toward them, nor did they find anything within themselves to cause them grief, for they lacked no good thing (as has already been shown). Neither did they experience discomfort from the things around them, for they took no notice of their circumstances.

Disregard of the world's derision

2. It is true that the evil world gives them no peace but does what it can to spite and ridicule them. It makes faces at them; tears, throws, and spits at them; trips them up; and whatever worse can be imagined. I saw many examples of such mistreatment but have learned that this happens by the command of the highest Lord, for those who wish to be righteous must wear cap and bells before the world.[146] For the way of the world is such that what is wisdom before God is sheer folly in its eyes.[147] I observed that many who were endowed with most excellent gifts of God were treated with nothing but contempt and derision, often even among their own people. Although this happens on occasion, I saw that they take no heed of this disdain. Instead they delight in the fact that the world holds its nose before them as if before a stench, averts its eyes from them as from an abomination, scorns them as fools, and executes them as criminals. For they have made it their watchword, by which they recognize each other as belonging to Christ, "not to

please the world." They also hold that whoever does not know how to suffer wrong joyfully does not yet fully possess the spirit of Christ. By speaking this way about matters, they strengthened one another. They also said that the world is equally merciless toward its own, and scratches, deceives, robs, and vexes them. Let it be done to us as well! What do we care? If we cannot be spared this torment, we wish to endure it so that the fortuitous injuries inflicted on us by the world can be recompensed by the bountiful goodness of God. In this way, the world's derision, hatred, wrongs, and injuries are turned to our profit.

To the true Christian all is one

3. I also understood that these true Christians did not even want to hear of the distinctions between what the world calls fortune and misfortune, riches and poverty, honor and dishonor. They say that everything that comes from the hand of God is good, felicitous, and beneficial. Therefore they do not grieve over anything, nor are they hesitant or evasive. Whether ordered to rule or to serve, to command or to obey, to teach others or to be taught by others, to have abundance or to suffer want, it is all the same to the true Christian. He will proceed with the same demeanor, caring only to be pleasing to God. They say that the world is not so onerous that it cannot be endured, or so valuable that it cannot be dispensed with. Therefore they are grieved neither by the longing for anything nor with the loss of anything. If someone slaps him on the right cheek, he cheerfully offers the other as well; if someone wants to argue with him about his cloak, he lets him have his coat as well. He leaves everything to God, his witness and judge, in the assurance that these affairs will, in due time, be reviewed and settled equitably.

What he sees outwardly

4. Neither does the godly person allow his peace of mind to be disturbed by the nations of the world. Indeed, many things displease him, but they do not worry or vex him internally. What will not go forward, let it go backward; what will not stand, let it

fall; what will not or cannot endure, let it perish. Why should a Christian be tormented by this if his conscience is clear and he has the grace of God in his heart? If people will not conform to our customs, let us conform to theirs, at least as far as conscience allows. It is true that the world is going from bad to worse, but will we improve it by our fretting?

He disregards the quarrels of the world

5. If the powerful of the world wrangle and quarrel over crowns and scepters, which leads to bloodshed and the destruction of countries and lands, the enlightened Christian is not troubled about this either. He considers it of little or no importance who rules the world. For just as the world cannot destroy the church even if Satan himself should hold its scepter, so also would it not cease to be the world even if a crowned angel should rule over it, for those who wish to be truly pious would still have to suffer. It is all the same to them, then, whoever sits on the throne of the world, except that when it is one of the godly (for this has been proven by experience), many flatterers and hypocrites mix into the company of the pious and by this mixture cause their piety to grow cold. In times of open persecution, on the other hand, the pious serve God with zealous ardor. It must also be considered that when the godly rule, many hide under the pretext of the common welfare, religion, honesty, and liberty. If one could see through them, however, it would be discovered that they seek not Christ, but rather their own kingdoms, liberties, and glory. A Christian is unconcerned about the outcome of all such affairs. He is content to dwell alone in his heart, finding sufficiency in God and his grace.

And the sufferings that befall the church

6. Nor do the temptations surrounding the church disquiet enlightened souls. They know that ultimately the triumph will be theirs. But they cannot obtain it without a victory, nor can there be a victory without a battle, nor a battle without enemies and a trying conflict with them. Therefore, they bravely contend with all that befalls them or others in the assurance that

the victory belongs to God, who will lead affairs where he intends them to go. Even if rocks, mountains, deserts, seas, or an abyss should obstruct the way, they must all finally yield. They also know that when enemies rage against God, it can only contribute to the increase of his glory. For if a matter undertaken for the glory of God should meet no resistance, it might be supposed that it was undertaken by people and accomplished by human force. On the contrary, however, the more fiercely the world with all its devils offers resistance, the clearer does the power of God appear.

The sorrows of the godly are easily driven away in a twofold manner

7. Finally, even if such accidents should occur that cause their hearts sorrow (of which I have seen examples), it cannot last long with them but is quickly diffused as a little cloud before the sun. This happens in two ways. First, they long for that happy eternity that awaits them after these present afflictions. That which takes place here is temporal; it occurs, passes again, dwindles, and disappears. Therefore, to yearn for one of these things or to grieve on its account is unworthy, for it is but the clatter of a moment. Second, they always have a guest at home; and by conversing with him, they are able to dispel all sorrow, no matter how great it may be. This guest is God, their Comforter, to whom they cling in their hearts and before whom they bring whatever troubles them, familiarly and openly. Their confidence is so bold that they hasten to the Lord God with every concern, pouring into his fatherly lap all their transgressions, shortcomings, deficiencies, weaknesses, pains, and longings, and entrusting themselves to him in everything. Since the Lord God cannot but delight in this filial and warm-hearted confidence that they have in him, he also cannot but grant them his comfort and impart to them strength to bear their sufferings. Thus the more their sufferings are renewed or multiplied, the more is God's peace, which passes all understanding, increased in their hearts.[148]

Chapter 49
The Godly Have Constant Joy in Their Hearts

A good conscience is a perpetual feast

1. Not only does pure peace dwell in true Christians but also constant joy and delight, which is diffused in their hearts from the presence and experience of God's love. For where God is, there is heaven; where heaven is, there is eternal joy; where eternal joy is, there a person knows not what more to desire. All worldly joy is but a shadow, a joke, a mockery compared with that joy. I do not even know with what words to describe or express it. I saw, perceived, recognized, and understood that to possess God with his heavenly treasures is so glorious that the glory, splendor, and brilliance of the whole world cannot be compared with it. It is so joyful that the whole world can neither add to nor detract from it. It is so great and lofty that the whole world can neither understand nor comprehend it.

N.B. [Nota bene]

2. How could it be otherwise for the person who perceives and feels within himself such divine light, such noble inner harmony that flows from God's Spirit, such freedom from the world and its slavery, such certain and abundant care from God, such security from enemies and accidents, and finally, as has been shown, such complete peace? That is the sweetness that the world does not understand; that is the sweetness that if anyone but tastes, he must boldly attempt everything for its sake; the sweetness from which no other sweetness can entice, no bitterness can drive away, no delight can allure, no disaster, not even death itself, can divert us.

3. Then I understood what it is that at times impels many of God's saints to so eagerly throw away honors, human favor, and their estates and possessions and makes them equally ready to give up the world if it were theirs. Others were ready to deliver their bodies joyfully to prison, scourging, and death. They were even prepared to suffer a thousand deaths—if the world could repeat them—in water, in fire, or by the sword, singing

through it all. Oh, Lord Jesus, how sweet you are to hearts that have tasted you! Blessed is the one who understands this delight!

Chapter 50
The Pilgrim Examines Christians According to Their Classes

1. Up to this point, I have described what is common to all true Christians. However, noticing various callings among them, just as in the world, I was eager to observe how they performed their functions. Again, I found an excellent order in everything, wonderful to behold. I do not want to describe this in detail but will only briefly touch on it.

What the marriage of Christians is like

2. I saw that their marriage is not much different from chastity; for among them there is moderation in their desires as in their attachments. In the place of those iron fetters, I saw here golden clasps; instead of pulling apart from each other, a joyful union of bodies and hearts. But if some lack of freedom still clings to this estate, it is more than recompensed by the increase of God's kingdom that results from it.

What kind of rulers they have

3. Those among them who are called to rule over others as magistrates behave toward the subjects entrusted to them with love and care as is the custom of parents with their children. This was pleasing to behold, and I saw how many of these rulers lifted up their hands and praised God. On the other hand, whoever finds himself under the rule of another seeks to govern himself such that he is a subject not only in word but also in deed. He honors God by rendering to whomever God sets over him, whatever the ruler's disposition, all honor and respect in thought, word and deed.[149]

What the learned are like

4. When I had proceeded further among them, I saw not a few learned people who, contrary to the custom of the world, surpassed others as much in humility as in learning and were the essence of kindness and affability. I managed to speak with one of them who was considered so learned that no aspect of human knowledge was hidden from him. Yet he carried himself as the most simple man, often sighing over his stupidity and ignorance. Among them the knowledge of languages is of little value if wisdom is not added to it. For they say that languages do not impart wisdom but are only a means by which we are able to communicate with the various groups of the earth's inhabitants, be they living or dead. Therefore, the learned one is not the individual who speaks many languages but rather the individual who is able to impart useful information. They consider all the works of God useful knowledge. They say that an understanding of the liberal arts helps somewhat,

N.B.

but the true source of knowledge is sacred Scripture. Its teacher is the Holy Spirit, and the goal of all is Christ, the One crucified. Therefore, I saw that all these people directed their learning to Christ, the center. Whatever they saw as an obstacle to approaching him, they rejected, even if it was most ingenious. I saw that they read books according to their needs, but they only perused the choicest, always considering human eloquence as but human.[150] They also wrote books but not to spread their own names. Rather they hope that they can share something useful with their neighbors, to assist the common good and defend against the wicked.[151]

What their priests and theologians are like

5. I saw here a certain number of priests and preachers according to the needs of the church. All were dressed simply, and their manner was as gentle and kind among themselves as it was to others. In prayer, reading, and meditation, they spent more time with God than with people. What time they do have, they spend teaching others, together in a group or privately.

N.B.

Their preaching, as their hearers assured me and as I myself experienced, was never heard without an inner moving of the heart and conscience, for the power of divine eloquence flowed from their mouths. From those listening, I saw joy when the mercy of God was described and tears when human ingratitude was discussed; for the preaching was full of truth, life, and fervor. The preachers considered it shameful to teach anything of which they themselves were not an example. Desiring to converse with them, I approached one of them who was a man of venerable grey hair and on whose countenance shone something divine.

N.B.

When he spoke to me, his speech was full of kindly severity, and it was clear in every way that he was God's ambassador, for he emitted absolutely no smell of the world. When I wished to address him by his title, in keeping with our custom, he did not permit it, calling this the foolishness of the world. He said that for him it was a sufficient title and honor that I address him as a servant of God or, if I wished, as "my father." When he gave me his blessing, I felt I know not what delight and what joy expanding in my heart,

N.B.

and I truly understood that genuine theology is something more powerful and more penetrating than what is generally experienced. Then I blushed at the remembrance of the haughtiness, pride, avarice, mutual quarrels, envy and hatred, drunkenness—in sum, the carnality—of some of our priests. Their words and deeds stand so far apart that they seem to speak about the virtues of the Christian life as if only in jest. If I may speak the truth, I was pleased with these men of fervent spirit and disciplined body, lovers of heavenly things while disregarding earthly ones, mindful of their flock but forgetful of themselves, sober with regard to wine but intoxicated with the spirit, modest in words but abundant in deeds. Each of them strove to be the first in work and the last in boasting. In short, in all their deeds, words, and thoughts, they had in mind the spiritual edification of all.

Chapter 51
The Death of Faithful Christians

For a Christian death is pleasant

1. When I had walked sufficiently among these Christians and observed their deeds, finally I saw that Death also walked among them. But she was not of a hideous, naked, and unpleasant appearance as in the world, but rather finely wrapped in the sheets that Christ left in his grave. Approaching now this one, now that one, she informed them that it was time for them to depart from the world. Oh, the joy and delight of those who received this news! They submitted to all kinds of pain, even the sword, fire, pincers, or anything else, only that it might come sooner. Each one fell asleep peacefully, quietly, and gladly.[152]

What happens to them after death

2. Watching what would happen with them next, I saw that angels, according to the divine command, sought out for each one a place where his body would have a little resting chamber. When it had been laid there by friends, enemies, or the angels themselves, the angels guarded the grave so that the bodies of the saints would be preserved in peace from Satan's attacks and not even the smallest speck of dust would be lost. Meanwhile, other angels, taking the soul, carried it upward in splendor and wondrous rejoicing. When I gazed after them with the eyes of faith (having adjusted my spectacles), I perceived indescribable glory.

Chapter 52
The Pilgrim Sees the Glory of God

1. Behold, the Lord of Hosts sat on a throne in the highest. Around him was a brilliant light that stretched from one end of

the heavens to the other. Beneath his feet was a splendor like crystal, emeralds, and sapphire. His throne was of jasper, and around him was a beautiful rainbow. Thousands of thousands and ten thousand times a hundred thousand angels stood before him, singing to one another: "Holy, holy, holy is the Lord of hosts! Heaven and earth are full of his glory."[153]

2. Likewise twenty-four elders, falling before the throne and casting their crowns at the feet of him who lives forever and ever, sang with a loud voice, "Worthy are you, O Lord, to receive glory and honor and power. For you have created all things, and by your will they exist and are created."[154]

3. I also saw before the throne another great multitude, which no one could count, from all nations and tribes and people and tongues, and because the angels carried up God's saints who had died in the world, the number was always increasing and the sound grew louder.[155] And they cried, "Amen! Blessing and glory and wisdom and thanksgiving and honor and power and might be to our God forever and ever. Amen!"[156]

4. In short, I saw lightning, brilliance, splendor, and indescribable glory, and heard inexpressible sounds and noises, all more joyful and more wonderful than our eyes, ears, and hearts can grasp.

5. Terrified by the sight of these glorious heavenly things, I fell before the majestic throne, ashamed of my sinfulness, for I am a man of unclean lips.[157] Then I cried, "The Lord, the Lord, the Lord God is powerful, merciful, and gracious, long-suffering and abounding in mercy and truth; showing mercy to thousands, forgiving iniquities, transgressions, and sins. Lord, have mercy on me, a sinner, for the sake of Jesus Christ."[158]

Chapter 53
The Pilgrim Is Received into God's Household

1. When I concluded speaking, my Savior, the Lord Jesus, addressed me from the midst of the throne and spoke these delightful words to me: "Fear not, my beloved. I, your Redeemer, am with you. I am your Comforter. Do not be afraid. Behold, your

unrighteousness is taken away from you, and your sin is blotted out. Rejoice and be glad, for your name is written among these, and if you serve me faithfully, you will become one of them. Whatever you have seen, use it in the fear of me, and in time you will see greater things than these. Only keep yourself in that to which I have called you, and walk in the path to glory that I have pointed out to you. Remain in the world as a pilgrim, a tenant, an alien, and a guest as long as I leave you there. But with me in my household you have been given the right of heavenly citizenship. Therefore, seek to have your associations here! Constantly lift your mind as high as possible to me, but incline as low as possible to your neighbor. Make use of earthly things as long as you are on earth, but delight in heavenly things. Be submissive to me, resistant and recalcitrant to the world and the flesh. Guard within yourself the wisdom I have imparted to you, and outwardly maintain the simplicity I have required of you. Have a vocal heart, but a silent tongue. Be sensitive to the miseries of your neighbors, but inured to the wrongs inflicted against yourself. With your soul serve me alone, with your body, whomever you can or must. What I command, do; what I lay on you, bear. Be unyielding toward the world, ever clinging to me. Be in the world with your body but with me in your heart. Blessed are you if you do these things, and it will be well with you. Depart now, my beloved, and remain in your calling until the end, fully enjoying the comfort I have brought you."

Chapter 54
The Conclusion of All

1. Then the vision disappeared from my eyes, and falling on my knees, I lifted my eyes and thanked my Redeemer as well as I knew, in the following words:

2. "Blessed are you, O Lord my God, worthy of eternal praise and exaltation, and blessed is your glorious name, worthy and most glorious from age to age. Your angels glorify you, and all your saints proclaim your praise. For you are great in power, your wisdom is unfathomable, and your mercy is above all your deeds. I

will glorify you, Lord, as long as I live, and sing to your holy name as long as I exist.[159] For you have made me glad by your mercy and have filled my mouth with rejoicing. You have snatched me from violent torrents, rescued me from deep whirlpools, and placed my feet in safety. I was far from you, Oh God, eternal sweetness, but you had mercy on me and drew near to me. I went astray, but you recalled me. I wandered, not knowing where to go, but you directed me to the right path. I had strayed from you and lost both you and myself, but you found me and returned me to myself and yourself. I approached even the bitterness of hell, but you pulled me back and led me to the sweetness of heaven. Therefore, bless the Lord, O my soul, and all that is within me bless his holy name![160] My heart is steadfast, O God, my heart is steadfast. I will sing and give praise to you.[161] For you are higher than every height and deeper than every depth, wonderful, glorious, and full of mercy. Woe to the foolish souls who leave you, imagining that they can find peace. Apart from you, neither heaven, nor earth, nor the abyss possesses it; for in you alone is eternal rest. Heaven and earth were created by you and are good, beautiful, and desirable because they are from you. But they are neither as good, nor as beautiful, nor as desirable as you, their Creator. Therefore, they cannot fulfill or satisfy souls seeking solace. You, O Lord, are the fullness of fullness, and our hearts are restless until they rest in you. Late have I come to love you, O eternal beauty, for late have I come to know you.[162] I recognized you, however, when you shone on me, O heavenly brightness. Let the one who has not known your mercy refrain from your praise. But may my innermost being confess the Lord. Oh, who will grant that my heart may be enraptured with you, O eternal fragrance, so that I may forget everything that is not you, O my God. Do not hide yourself from my heart, O beauty most beautiful! If earthly things overshadow you, let me die that I may behold you, and being with you, may not lose you again. Restrain me, Lord, lead me, hold me, that I may not stray and fall. Grant that I may love you with an eternal love and love nothing beside yourself except in you and for your sake, O endless love! But what else shall I say, my Lord? Here I am, I am yours; I am your own, yours eternally. I renounce heaven and earth that I may have you alone. Only do not withhold yourself from me, and I have enough. To all eternity, unchangeably, I have enough in you alone. My soul and body delights in you, O living God. Oh, when will I come and appear before your face? Whenever you wish, my Lord God, take me. Here I am, I stand ready. Call me whenever you desire, wherever you desire, however you desire. I will go wherever you order and will do whatever you command. Only may your good Spirit guide me and lead me through the snares of the world as on level ground, and may your mercy accompany me on my way. Lead me through this mournful darkness of the world to the eternal light. Amen and amen."

Gloria in excelsis Deo et in terra
pax hominibus bonae voluntatis.[163]

Notes to Text

1. The Žerotíns were one of the leading families of Moravia. Though Charles the Elder was Comenius's generous benefactor and a member himself of the *Unitas Fratrum*, the noble remained a loyal supporter of Habsburg Emperor Ferdinand II during the Bohemian rebellion. For more on Žerotín see Otakar Odložilík's classic study, *Karel starší z Žerotína* (Prague, 1936).

2. For the historical context and personal background to the treatise, see the Introduction, pp. 9–17.

3. Comenius meant these words seriously, for he returned to the *Labyrinth* twice during the course of his life to correct, expand, and modernize the text. The first version was written in 1623. As the present letter indicates, it was dedicated to Comenius's co-religionist Count Charles the Elder of Žerotín on whose estates he had found refuge after being expelled from his home during the Thirty Years' War. The two enlarged versions of the work were published while Comenius was in exile. The first edition was printed in Leszno, Poland, in 1631, and the final edition in Amsterdam in 1663. For a full description of the original texts, see *Johannis Amos Comenii Opera Omnia*, vol. 3 (Prague, 1978), 398.

4. For Comenius's linguistic innovations in the *Labyrinth*, see Karel Kučera, "An Analysis of the Vocabulary of the Labyrinth of the World and the Paradise of the Heart," *Acta Comeniana* 4 (1979), 327–352.

5. On the history of the doctrine of the *summum bonum* in spirituality, see the seminal work of Kenneth E. Kirk, *The Vision of God: The Christian Doctrine of the Summum Bonum* (New York, 1931).

6. Eccl. 2:17.

7. Eccl. 12:13.

8. Ps. 73.

9. The futility of seeking happiness in external things, i.e., things of the created world, in contrast to seeking rest in God, is an Augustinian theme to which Comenius will return time and time again in this treatise. For a fuller discussion of this emphasis in Comenius's spirituality, see the Introduction, pp. 29–31.

10. See the Introduction, pp. 9–17.

11. In all likelihood this is a reference to Comenius's early years

before he entered the Latin school at Přerov at age 16. Growing up in the Moravian village of Nivnice, he had the opportunity to sample the various options of rural life, including the maintenance of a local mill. See Milada Blekastad, *Comenius* (Oslo, 1969), 16–17.

12. The science of optics underwent a major revolution in Comenius's day. The contributions of Comenius's acquaintance René Descartes were particularly important in the development of spectacles. In general, see David Lindberg, *Studies in the History of Medieval Optics* (London, 1983). On Descartes in particular, see John G. Burke, "Descartes on the Refraction and the Velocity of Light," *American Journal of Physics* 34 (1966), 390–400.

13. Comenius uses the image of the marketplace in a similar fashion in his later work *Unum necessarium.* In his letter of dedication to Prince Ruprecht, son of the winter king of Bohemia, Frederick of the Palatinate, he describes the world as a marketplace full of deception. Here people stumble about blindly, purchasing goods with no lasting value. *Unum necessarium* (Amsterdam, 1668); reprinted in *Johannis Amos Comenii Opera Omnia,* vol. 18 (Prague, 1974), 75–76.

14. The tension that Comenius sets up here between the *homo animalis* and *homo spiritualis* is explored by Jan Lehár in "'Labyrint Světa' and its Characters," *Acta Comeniana* 4 (1979), 230.

15. A Czech proverbial expression. For Comenius's extensive use of Czech proverbs see Jaroslav Kolár, "Komenskýs Labyrinth in der Beziehung zur literarischen Produktion des 16. Jahrhunderts," *Acta Comeniana* 7 (1987), 121–126.

16. "And death's craftsman is itself." Sallust, *Duae epistolae de republica ordinanda* I,1.

17. On the tragic experience of Comenius's first marriage see the Introduction p. 13.

18. Spinka *Labyrinth,* p. 136, n. 8, notes that the remainder of this chapter is not found in earlier versions of the text. It was added to the 1663 edition published in Amsterdam. The description was based on Comenius's voyage to England in 1641. In a letter to his friends in Leszno, Comenius reported, "That my first voyage succeeded not according to my wishes, and that I was driven back from the coast of Norway over the whole Baltic Sea for nearly a hundred miles by the force of gales, I believe you know." Reprinted in *Comenius in England,* ed. R. F. Young (London, 1932), 64.

19. For the terms used in this technical passage, we have borrowed Spinka's translation.

20. By "mirror" Comenius implies imagination or creative and critical thought.

21. "Not all manage to reach Corinth." Horace, *Epistolae* I,19,36.

22. Comenius was particularly sensitive to contemporary pedagogical issues. For more on his views on education see the Introduction, pp. 17–26.

23. This seems to be an allusion to Isocrates' well-known aphorism, "The root of education is bitter, but its fruit is sweet." On this classical educator, see H. I. Marrou, *A History of Education in Antiquity* (New York, 1956), 79–91.

24. Comenius uses the same metaphor for books in *Unum necessarium*. He notes how dangerous it is to eat them indiscriminately *(Unum necessarium*, 103). Also see Comenius's comments in *Centrum securitatis* (Leszno, 1633), reprinted in *Johannis Amos Comenii Opera Omnia*, (Prague, 1978), 3:518–519.

25. For the prodigious feats of memory common in medieval and early modern Europe, see Frances Yates, *The Art of Memory* (Chicago, 1966). Also of use is a more recent study, Mary Carruthers, *The Book of Memory: A Study of Memory in Medieval Culture* (New York, 1990).

26. I.e., ink.

27. The ancient Greek philosopher Plato (428/427–348/47 B.C.) developed a wide-ranging philosophical system based on a theory of eternal Ideas or Forms that represent universals or absolutes. In his logical treatises, Aristotle (384–322 B.C.) criticized Plato's theory of Forms. Aristotle claimed that individual things such as particular people and animals are substances or primary realities. This theory contradicted Plato's notion that sensible particulars are only partly real, pale reflections of the full reality of the Idea. The rediscovery of Aristotle in the Latin West and the application of his ideas to Christian theology in the thirteenth century gave rise to a long-standing debate between theologians and other scholars influenced by Aristotelianism and those of a neo-Platonist inclination. In Comenius's day, an anti-Aristotelian spirit reigned, partly in reaction to scholasticism.

28. Marcus Tullius Cicero (106–43 B.C.) was a Roman statesman, lawyer, scholar, and writer, perhaps best known in modern times as the greatest Roman orator. In the political arena, Cicero vainly attempted to preserve republican ideals during the final civil wars that ultimately destroyed the Roman republic. Sallust (86–35/34 B.C.), a Roman historian and Latin literary stylist, is particularly noted for his censorious writings on the personalities, corruption, and conspiracies of contem-

porary Roman politics. Although Sallust is known to have hated Cicero, the alleged dispute between the two men is based on a forged first-century text, *Invective against Cicero*, in which the author decries his opponent's political views.

29. Thomas Aquinas (1224/25–1274), the great Dominican scholastic theologian, sought to employ the thought of Aristotle as the philosophical basis for Christian theology. John Duns Scotus (ca.1265–1308) was the most formidable critic of the Thomist system. Scotus argued against the Thomistic proofs for the existence of God, opposed Thomist "intellectualism" (predominance of the faculty of reason) with "voluntarism" (predominance of the will), and diverged sharply from the Dominican's doctrine of grace and salvation. His own system was based on the unconditional freedom of an omnipotent God, which Scotus considered irreconcilable with the determinist features of Aristotelian and even Thomist thought. In keeping with his emphasis on the limits of human reason, he exalted the authority of the church as the supreme interpreter of God's revelation.

30. Bartolus of Saxoferrato (1313/14–1357) was a prominent jurist and commentator on Roman civil law. As a law professor at Perugia Bartolus was known for his dialectical method of teaching law. His student, Petrus Bardus de Ubaldis (1327–1406), was known to have opposed Bartolus's teaching methods.

31. Desiderius Erasmus (1469–1536), the great humanist scholar of the northern Renaissance, emphasized the role of education in his plea for the reform of the church. However, he strongly opposed the rigid system of scholastic theology traditionally taught at the Sorbonne, the theological faculty of the University of Paris.

32. Peter Ramus (1515–1572) was a French philosopher, logician, and rhetorician whose reformed version of Aristotelian logic was enormously popular in Europe during the sixteenth and seventeenth centuries. Tommaso Campanella (1568–1639), a Dominican friar, philosopher, and poet, called for an empirical approach to philosophy, stressing the need for human experience as a foundation for philosophy. By their critique of scholastic Aristotelianism, both men provoked the opposition of the Peripatetics, the orthodox Aristotelian philosophers of the day.

33. Nicholas Copernicus (1473–1543) was the leading proponent of the new, and for some time controversial, view of a heliocentric universe. The ancient astronomer, geographer, and mathematician Ptolemy (2nd c. C.E.) had constructed a system in which the earth was the center of the

universe. Comenius himself rejected the Copernican view. For his scornful remarks on the Copernican system, see the *Labyrinth*, chapter 11.13.

34. Theophrastus Bombastus von Hohenheim (1493–1541), better known as Paracelsus, was an innovative German-Swiss physician and alchemist. He rejected the theories of Galen (129-ca.199 C.E.) and Avicenna (980–1037), the recognized Greek and Arab medical authorities of his day, in favor of more empirical methods of investigating and treating diseases.

35. Jan Hus (1372/73–1415), the Czech religious reformer whose work anticipated the Protestant Reformation, and Martin Luther (1483–1546) were both well known for their attack on ecclesiastical abuses of their day. Both men vigorously opposed the sale of indulgences, insisted on the authority of Scripture, and challenged the authority of the papacy. The Society of Jesus (Jesuits) was founded by Ignatius of Loyola in 1540. The Jesuits were the chief agents of the Counter-Reformation and were known for their fierce loyalty to the pope.

36. Johannes Brenz (1499–1570) was the principal organizer of the Lutheran Reformation in Württemberg, while Theodore Beza (1519–1605) assisted and later succeeded John Calvin as the leader of the Reformation in Geneva. According to Spinka (p.138, n.23), the dispute to which the text alludes probably refers to their opinions on the burning of Michael Servetus in 1554. Brenz was thought to have opposed the death penalty for heretics, albeit in a work mistakenly attributed to him. Beza responded to this work in a treatise that defended the persecution of heretics.

37. Jean Bodin (1530–1596) was a French political philosopher best known for his writing on the theory of ideal government. Bodin also wrote a lesser known treatise, *De la demonomanie des sorciers* (1580), in which he supported the burning of witches and sorcerers. The leading continental opponent of witch hunting was the German physician Johann Wier (1515–1588), who denounced the death penalty for those convicted of witchcraft. In his work *De praestigiis daemonum* (1563), he "urged that many supposed witches were innocent melancholics and that even the guilty ones were mere tools of Satan, incapable of doing harm by their own activities" (Keith Thomas, *Religion and the Decline of Magic* [New York 1971], 580).

38. Johannes Sleidanus (1506–1556), a German Lutheran annalist, wrote the earliest and most objective Protestant account of the Reformation era, entitled *Commentariorum de statu religionis et reipublicae, Car-*

olo Quinto Caesare, libri XXVI (Strassburg, 1555). In grudging tribute, even Emperor Charles V admitted that "the rogue has certainly known much...he has either been in our privy council or our Councilors have been traitors." However, Laurentius Surius (1522–1578), a Carthusian monk and convert from Lutheranism to Roman Catholicism, vigorously opposed Sleidanus's work in his *Commentarius brevis rerum in orbe gestarum ab anno 1500 usque in annum 1568* (Cologne, 1568).

39. Schmiedlein was the name given to Jacob Andreae (1528–1590) of Tübingen, a Lutheran theologian and the grandfather of John Valentine Andreae, whose works had a great influence on Comenius's thought and writing. Jacob Andreae played a major role in the preparation and acceptance of the Formula of Concord (1577). This last great Lutheran creed unified and defined Lutheranism in contradistinction to both the more extreme position of the "Gnesio-Lutherans" and the more moderate views of the "Philippists," who were suspected of Calvinism. It was in this connection that Andreae was considered an opponent of Calvinism.

40. Franciscus Gomarus (1563–1641), a Calvinist theologian and professor at Leyden, was an extreme representative of the "supralapsarian" view of predestination. Jacobus Arminius (1559/60–1609), a Dutch theologian and reformer who joined the faculty at Leyden in 1603, espoused a notion of "cooperating grace" in the act of believing that diverged sharply from the strict Calvinist doctrine of predestination. The acrimonious dispute between the two theologians embroiled the entire Dutch Reformed Church in controversy. Arminianism was eventually condemned at the Synod of Dort (1618–19), where Gomarus played a leading role.

41. The Rosicrucians were members of a fraternity claiming to possess esoteric wisdom handed down from ancient times. For more on their questionable origin and teachings, see notes 59 and 60. The reference to philosophasters alludes to the work of the English scholar, writer, and clergyman, Robert Burton. His first work, a Latin comedy entitled *Philosophaster* (1606), is a lively exposure of charlatanism akin to Ben Jonson's *Alchemist*. The play was performed at Christ Church in 1618.

42. Spinka, *Labyrinth,* p. 139, n. 29, observes that Comenius takes this list from J. V. Andreae's *Mythologiae christianae sive virtutum et vitiorum vitae humanae imaginum* (Strassburg, 1619), III, Chapter 40.

43. 1 Cor. 3:18–20.

44. According to Spinka, these were poems included in school chil-

dren's textbooks that Comenius considered morally suspect. *De Culice* (Concerning a Gnat) was ascribed to Virgil; *De Passere* (Concerning a Sparrow) was written by Catullus; *De Lesbia* (Concerning Lesbia), also by Catullus, was written in honor of the woman he loved; *De Priapo* (Concerning Priapus) was one of a number of odes dedicated to this god of fertility; *De arte amandi* (On the Art of Loving) probably refers to Ovid's *Ars amatoria*, a work that was one of the major reasons for the author's banishment; Ovid's *Metamorphoses,* a poem in 15 cantos, explored the range of human passions revealed in the behavior of the gods; *Encomia* refers to various eulogies of famous individuals; *Satirae* were witty and biting critiques of contemporary society. Those written by Horace and Juvenal were most famous.

In Comenius's *Great Didactic,* he explicitly condemns certain ancient writers that he considered immoral: "Should we not blush, therefore, when we confide the education of the sons of the King of kings, of the brothers of Christ and heirs of eternity, to the jesting Plautus, the lascivious Catullus, the impure Ovid, that impious mocker of God, Lucian, the obscene Martial, and the rest of the writers who are ignorant of the true God? Those who, like them, live without the hope of a better life, and wallow in the mire of earthly existence, are certain to drag down to their own level whoever consorts with them." Keatinge's translation (London, 1910), 235–6.

45. Concerning Comenius's ambivalent relationship with seventeenth-century science, Hans Aarslef has commented, "Comenius made no contribution to natural science, and he was profoundly alienated from the developments in science that occurred during his lifetime... On the other hand, it is also clear that several men who later figured prominently in the Royal Society showed close affinity with much of his thought. The motto of the Royal Society—*Nullius in Verba*—occupied a significant place in Comenius's *Natural Philosophy Reformed by Divine Light; Or, A Synopsis of Physics*, and in both contexts it had the same meaning. It was a reminder that tradition and authority were no longer the arbiters of truth; they had yielded to nature and autopsy as the sole sources of certain knowledge" (*Dictionary of Scientific Biography* [New York, 1971], 3:362).

46. Comenius is referring to the French humanist Peter Ramus, one of the most important pedagogical reformers of early modern Europe. Best on Ramus is Walter Ong, *Ramus: Method and the Decay of Dialogue: From the Art of Discourse to the Art of Reason* (Cambridge, 1958).

47. The contrast between Descartes and Comenius is useful here.

Reflecting on his quest for a certain basis of knowledge, Descartes writes in the *Discourse on Method*: "I was especially delighted with the Mathematicians, on account of the certitude and evidence of their reasonings" (Part I, section 10). He goes on to explain how the mathematicians alone have been able to find any certainty.

48. For an overview of medieval mathematics, see Michael S. Mahoney, "Mathematics," in *Science in the Middle Ages*, ed. David Lindberg (Chicago, 1978), 145–178.

49. "Let no one but geometricians enter."

50. "The main controversy among the geometricians, concerning squaring the circle."

51. The controversy described in this passage involved Joseph Justus Scaliger (1540–1609), a Dutch Protestant philologist and historian of Italian descent, and Christopher Clavius, a German Jesuit and mathematician. Scaliger is most noted for his works on chronology. However, in 1594 he published a book, *Cyclometrica elementa duo*, in which he attempted to demonstrate that circles could be squared. Clavius, known for his role in correcting the Julian calendar and issuing the Gregorian calendar in 1582, attacked Scaliger's work. Best on Clavius is James Lattis's new study, *Between Copernicus and Galileo: Christoph Clavius and the Collapse of Ptolemaic Cosmology* (Chicago, 1994).

52. Though there was a general bias against some church music among the Brethren, the *Unitas Fratrum* did establish a rich tradition of hymn music. Comenius himself translated a number of Luther's songs, and in 1659 he published a Czech hymnal (Blekastad, 234, 589).

53. In a later edition, Comenius added the name Copernicus in the margin—an addition that demonstrates his opposition to Copernicus's heliocentric system.

54. This is a verbal pun in Czech. Comenius plays on the word astronomers (*hvězdáři*) in order to create the word astro-liars (*zhvězdlháři*).

55. It is important to remember that the pseudoscience of astrology was taken very seriously by many in the humanist community of the early seventeenth century. For the influence of astrology in the early modern period, see *Astrology, Science and Society*, ed. Patrick Curry (Bury St. Edmunds, 1987).

56. Comenius also explores the folly of the historians in *Centrum securitatis*, 518–519.

57. There is a new edition (Darmstadt, 1987) of K. C. Schmieder's classic *Geschichte der Alchemie* (Halle, 1832). On alchemy in Central

Europe during this era, see Bruce Moran, *The Alchemical World of the German Court* (Stuttgart, 1991) and Pamela Smith, *The Business of Alchemy: Science and Culture in the Holy Roman Empire* (Princeton, 1994).

58. The philosopher's stone.

59. On this mysterious group, see Will-Erich Peuckert, *Das Rosen-kreutz* (Berlin, 1973). Also useful, but with some discretion, is Frances Yates, *The Rosicrucian Enlightenment* (London, 1986).

60. *Fama Fraternitatis,* Latin and German edition of 1612. The *Fama Fraternitatis* is the earliest extant document that refers to this secret fraternity. It recounts the travels of Christian Rosenkreuz, the supposed founder of Rosicrucianism. Rosenkreuz was purportedly born in 1378 and lived to the age of 106. His interest in hermeticism led him on extensive trips to Morocco, Egypt, Syria and Arabia. Upon his return to Europe, he imparted his knowledge to three disciples.

The *Fama* has been attributed to Johann Valentin Andreae. There are many, however, who doubt his authorship. Andreae himself claimed to have no connection with the Rosicrucians. Spinka explores this issue in more depth in *Labyrinth,* on p. 141, n. 49.

61. For the shadowy figure of Hugo Alverda, see Peuckert, 136–137.

62. Various judgments about the Fama.

63. Candidates for the Fraternity.

64. Continuation of the Fama Rosaeorum.

65. The outcome of the Fama.

66. Spinka, *Labyrinth,* p. 141, n. 50, notes that Comenius's contemporary Johannes Jessenius (1566–1612) was the first to introduce anatomical studies at the university in Prague. On Jessenius, see J. V. Polišenský, *Jan Jesenský-Jessenius* (Prague, 1965).

67. The practice of medicine.

68. The purpose of law.

69. The concerns of law.

70. The foundation of law.

71. Perplexity of the law.

72. I.e., the rector's canopy.

73. A licentiate was someone who had obtained a license, an academic degree ranking below that of the doctorate. The degree permitted him to lecture at the university.

74. There was a substantial Jewish community in Prague during this period. See *The Prague Ghetto in the Renaissance Period*, ed. O. Muneles (Prague, 1965).

75. I.e., people.

76. Inventions of the Talmud. The Talmud is a collection of scholarly interpretations and annotations on Jewish oral law. There are two recensions of the Talmud, the Palestinian and the Babylonian. The former was first printed in Venice in 1523–24, and the latter in Spain ca.1482.

77. Comenius is obviously referring to the major division of Islam, the divide between the Shiite and Sunnite sects.

78. Comenius employs a clever play on words here, contrasting spiritual (*duchovní*) fathers with fathers of revenue (*duchodní*).

79. Acts 6:2–4.

80. The emphasis on church order and discipline was an important characteristic of the *Unitas Fratrum*. The distinctions between the Bohemian Brethren and other Protestant groups were less doctrinal than organizational. For more on this subject, see Peter Brock, *The Political and Social Doctrines of the Unity of Czech Brethren in the Fifteenth and Early Sixteenth Centuries* (The Hague, 1957).

81. By "reformed" he means both Lutherans and Calvinists.

82. Comenius was not only concerned for the unification of Protestantism but also worked out a scheme for the unification of all Christendom based on universal "pansophic" education. See Matthew Spinka, "Comenian Pansophic Principles," *Church History* 22 (1953), 155–165.

83. "He who knows not how to pretend, knows not how to rule."

84. This is likely an allusion to the famous, though probably apocryphal, words of Martin Luther before the Diet of Worms in 1521.

85. Here Comenius plays on the Czech phrase, *Práva a zřízení zemská*, the harsh new constitution that the Habsburgs imposed on the Bohemian kingdom.

86. This entire section is an allusion to the Bohemian revolt that started the Thirty Years' War. For a fuller discussion of its significance see the Introduction, pp. 12–13.

87. Comenius's pacifist ideas are well documented. Especially important in this regard is his *Angelus Pacis* (1667). This tract urged the immediate cessation of hostilities between the Dutch and the English. Comenius actually attended the peace conference at Breda that was convened to end this commercially inspired conflict.

88. The "limping messenger" was a proverbial expression referring to later news, which often contradicted earlier reports. In this regard, see A. Dressler, *Studien zur Frühgeschichte der Presse* (Munich, 1952).

89. The kingdom of Venus.

90. The heat of lechery.

91. Syphilis.

92. Lechery, the precipice of despair.

93. Fame generally depends on the opinion of the masses.

94. Also conferred on the unworthy.

95. This is a reference to Herostratus, who burned down the temple of Artemis in 356 C.E.

96. In the 1623 manuscript edition and the first printed edition in 1631, Comenius included Alexander the Great, Julius Caesar, and the Duke of Alba, as well as the names in the following four endnotes, in his own margin notes. The references to the first two conquerors in this context are obvious. The third, the Duke of Alba (1508–82), was a Spanish general dispatched by Philip II to quell the revolt of the Low Countries. His infamous reputation for harsh and repressive policies spread quickly throughout the continent.

97. Arius (ca.260–336) was a presbyter in Alexandria whose teaching sparked the greatest theological controversy of the fourth century. Arius taught that the Logos is a creature called into being by God "out of nothing." The Son, then, is not eternal or equal to the Father but is created as the principle of all things. Moreover, Arius affirmed, "there was once when he [the Son] was not," i.e., a time when the Logos did not yet exist. Arius was first opposed by Bishop Alexander of Alexandria. The dispute eventually led to the Council of Nicaea (325) where Arius and his teachings were condemned. The Nicene Creed promulgated by this council included a number of explicitly anti-Arian phrases. The decisions of the council by no means settled the matter, however, for the Arian controversy raged for decades. The Council of Constantinople (381) reaffirmed the decisions of Nicaea.

98. Pontius Pilate was the Roman prefect of Judaea from 26 to 36 C.E. under the emperor Tiberius. He presided at the trial of Jesus and sentenced him to death by crucifixion.

99. On Copernicus see note 33.

100. Ignatius Loyola (1491–1556) was the founder of the Society of Jesus. The Jesuits helped stay the progress of Protestantism. Despite his generally irenic spirit, Comenius on several occasions expressed his antipathy toward the Jesuit Order. During the Moravian uprising of 1619–1620, Comenius wrote a vitriolic tract against the order. This treatise, however, has not survived. See Josef Polišenský, "Comenius and the Revolutions of the 16th and 17th Centuries," *Acta Comeniana* 5 (1983), 64.

101. The apex of wisdom is despair of the affairs of the world.

102. There were, of course, a number of women regents in the second half of the sixteenth century: Catherine de Medici in France, Elizabeth in England, and Mary in Scotland.

103. This chapter marks the introduction of a new theme. For a fuller discussion of Comenius's treatment of "wisdom expelled" see the Introduction, pp. 33–34.

104. The root of black hellebore was made into a powder and used to treat cases of insanity in early modern Europe.

105. Count Lützow (p. 179) notes that in Comenius's time the custom of repeating a title twice was a demonstration of respect. An example of this practice is found in Comenius's letter of dedication to Count Charles the Elder of Žerotín, p. 57.

106. Paracelsus (1493–1541) was a controversial German/Swiss physician who despite his bombastic claims established the role of chemistry in medicine. See also note 34.

107. An arbitrary interpretation of the law in the eyes of the judge.

108. We have followed Count Lützow's translation, rendering *mužatka* 'amazon'. The literal meaning is 'manness.'

109. See note 102.

110. The whole world is guided by the example of the ruler.

111. Ecclesiasticus 26:26.

112. This is an error in the text. The reference should read Eccl. 1:2 and 15.

113. 1 Kgs 4:34.

114. Eccl. 12:11.

115. 1 Kgs 4:33.

116. 1 Kgs 11:3.

117. Baruch, a book of the Apocrypha, was included in the Kralice Bible, the standard Czech Bible of Comenius's day.

118. Ex. 32:27.

119. 1 Kgs 18:38.

120. 2 Kgs 18:4.

121. Comenius seems to be drawing on the imagery of Hebrews 11:35–38.

122. Although there are no breaks in the original, this chapter marks the beginning of the second part of the treatise, *The Paradise of the Heart*.

123. Spinka, *Labyrinth*, p. 145, n.95, observes that much of this pas-

sage, and particularly this section, follows Andreae's *Civis christianus*, chapter 1.

124. Augustine, *Confessions* X.29.

125. John 14:27.

126. Comenius expresses a similar sentiment in *Centrum securitatis*, 545, 546.

127. The view that the Bible contained all the liberal arts was common in Comenius's time. It was defended in particular by his teacher at Herborn, J. H. Alsted, in his *Triumphus bibliorum sacrorum* (Frankfurt, 1647).

128. Mt. 5:39–40.

129. Here again we find a classic Augustinian theme that recurs in Comenius' spiritual thought. It is treated more fully in the Introduction, pp. 28–31.

130. For Comenius's use of the clock metaphor, see Otto Mayr, *Authority, Liberty and Automatic Machinery in Early Modern Europe* (Baltimore, 1986), 42.

131. For this incident, see chapter 17, 17.

132. Comenius uses the same clock metaphor in *Centrum securitatis*, 490.

133. Acts 17:28.

134. This section clearly parallels Martin Luther's treatment of the theme of Christian liberty in his 1520 tract, *On the Freedom of the Christian*. Luther himself summarizes his thesis in the following terms: "A Christian is the most free lord of all, and subject to none; a Christian is the most dutiful servant of all, and subject to everyone."

135. Rom. 8:17.

136. Ex. 20:1–17.

137. Lk. 10:25–27.

138. Rom. 12:15.

139. Acts 4:32–35.

140. Ezek. 11:19.

141. Acts 5:41.

142. Gal. 2:20.

143. Phil. 4:11–12.

144. For a similar treatment of the Mary-Martha theme, see *Unum necessarium*, 89. On the use of Mary and Martha in the history of medieval spirituality, see the recent treatment of Giles Constable, *Three Studies in Medieval Religious and Social Thought* (Cambridge, 1995).

145. Comenius believed in prophetic revelation. Of particular inter-

est is his *Lux e Tenebris* (Leyden, 1657). Blekastad traces his relationships with a number of prophets including Nicholas Drabík, Christoph Kotter, and Christina Poniatowski. Also of use is Klaus Schaller, "E labyrinthis exitus in planum-Komenskys Selbstkritik gegenüber seinen didaktischen Erfindungen und sein Einsatz für die göttlichen Offenbarungen," *Acta Comeniana* 6 (1985), 45–57.

146. Caps and bells were part of the costume of medieval fools. Comenius, of course, is implying that true Christians will often be mocked by the world.

147. 1 Cor. 1:18–24.

148. Phil. 4:7.

149. Rom. 13:7.

150. Also relevant is *Unum necessarium*, 103.

151. For the role of the Christian humanist and scientist see *Unum necessarium*, 101–108.

152. Also see *Centrum securitatis*, 526–527.

153. Rv. 4:2–4 and 8.

154. Rv. 4:10–11.

155. Rv. 7:9.

156. Rv. 7:12.

157. Is. 6:5.

158. Ps. 103:8.

159. Ps. 104:33.

160. Ps. 103:1.

161. Ps. 57:7.

162. Augustine, *Confessions* I.1 and X.27. This final section of the *Labyrinth* draws heavily from the *Confessions* as well as from the Psalms.

163. Luke 2:14: "Glory to God in the highest, and on earth peace to people of good will."

Selected Bibliography

Text used for translation

Labyrint světa a ráj srdce. In Johannis Amos Comenii Opera Omnia, vol. 3: 271–397. Prague, 1978.

Selected texts and translations[1]

Blekastad, M., ed. Unbekannte Briefe des Comenius und seiner Freunde 1641–1661. Kastellaun, 1976.

Comenius, J. A. Bequest of the Unity of Czech Brethren. Ed. M. Spinka. Chicago, 1940.

——. Centrum securitatis. In Johannis Amos Comenii Opera Omnia, vol. 3. Prague, 1978.

——. De rerum humanarum emendatione consultatio catholica. 2 vols. Eds. J. Červenka and V. T. Miškovská. Prague, 1966.

——. Duchovní Písně. Ed. A. Škarka. Prague, 1952.

——. Janua lingua reserata. Prague, 1959.

——. The Labyrinth of the World and the Paradise of the Heart. Trans. Count Lützow. London, 1905.

——. The Labyrinth of the World and the Paradise of the Heart. Trans. M. Spinka. Ann Arbor, 1972.

——. Opera didactica omnia. Prague, 1957.

——. Orbis sensualium pictus. Sydney, 1967.

——. Unum necessarium. In Johannis Amos Comenii Opera Omnia, vol. 18. Prague, 1974.

[1]This is by no means a comprehensive list of Comenius's writings. We have included here works related to spirituality or those frequently cited in the Introduction.

SELECTED BIBLIOGRAPHY

———. *The Way of Light.* Trans. E. T. Campagnac. Liverpool, 1938.
Kvačala, Jan, ed. *Korespondence J.A. Komenského.* 2 vols. Prague, 1898–1902.
Molnár, Amedeo, ed. and trans. *John Amos Comenius: A Perfect Reformation.* Prague, 1957.
Molnár, A., and Rejchrtová, N., eds. *Jan Amos Komenský O Sobě.* Prague, 1987.
Patera, A., ed. *J. A. Komenského korespondence.* Prague, 1892.
Ryba, B., ed. *Listy přátelům a příznivcům.* Prague, 1970.
———. *Sto listů Jana Amose Komenského.* Prague, 1942.
Šafránek, M., ed. *The Angel of Peace.* New York, 1944.

Studies

Balcar, Lubomír. "Theologické srovnání Komenského 'Labyrintu světa's Bunyanovou knihou 'Pilgrim's Progress.'" *Archiv pro bádání o životě a spisech J.A. Komenského* 14 (1938): 113–125.
Blekastad, Milada. *Comenius: Versuch eines Umrisses von Leben, Werk und Schicksal des Jan Amos Komensky.* Oslo, 1969.
Brambora, Josef. "La place de la Consultation parmi les corpus littéraires de Komenský." *Acta Comeniana* 1 (1970): 195–202.
———. "Results and Tasks of Literary Scholarship on Comenius." *Acta Comeniana* 4 (1979): 179–197.
Bušek, Vratislav, ed. *Comenius.* Chicago, 1972.
Čapková, Dagmar. "On the New Image of Comenius." *Acta Comeniana* 3 (1973): 470–481.
———. "Some Comments on the Interrelation between Comenius's Concept of History and His Concept of Education." *Acta Comeniana* 3 (1972): 107–115.
———. ed. *Consultationes de Consultatione.* Prague, 1970.
Červenka, Jaromír. "Die Grundlagen der pansophischen Idee des Johann Amos Comenius." *Acta Comeniana* 1 (1970): 77–84.
Čiževsky, Dmitri. "Comenius' *Labyrinth of the World:* Its Themes and Their Sources." *Harvard Slavic Studies* 1 (1953): 85–135.
Crews, C. Daniel. "Through the Labyrinth: A Prelude to the

SELECTED BIBLIOGRAPHY

Comenius Anniversary of 1992." *Transactions of the Moravian Historical Society* 27 (1992): 27–52.

Erlenbusch, Fritz. "Komenský a němečtí pietisté." In *Co daly naše země Evropě lidstvu*. Prague, 1940, 185–188.

Floss, Karel. "Comenius, die Trinität, und das dritte Jahrtausend." *Communio viatorum* 34 (1992): 19–32.

Hrbek, J. "Comenius and His Endeavors to Reform Human Society." *Acta Comeniana* 3 (1972): 17–20.

Kalivoda, Robert. "The Significance of J. A. Comenius for Modern Philosophy." *Communio viatorum* 28 (1985): 59–66.

Kučera, Karel. "An Analysis of the Vocabulary of the *Labyrinth of the World and the Paradise of the Heart*." *Acta Comeniana* 4 (1979): 327–352.

Kurdybacha, Łukasz. "The Influence of the Early Enlightenment on John Amos Comenius." *Acta Comeniana* 1 (1970): 93–99.

Kvačala, J., ed. *Archiv pro badání o životě a spisech J. A. Komenského*. Brno, 1910–1937; new series, Prague, D. Chlup, ed., 1957–.

Lee, Sook Jong. "The Relationship of John Amos Comenius' Theology to his Educational Ideas." Ph.D. diss., Rutgers University, 1987.

Lehár, Jan. "'Labyrint světa' (The Labyrinth of the World) and its Characters." *Acta Comeniana* 4 (1979): 225–249.

Lentzen-Deis, Heinrich Bodo. *Die Rolle und Bedeutung der Religion in der Pädagogik des Jan Amos Comenius*. Düsseldorf, 1969.

Lochman, J.M. "Chiliasmus verus: Eschatologie und Weltgestaltung in der Perspektive des Comenius." *Theologische Zeitschrift* 35 (1979): 275–282.

———. *Comenius*. Hamburg, 1982.

———. "Der Mensch im ganzen der Schöpfung (zur ökumenischen und ökologischen Aktualität von J.A.C.)." *Communio viatorum* 34 (1992): 59–67.

———. "Jan Amos Komensky—ein Theologe der Sehnsucht und der Hoffnung." *Unitas Fratrum* 32 (1992): 5–17.

Matar, N. I. "The Comenian Legacy in England: The Case for the Conversion of the Muslims." *Seventeenth Century Journal* (Autumn 1993): 203–215.

Molnár, Amedeo. "Comenius et l'Unité des Frères tcheques." *Communio viatorum* 1 (1958): 110–115.

——. "Comenius und die Gegenreformation." *Communio viatorum* 19 (1976): 97–108.

——. "Die Theologie der Brüder." In Říčan, *Die Bömischen Brüder*. Berlin, 1961, 283–321.

——. "Zum Theologieverständnis des Comenius." *Communio viatorum* 27 (1984): 227–241.

Mout, Nicolette. "Comenius, Descartes and Dutch Cartesianism." *Acta Comeniana* 3 (1972): 243–245.

——. "The International Calvinist Church of Prague, the Unity of Brethren and Comenius 1609–1635." *Acta Comeniana* 4 (1979): 65–75.

Nováková, Julie. "Bible Quotations in the Works of Comenius." *Communio viatorum* 28 (1985): 225–238.

Needham, J., ed. *The Teacher of Nations: Comenius, 1641–1941*. Cambridge, 1942.

Odložilík, O. "Bohemian Protestants and the Calvinist Churches." *Church History* 8 (1939): 342–355.

——. *Jan Amos Komenský*. Chicago, 1942.

Patočka, Jan. "Les antécédents Hussites de Comenius." In *Jan Amos Komenský. Gesammelte Schriften zur Comeniusforschung*. Bochum, 1981, 276–286.

——. "Cusanus and Comenius." *Pädagogik* 4 (1954): 508–523.

——. *Jan Amos Komenský (II). Nachgelassene Schriften zur Comeniusforschung*. Schriften zur Comeniusforschung, Band 15. Sankt Augustin, 1984.

Pelikan, J. "The Place of J. A. Comenius in the History of Christian Theology." *Communio viatorum* 34 (1992): 5–18.

Polišenský, Josef. "Comenius and the Development of European Thought." *Acta Comeniana* 1 (1970): 241–245.

——. "Comenius and the Revolutions of the 16th and 17th Centuries." *Acta Comeniana* 5 (1983): 59–73.

——. *Jan Amos Komenský*. Prague, 1963.

Říčan, Rudolf. *The History of the Unity of Brethren*. Bethlehem, 1992.

——. "Motifs et modèles de l'Unité des Frères dans la Consultation." *Acta Comeniana* 1 (1970): 47–57.

——. *Jan Amos Komenský, muž víry, lásky a naděje.* Prague, 1971.

Riemeck, Renate. *Der andere Comenius: Böhmischer Brüderbischof, Humanist, und Pädagoge.* Frankfurt am Main, 1970.

Rood, Wilhelmus. *Comenius and the Low Countries: Some Aspects of the Life and Work of a Czech Exile in the Seventeenth Century.* New York, 1970.

Sadler, John Edward. *J. A. Comenius and the Concept of Universal Education.* London, 1966.

Schaller, Klaus. "Das Menschenbild des Johann Amos Comenius als Pädagoge." *Unitas Fratrum* 32 (1992): 18–34.

——. "E labyrinthis exitus in planum—Komenskýs Selbstkritik gegenüber seinen didaktischen Erfindungen." *Acta Comeniana* 6 (1985): 45–57.

——. *Pan. Untersuchungen zur Comenius-Terminologie.* The Hague, 1958.

——. *Die Pädagogik des Johann Amos Comenius und die Anfänge des pädagogischen Realismus im 17. Jahrhundert.* Heidelberg, 1967.

——. ed. *Comenius. Erkennen, Glauben, Handeln.* Sankt Augustin, 1985.

——. *Comenius 1992. Gesammelte Beiträge zum Jubiläumsjahr.* Sankt Augustin, 1992.

Schurr, Johannes. *Comenius: Eine Einführung in de Consultatio catholica.* Passau, 1981

Smolik, Joseph. "Das eschatologische Denken des Johann Amos Comenius." *Evangelische Theologie* 43 (1983): 191–202.

Spinka, Matthew. "Comenian Pansophic Principles." *Church History* 22 (1953): 155–165.

——. "The Irenic Program and Activity of John Amos Comenius." Ph.D. diss., University of Chicago, 1923.

——. *John Amos Comenius, That Incomparable Moravian.* Chicago, 1943; reissued, 1967.

Škarka, Antonín, "Komenský—Básník Duchovních Písní." *Archiv pro badání o životě a spisech J. A. Komenského* 14 (1938): 11–76.

Trevor-Roper, H.R. "Three Foreigners: The Philosophers of the

Puritan Revolution." In *Religion, the Reformation and Social Change, and Other Essays*, 237–293. New York, 1967.

Trojan, J. "Comenius on Power." *Communio viatorum* 34 (1992): 68–77.

Unitas Fratrum 32 (1992).

Van der Linde, Jan Marinus. "Der andere Comenius." *Unitas Fratrum* 8 (1980): 35–48.

Voeltzel, René. "Les trois conseils oecuméniques de Comenius." *Revue d'histoire et de philosophie religieuse* 62 (1982): 443–445.

Vorländer, Herwart. "Der Theologe Johann Amos Comenius." *Zeitschrift für Kirchengeschichte* 79 (1968), 159–179.

Young, Robert F. *Comenius in England*. London, 1932.

Index

Other Volumes in This Series

Other Volumes in This Series

Other Volumes in This Series

DATE DUE

DEC 1 2 2001			
GAYLORD			PRINTED IN U.S.A